T0156544

Also by Paul Begala

It's Still the Economy, Stupid:
George W. Bush, the GOP's CEO

Is Our Children Learning?
The Case Against George W. Bush

with James Carville

Take It Back:
Our Party, Our Country, Our Future

Buck Up, Suck Up . . . and Come Back When
You Foul Up:
12 Winning Secrets from the War Room

WHY
GEORGE
W. BUSH

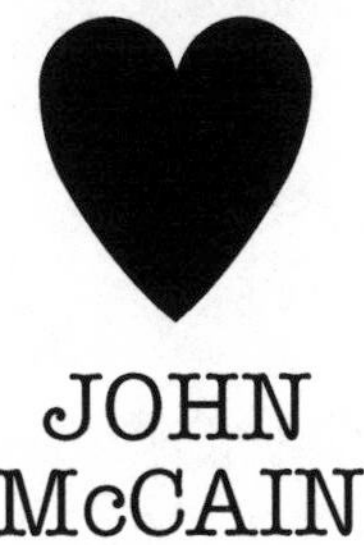

JOHN
McCAIN

PAUL BEGALA

Simon & Schuster Paperbacks
New York ★ London ★ Toronto ★ Sydney

Simon & Schuster
1230 Avenue of the Americas
New York, NY 10020

First Simon & Schuster trade paperback edition September 2008

Designed by Nancy Singer

Manufactured in the United States of America

10 9 8 7 6 5 4 3 2 1

Library of Congress Cataloging-in-Publication Data
Begala, Paul.
Third term : why George W. Bush [loves] John McCain / Paul Begala.
p. cm.
On t.p. "[loves]" appears as a graphic heart.
1. McCain, John, 1936– —Political and social views. 2. Bush, George W. (George Walker) 1946– —Political and social views 3. United States—Politics and government—2001– 4. United States—Foreign relations—2001– 5. United States—Economic policy—2001– 6. United States—Social policy—1993– 7. Presidents—United States—Election—2008 8. Conservatism—United States. 9. Legislators—United States—Biography. 10. Presidential candidates—United States—Biography. I. Title.
E840.8.M26B44 2008
973.931092—dc22 2008029421

ISBN-13: 978-1-4391-0213-8

To Harold & Ethel Cass

And Eddie & Emma Begala

Who bequeathed to me the American Dream.

★ ★ ★

CONTENTS

★ ★ ★

INTRODUCTION

A wealthy and hot-tempered rebel, encouraged always by an indomitable mother, he spent half his life fighting to live up to a famous father and grandfather. A self-described moderate on the campaign trail, he courts ultra–right-wing preachers behind the scenes and promises to appoint stridently conservative judges. A multimillionaire who supports more tax cuts for more millionaires, he surrounds himself with supply-siders and calls for policies that would drive us deeper into debt. The chief cheerleader for the war in Iraq, he said we'd be "welcomed as liberators" and angrily challenges anyone who questions his distorted and out-of-touch view of reality. A self-styled reformer, his kitchen cabinet is stocked with Washington lobbyists. Deeply out of touch on economic issues, he repeats nostrums like "The fundamentals are strong" even as the fundamentals are deteriorating. He carefully courts members of the press, who suck up to him even though he supports authoritarian policies like wiretapping Americans without a court order. He is supported by oil company lobbyists, and he supports drilling in some of our most sensitive ecosystems. Although he gladly accepts government health care for himself, he opposes government-guaranteed health care for you—abandoning you to take on colossal insurance corporations on your own. Charming and disarming at first blush, his wit masks a petulant temper and a self-righteous streak that even members of his own party worry about.

Every one of those sentences describes George W. Bush. And every one of them describes John McCain.

The biggest myth of Campaign 2008 is that John McCain is fundamentally different from George W. Bush. This book sets out to explode that myth.

In ways both big and small, frightening and funny, on matters of both style and substance, and on issues of policy and politics, John McCain represents a continuation of the Bush years. His defenders—and they are legion in the national press corps he accurately calls his "base"—will howl, but a clear-eyed reading of the record makes a compelling case that on nearly all of the things that matter most, John McCain would be more of the same.

To be sure (you knew there had to be the obligatory "to be sure" paragraph), McCain distinguished himself in wartime in ways that Bush did not. While Bush was failing even to show up for the Alabama National Guard, McCain was seeking out the most dangerous assignments in the navy. John McCain's suffering at the hands of torturers in North Vietnam, his heroism and devotion to country—they are all real. Every schoolchild should study McCain's POW experience to appreciate a man of such extraordinary valor. You will be disappointed if you are looking for a book that will answer the Swift Boat Veterans' lies about John Kerry with lies about John McCain.

Nor will I stoop to the politics of personal destruction as was practiced against my former boss Bill Clinton. Personal failings rarely predict presidential failings. FDR was an unfaithful husband; George W. Bush is a model of marital fidelity. Who would you rather have leading our country? Instead, this is a study of politics, policy, and personality—and the stunning similarities between George W. Bush and John McCain in each area.

In writing this book I have put a premium on accuracy. I have tried to cite the source for every vote and every quote. I am, of course, a man of strong opinions. But I believe it is essential for me to back those opinions up with facts. As Casey Stengel said, "You can look it up."

This book examines how George W. Bush and John McCain came to initially loathe each other—perhaps because they were more alike than either could bear to admit—and then how, in one painfully awkward hug, they lashed their fates together. It examines the issues of war and peace, of the economy and health care, of the environment and special interests—and returns damning proof that, despite what McCain and his apologists would have you believe, a vote for John McCain is a vote for a third term for George W. Bush.

★ ★ ★

THIRD TERM

★ ★ ★

WHY
GEORGE
W. BUSH

JOHN
McCAIN

★ ★ ★

Doug Mills/*The New York Times*/Redux

1

THE HUG

He has earned our admiration, and our love.

—John McCain on George W. Bush[1]

I love you, man!

—George W. Bush on John McCain[2]

It is the defining moment of John McCain's political career: The Hug. George W. Bush's 2004 reelection campaign needed help. After four years of a surprisingly radical brand of conservatism, Mr. Bush needed some moderate bona fides. After a campaign of fiction and falsehoods that led us to war, Bush needed a credibility transfusion. After the Democrats nominated a certified war hero, John Kerry, Mr. Bush (who famously avoided serving not only in Vietnam but even in the Alabama National Guard) needed a warrior's support.

And so John McCain gave him The Hug.

In embracing George W. Bush that August afternoon in Pensacola, Florida, John McCain embraced Mr. Bush's agenda, his policies, his principles, and his manipulative, mendacious brand of politics. And McCain embraced him with gusto.

This wasn't an irrationally exuberant Sammy Davis, Jr., spontaneously wrapping his arms around Richard Nixon. This was a calculated, choreographed commitment. The John McCain most people thought they knew would never have hugged George W. Bush. More likely, he'd have punched him in the nose. And for good reason.

THE SMEAR

The South Carolina Republican Party has long been the putrid petri dish of right-wing sleaze, and in the 2000 GOP primary, the slime oozed from Team Bush all over John McCain and his family. South Carolina became Ground Zero for the Republican presidential nomination after John McCain stunned George W. Bush in New Hampshire, beating him by 19 percent.

We show our character in defeat, and in response to the humiliation of New Hampshire, George W. Bush's true character emerged. He went hard right and he went down and dirty. Suddenly whisper campaigns sprouted up like kudzu all across the Palmetto State:

- **McCain is crazy.** Here's how the *Dallas Morning News* reported the rumors: "In recent weeks, the Bush campaign has been accused of—and has denied—spreading rumors that Mr. McCain may be unstable as a result of being tortured while a prisoner of war in North Vietnam. Several Senate Republicans, among them party leaders who favor Mr. Bush for president, have been identified in published reports as being responsible for privately pushing the allegations. Also, James B. Stockdale, a former prisoner of war in Vietnam who ran as Ross Perot's running mate in 1992, said he got a call from a friend close to the Bush campaign soliciting comments on Mr. McCain's 'weakness.' "[3]

- **McCain is "the fag candidate."** This gem came from push-polling, a despicable tactic wherein a voter is called by someone pretending to be a pollster but who is in fact spreading dirt. Anonymous push-pollers called South Carolina Republicans and described McCain as "the fag candidate"[4]—perhaps because he met with the pro–gay-rights Log Cabin Republicans.

- **McCain's wife is a drug addict.** Cindy McCain, like millions of Americans, from the late Chief Justice William Rehnquist to radio gasbag Rush Limbaugh, had been treated for dependency on prescription drugs. Rather than saluting her courage and recovery, leaflets surfaced in South Carolina calling Mrs. McCain "a drug addict."[5]

- **McCain abandoned his "crippled first wife."** Carol Shepp, McCain's first wife, was badly injured in a 1969 auto accident while McCain was a POW. Seven years after he returned from Vietnam, McCain's marriage to Carol fell apart. McCain has accepted responsibility for the marriage's failure, but it was hardly fair to say McCain "abandoned" Carol, or that Carol was "crippled."[6] Like half of all marriages, this one did not work out.

- **McCain fathered children out of wedlock.** Richard Hand, a professor at the racist, anti-Catholic Bob Jones University, wrote a now-infamous email in which he alleged that McCain "chose to sire children without marriage." When Hand was told on CNN that there was no evidence that his charge was true, he replied, "That's a universal negative. Can you prove that?"[7]

- **McCain's dark-skinned, adopted daughter was the product of a McCain extramarital affair.** This was the worst. Anonymous callers alleged that McCain had fathered "a black baby"[8] with a prostitute. In truth, Cindy McCain had brought a dark-skinned baby home from Mother Teresa's orphanage in Bangladesh. She and John adopted her and named her Bridget. In 2006, Bridget Googled her name and learned of how she'd been smeared when her father had been losing to George W.

Bush. A teenager today, she is still owed an apology that will never come.

So there was, one might say, some baggage in the Bush-McCain relationship. But perhaps I understate. To paraphrase a friend of mine, if Paris Hilton were to check into the Plaza hotel for a two-month stay with a full retinue of hairdressers, masseurs, manicurists, florists, bartenders, and aromatherapists, the entire entourage would have less baggage than the Bush-McCain relationship.

Think about it. Put yourself in McCain's shoes. Someone benefited from (and, some believe, orchestrated) the most savage attack on your sexuality, your sanity, your marriage, your wife, and your daughter. He smirked as his supporters attacked your honor, your dignity, your manhood, and your innocent child. What would you do? Seriously. Some of us might have shunned someone who'd treated us that way. Others might have cursed them. Still others might have kicked them in the shin or kneed them in the groin. But not John McCain.

John McCain hugged George W. Bush.

What about forgiveness? you may ask. Good point. But forgiveness starts with confession and contrition, and neither Mr. Bush nor his top advisers have ever manned up and confessed to smearing McCain. Indeed, as recently as 2007, Karl Rove aggressively challenged a questioner who alleged he had "helped spread the false story" about McCain's daughter. "That is absolutely not true, and I take offense," Rove replied to the questioner at Troy University in Alabama. "If you have any bit of evidence that anybody connected with the Bush campaign was involved in that, you bring it forward, because it is a reckless charge."[9]

So why would John McCain embrace George W. Bush? Not to be too simplistic: He wanted to. He believed in the Bush agenda and wanted to advance it into a second term.

THE WEAVER-ROVE RIFT

The McCain-Bush split probably began before they knew each other. Its roots lie in the caliche soil of central Texas, where two up-and-coming Republican operatives got their start. Karl Rove and John Weaver were instrumental in capitalizing on the disaffection some Texans felt with the Democratic Party after LBJ embraced racial equality. After Johnson signed the Civil Rights Act of 1964, he prophesied to Bill Moyers, "I think we've just delivered the South to the Republican Party for the rest of my life, and yours." [10]

It took a while, but LBJ's prophecy came true in his beloved Texas—and Karl Rove and John Weaver were central to that historic shift. In the mid-1980s, Rove and Weaver were friends and partners in a successful political consulting firm. As so often happens, there was a dispute—some say about money (it almost always is). In any event, Weaver decided to strike out on his own. This happens in business—especially the political consulting business—every day. Weaver lured away one of Rove's top employees and was named executive director of the Texas GOP by Rove-Weaver client Gov. Bill Clements. Then, according to the *Atlantic*'s Joshua Green, "Rove spread a rumor that Weaver had made a pass at a young man at a state Republican function." [11]

The rumors persisted, Weaver's business faltered, and in time Weaver quit Texas, leaving Rove the dominant GOP consultant in the Lone Star State. Although he'd departed Texas, Weaver carried some heavy Rovian baggage with him; baggage he brought aboard the Straight Talk Express.

A BRIEF FLIRTATION

Doubtless nursing a grudge from the vicious campaign in South Carolina, McCain spent much of the first Bush term taking well-timed jabs at the new president. He voted for an initial Senate version of the $1.35 trillion Bush tax cuts, but when the bill came up for final passage, McCain voted no. Echoing Democratic denunciations of a giveaway to the rich, McCain told his Senate colleagues, "I cannot in good conscience support a tax cut in which so many of the benefits go to the most fortunate among us, at the expense of middle-class Americans who most need tax relief."[12]

There were other apostasies, and even a brief flirtation with switching parties. At the center of the talk, of course, was Weaver. On March 31, 2001, Weaver had lunch at a Chinese restaurant in Bethesda, Maryland, with Tom Downey. A former congressman from New York, Downey was still as well connected as anyone in the Democratic Party. Downey insists the lunch was at Weaver's request. But the courtship was mutual and intense. Weaver suggested that McCain might bolt the GOP "if the right people asked him." Downey immediately contacted Democratic Senate leader Tom Daschle, who recruited Senators Harry Reid, John Edwards, and Ted Kennedy to join in the effort to persuade McCain. At various points over the next two months, members of the group spoke with McCain on the Senate floor, in his office, at a gathering in Senator Kennedy's office—wherever they could buttonhole him. The talks got pretty specific. "We talked about committees and his seniority . . . [a lot of issues] were on the table,"[13] Daschle recalled.

As the courtship of McCain heated up at the senatorial level, Weaver and four other McCain confidants gathered for lunch; leaving the GOP was on the menu. McCain had just voted against the Bush tax cuts, and Weaver (who reportedly coined the 2000 campaign's most incendiary slogan, "Burn It Down!") was thinking about new ways to light the fire. "Did it [leaving the GOP and running as an independent in 2004] come up? Sure," Weaver told CNN. "Some people want him to do it, but as far as we know, it is not an option on the table." The conservative writer and editor Bill Kristol was also at the lunch. "I believe that McCain thinks about it a little bit," he said. "But he's been very discreet. All the talk has been among aides and friends."[14]

The talks collapsed on May 24, 2001, when Vermont's Republican senator, Jim Jeffords, became an independent, thus swinging control of the Senate to the Democrats. In the wake of Jeffords's move, McCain was quick to renounce all talk of leaving the GOP. "I have no intention of running for president, nor do I have any intention of, or cause to, leave the Republican Party," he told CNN.

For John McCain, the die was cast. His future was with the Republican Party—and the Republican Party was with George W. Bush.

The attacks of September 11, 2001, caused a rally-round-the-president phenomenon that boosted Bush's anemic approval rating into the stratosphere. McCain could have shown his maverick bona fides then. He could have pointed out that Bush was derelict in his duty when he ignored the CIA's warning that BIN LADEN DETERMINED TO STRIKE IN U.S. He could have noted that a real leader would not have panicked, as Bush did; a real leader would not have run and hid, as Bush did; a real leader would not have hesitated, as Bush did. McCain could have told the nation that a real president would not have sat frozen in front of schoolchildren for over five minutes after being told, "America is under attack." But McCain did not. He joined the chorus of Bush suck-ups, feeding the false story that this incompetent man was somehow the strong, brave, wise leader we needed.

John McCain would remain a Republican. And a Bush Republican at that.

CAVING IN OVER COFFEE

And so in early 2004, John Weaver reached out to Team Bush. He called Mark McKinnon, Bush's media adviser (and my friend since college). It was a smart choice. A conciliator by nature, McKinnon was among the least anti-McCain members of the

Bush inner circle. McKinnon had traveled a long and difficult route in American politics: from the far fringes of the student left when he was in college (he considered me a sellout for supporting student government and serving as student body president), McKinnon moved from his first job with the stalwart progressive Texas Democrat Lloyd Doggett, to Ann Richards. Then, in the late '90s, he fell in love with George W. Bush. Perhaps in an ironic tribute to his formerly iconoclastic views, McKinnon named his firm Maverick Media, and the Maverick began making ads for George W. Bush. McKinnon is gifted, and soon the Yale frat boy with the Harvard MBA was seen droppin' his *g*'s and wearin' jeans and boots and swingin' on the front porch with his beloved Laura: just a regular Texas good ol' boy.

Still, it wouldn't have been surprising if McKinnon had retained some deep-hidden respect and affection for another self-styled maverick. Besides, Weaver could hardly have stomached picking up the phone and calling Rove directly. McKinnon called Rove and brokered a date for him with Weaver. They met at Caribou Coffee, at 1701 Pennsylvania Avenue—a short walk from Rove's office at the White House. Weaver made the first move. "Time to put this behind us," he told Rove. There was no need to define "this": the years of bitterness and backstabbing needed no reiteration. Rove was gracious, as gracious as McCain's grandfather was as he stood on the deck of the USS *Missouri* to help receive the Japanese surrender. It's easy to be gracious when the other side offers total capitulation. "I know how hard this must be for you," Rove said. "And I appreciate it."[15]

Rove then posed the question: would McCain come out and campaign with Bush? The two had suffered through an exquisitely awkward joint appearance in Pittsburgh in the 2000 campaign. McCain left the 2000 convention early. Some believed he could not bear the Bush coronation; others reported he was being treated for cancer. Rove knew just what to ask for—a little of the McCain magic on the campaign trail. "All you had to do was ask," Weaver replied.[16] McKinnon paid the bill, but both sides walked away buzzing from more than the caffeine.

One person who knows both McCain and Bush well suggested the rift was more driven by aides than personal animosity. "McCain and Bush like each other's toughness," this person told me. "Always have." The ease and speed of the reconciliation suggests there is much truth to the point.

"Listen, we had a very tough, intrafamily fight [in the 2000 primaries]," Weaver recalled in a 2007 interview with the *Washington Post*'s Peter Baker. "These are always tougher, the fights between families. McCain was over it before everybody else was. Like a lot of these things, some of the lower-level soldiers didn't come out of the hills for a long time."

It is interesting that Weaver used a military analogy. Of course, all of us campaign hacks fall back on that—even the word *campaign* comes from the world of warfare. John Weaver, ever the loyal soldier, was offering his most bitter enemy—and his boss's—an unconditional surrender.

THE FIRST DATE

On June 18, 2004, McCain accompanied Bush to Fort Lewis, Washington. Before a Bush campaign rally, they met briefly in the lodge where Bush had stayed the night before. Then the old warrior introduced the old draft dodger to the crowd. The staff of the independent, bipartisan 9/11 Commission had just reported that there was no evidence of any "collaborative relationship" between Saddam Hussein and the al Qaeda terrorist networks, making Bush a liar: One of his principal arguments for invading Iraq was the fact that Saddam was somehow linked to al Qaeda. Again and again Mr. Bush and his vice president sought to associate Saddam Hussein with the terrorism of 9/11. And now Bush's lie was shattered—and John McCain was there to pick up the pieces. McCain vouched for Bush. He did so with gusto, with relish. McCain said the president "led this country with moral clarity." He said Mr. Bush "heard the call to action on that terrible morning in September and summoned the rest of us to this long and difficult task."

I do not know—indeed, cannot know—what was going through McCain's mind at the time. He already knew Bush was a liar; he'd said as much in the 2000 campaign. And he knew that no lie was beyond this man and his supporters—just ask young Bridget McCain. McCain also knew, must have known, that Bush's mendacity violated every sense of honor in McCain's Naval Academy DNA.

As if that wasn't enough, McCain defended Bush's incompetent handling of the Iraq War, which McCain would later pretend he'd been consistently critical of. "There have been ups and downs," McCain told the soldiers of Fort Lewis. "As there are in any war, but like you, he has not wavered in his determination to protect this country and to make the world a better, safer, freer place." McCain closed with a suck-up that would have made the McCain of 2000 gag. He actually drew a moral parallel between the lying coward he was sharing the stage with and the six thousand heroic military men and women he was speaking to. "You will not yield, nor will he."[17]

It was a stunning performance, even for someone used to the phoniness of politics. Tellingly, Bush didn't even try to return the compliment. After McCain's sycophantic introduction, the man who became president in part by smearing McCain and his family dismissed the vanquished with a perfunctory thanks and boilerplate compliments: "It is a privilege to be introduced to our men and women in uniform by a man who brought such credit to the uniform. When he speaks of service and sacrifice, he speaks from experience. The United States military has no better friend in the United States Senate than John McCain."[18]

When Bush finished, he embraced McCain. The *Washington Post* said, "Bush, waving repeatedly to the crowd as he strode onto the stage amid applause, walked straight toward McCain and put his arms around him. The Arizonan leaned his head toward Bush's cheek, and then the president grinned as the senator whispered in his ear."[19]

How sweet. McCain's admirers probably would like to believe that their hero whispered a four-letter–filled entreaty for Mr. Bush to commit an unnatural act on himself. But no dice. Whatever whispered words were shared by the pair, the two amigos continued their hug-a-thon later that day in Reno. After McCain introduced Mr. Bush there, he gave Bush a hug and patted his back six times.

THE HUG THAT WILL LIVE IN INFAMY

But The Hug—the legendary embrace that appears at the beginning of this chapter—came a few months later in Pensacola, Florida, on August 10, 2004. The location could not have been more fraught with significance for McCain. Pensacola is the home of the oldest naval air station in America, the cradle of naval aviation. It was there that a newly minted Ensign John McCain reported for his first assignment after graduating from the Naval Academy. It must have been a bitter moment for McCain to return there forty-six years later to introduce a man who'd refused to report for duty in the Alabama Air National Guard while John McCain was being held as a POW in the Hanoi Hilton.

But McCain rose to the occasion—or, rather, sank to it. "He was determined and remains determined to make this world a better, safer, freer place," McCain said. "And he has more than earned our support—he has earned our admiration and our love."[20] And then McCain did it. There was no sneaking up, no surprise gotcha-grab from behind. McCain strode over to Bush. Both men had removed their coats and ties and had rolled up their sleeves in deference to the August heat in the "Redneck Riviera." As he approached Bush, McCain shifted his body ever so slightly to his right, extended his arms—first the right, then the left—and pulled Bush in for a massive bear hug. Bush at first seemed to want to continue waving to the crowd, but McCain's embrace was so all-encompassing that Bush could only give in.

As they embraced, Bush patted McCain's back, and then

McCain gently nestled his head on Bush's chest. It was as submissive a posture as one could imagine: the defeated beta wolf offering his jugular to the alpha male. To complete the tableau, Bush gave McCain a peck on the temple.

That's right—the younger, feckless playboy dismissed the older, fearless flyboy with the kind of peck on the head you use for shooing away a cloying, annoying little nephew.

Weaver was ready to spin The Hug into political gold. "I wouldn't characterize either man as a hug victim," he told the *New York Times.* "I think they were mutual hugs, and mutual looking forward."[21] Rick Davis, McCain's longtime right-hand man, eagerly reinforced the argument that Bush and McCain were essentially identical ideologically, telling the *Times,* "I think what they [the Bush campaign] have found is McCain doesn't upset their conservative base because he's a conservative. He's both a religious conservative, he's pro-life—you couldn't run a thread between his position on abortion and Bush's—and yet at the same time he speaks to a much broader audience politically. So why not hang around with that guy?"[22]

Why not indeed? The truth is, The Hug was probably not as painful for McCain—nor as emotional, nor as difficult—as I would have thought. The truth is, John McCain was merely reverting to form, as Davis said. McCain was, is, and ever shall be a Bush Republican. His occasional forays into Bush-bashing were simply expressions of ambition, an attempt to beat another right-wing corporate tool to the top of the greasy poll. But there is no ideological difference between them, and the combination of their shared policy agenda and their equally fanatical ambition made it easy for McCain to embrace George W. Bush—embrace him personally and politically; embrace his values and his principles; his agenda and his priorities; his war and his economic policy; nearly all things Bush both foreign and domestic. Perhaps that's why loyal Bush spokesperson Nicole Devenish vouched for the authenticity of The Hug, saying, "I don't think either man is capable of pretense." Devenish is now known by her married name, Nicole Wallace—and by her new professional role, coordinating strategy and communications for the John McCain campaign.[23]

The Hug was real; it was the "Straight Talk" that was phony.

★ ★ ★

★ ★ ★

2

McSAME OLD THING

George W. Bush is "one of the great presidents of the United States."

—John McCain[1]

I'm proud to be up here with a fine American, a great friend, John McCain.

—George W. Bush on John McCain[2]

MEET THE NEW BOSS, SAME AS THE OLD BOSS

John McSame. George W. McCain. McBush. There are endless word games you can play with the names of these two birds of a political feather. "But, ahh," you say (that is, if you're in the tank for McCain, like so many in the national media), "McCain is completely different than Bush."

Not if you base your analysis on two things the right wing is not big on: math and facts.

John McCain usually votes the exact same way as George W. Bush. Over the years Bush has been in office, McCain has voted the way Bush wanted over 90 percent of the time.[3] Let me give you a handy table to look over while you listen to the squealing of the so-called Straight Talk Express taking a sharp screeching turn to the right.[4]

John McCain: Votes with Bush Through the Years		
YEAR	SUPPORT	OPPOSE
2008 (through May 15, 2008)	100%	0%
2007	95%	5%
2006	89%	11%
2005	77%	23%
2004	92%	8%
2003	91%	9%
2002	90%	10%
2001	91%	9%

91 PERCENT OF THE TIME HE'S JUST LIKE BUSH

I was a liberal arts major, but even I can do simple math. From the day George W. Bush was installed as president (by five thieves in black robes) to the day I wrote this chapter, John McCain has voted with George W. Bush an average of 91 percent of the time.

What would you call someone at work who agreed with the boss 91 percent of the time? A suck-up, that's what. Or, if you're a little more earthy, a brownnoser. More elegantly, one might say a sycophant. In an Elizabethan frame of mind, you would call such a person a courtier, or a throne-sniffer. In Texas we might say a bootlicker. But you wouldn't call him a maverick. If a baseball player bats righty 91 percent of the time, sportswriters don't call him a lefty. That's because sportswriters are a lot less gullible than political reporters.

The fact that political reporters fall for John McCain's spin does not obscure the fact that on almost all of the important issues, John McCain would represent a third term of George W. Bush. The subsequent chapters of this book carefully document how John McCain would extend Bush's failed policies in Iraq, on the economy, health care, the judiciary, and more.

A FAMOUS FATHER, AN INDOMITABLE MOTHER, A YOUTHFUL REBELLION, JUST LIKE BUSH

The pro-McCain press likes to point out the obvious contrast between Bush and McCain's, umm, war records. While McCain was suffering in the Hanoi Hilton, Bush was partying in every bar from Beaumont to Birmingham. But at many other points, their biographies are more similar than either would like to admit.

They're both the firstborn, namesake sons of dynasties. George W. Bush's father was, of course, president, vice president, UN ambassador, CIA chief, envoy to China, congressman, chairman of the Republican National Committee, World War II hero, and Phi Beta Kappa while lettering in baseball at Yale.[5] That's a lot to live up to. And his grandfather, Prescott Bush, was a man of great accomplishment as well—senator, banker, millionaire, leader of the GOP's moderate wing (back when it had one).

John McCain, for his part, is from navy royalty. His father, John Sidney McCain, Jr., was a Naval Academy graduate, a four-star admiral, and commander of the Pacific Fleet. He commanded two submarines in World War II and earned the Silver Star. McCain's grandfather, John Sidney "Slew" McCain, Sr., was also an Annapolis grad (where he was friends with fellow navy legends "Bull" Halsey and Chester Nimitz). He went on to become a four-star admiral. (The McCains were the first father-son four-stars in the storied history of the U.S. Navy.) Slew was on the deck of the USS *Missouri* on September 2, 1945, one of the senior commanders who received the Japanese surrender at the end of World War II.[6] Within days he would die of a heart attack. There is speculation he'd had an earlier heart attack but hadn't told anyone. He'd wanted to gut it out until the war had been won.[7]

Just as interesting, both Bush and McCain have mothers who are forces to be reckoned with. Barbara Bush was raised in a time and a place and a class where women were often seen and not heard, yet she never took any crap from anyone. Similarly, as an admiral's wife, Roberta McCain was well-known for her vivacity, energy, and independence.[8]

So both young George and young John had a lot to live up to. Too much, perhaps. Interestingly, neither chose to play the part of the dutiful son. Instead, each chose the path of the prodigal son. And, frankly, it looks like they both had a damn good time.

Bush famously drank his way through half his life. By his own admission, when he was young and irresponsible, he was young and irresponsible.[9] He was good looking and popular, from a powerful and wealthy family, possessed of a name that opened doors. What wasn't to like? He became a rebel without a risk. After he performed badly in an elite private academy in Houston, he was shipped off to an even more elite private academy: Andover. His rebellion at Yale was pathetic. While others were protesting the war, staying up late cramming for exams, and debating the meaning of life and the duties of privilege, Bush was partying his ass off at the Deke House. His average grade was a 77.[10] Rumors abound, largely undenied by Bush. Mind-altering chemicals of the '60s were okay, and he got arrested—not for protesting the war that was killing the kids whose daddies couldn't get them into Yale but for stealing a Christmas wreath on a drunken night out.[11] Later, of course, he was arrested for driving under the influence[12] and even challenged his war hero dad to a fistfight while hammered on the family front lawn.[13]

McCain, too, has been candid about his youthful excesses—and they weirdly parallel Bush's. His version of Bush's "young and irresponsible" dodge is to say he succumbed to the "unruly passions of youth."[14] His nicknames at Episcopal High School in Alexandria, Virginia, were "Punk" and "McNasty."[15] At the Naval Academy, McCain was semi-famous—not only for his pedigree and quick temper but also for his legion of demerits. In the academy yearbook, Midshipman McCain is described as a "sturdy conversationalist and party man."[16] He was fifth from the bottom of his graduating class, 894 in a class of 899.[17]

Later, as a navy liaison to the Senate, McCain kept time with legendary senator (and drinker) John Tower.[18] According to the *New York Times,* drinks were drunk, women were chased, and a good time was had by all.[19]

Let me be clear. I don't think John McCain is a bad man. In fact, I think he's a good man—a man whom I admire in many ways. But he is also more like George W. Bush than you might have thought. Black sheep of a feather, as George W. Bush himself might say.

A VAST FORTUNE, JUST LIKE BUSH'S

Don't get me wrong, there's nothing wrong with being rich. I am all for it. I just think it's interesting that both George W. Bush and John McCain have vast family fortunes—and both support economic policies that would greatly benefit their fellow millionaires and hammer the hell out of poor and working Americans. Coincidence? You decide.

I'm sure you know about Bush's fortune. How he made $14 million by investing $600,000 in the Texas Rangers (can you say "sweetheart deal"?).[20] And you probably know about the sixteen-hundred-acre ranch in Crawford, Texas, complete with a creek, a canyon, waterfalls, and a private lake, stocked with private fish.[21] You almost certainly have seen Bush at his family's beautiful compound on the surf-pounded cliffs of Kennebunkport, Maine, and have no doubt seen the photos of him tooling around on his father's twenty-eight-foot cigarette boat. The name Bush equals wealth in the public perception.

But while I'm sure you already knew about Bush's wealth, this may be the first time you've learned that John McCain is rich. Really rich. Get this: John McCain is richer than George W. Bush. A lot richer.

The Senate is famously known as a millionaires' club. But even within that club, McCain's wealth stands out. According to the Center for Responsive Politics, John McCain was the eighth-wealthiest senator in 2006, based on his Senate personal financial disclosure. McCain's minimum net worth was listed at $27,817,187, and his maximum net worth was listed at $45,045,011.[22] He filed those reports publicly, but since his enormous wealth doesn't fit the McCain-friendly media's narrative, it is rarely mentioned.

Almost all of that wealth comes from Cindy McCain. She inherited an enormously successful beer distributorship from her father, and I myself have done all I can to increase her wealth every time I've visited Arizona. I am definitely pro-beer. So is Cindy McCain. Experts consulted by the *Wall Street Journal* say her stake in the beer distributorship is worth about $100 million.[23]

John and Cindy McCain own a plethora of houses and condos throughout the western United States. (I've always wanted to use *plethora* in a book. Somewhere, my ninth-grade English teacher, Ms. Gloria Rinehimer, is smiling.) Anyway, that plethora cost an estimated $13,123,269 and includes:

- Two beachfront condos in Coronado, California[24]
- A condo in La Jolla, California[25]
- Two high-end condos in Phoenix, Arizona. The condos have been combined into one mondo condo of up to 7,000 square feet, worth $4.6 million[26]
- Three ranch houses located outside of Sedona, Arizona[27]
- A high-rise condo in Arlington, Virginia[28]
- A loft they bought for their daughter, Meghan[29]

Oh, yeah. McCain also owns a parking lot worth $1 million, according to the 2006 U.S. Senate Personal Finance Disclosure.

A parking lot worth $1 million. I thought I was rich when I no longer had to drink Buckhorn beer just because it was on sale, but a $1 million parking lot? Man, that is r-i-c-h.

For perspective—as if you needed it—the average American family's home is worth $217,800.[30] The McCains have nine homes worth a total of $13 million. That's enough to house sixty average families in sixty average homes.

There is also money on McCain's side of the marriage. His redoubtable mother, Roberta, is the daughter of an oil wildcatter. When visiting Europe, she was told she was too old to rent a car (she was in her nineties). So she bought one—a new Mercedes-Benz.[31] I admire Mrs. McCain's spunk. We should all be as vigorous and well-off in our nineties. Trouble is, with the Bush-McCain economic policies making us poorer, with the Bush-McCain health-care policies making us sicker, and with the Bush-McCain Social Security privatization threatening that sacred trust, there's very little chance of that happening.

DANGEROUSLY IGNORANT, JUST LIKE BUSH

If you are calling for placing American troops in a country for one hundred years,[32] you should probably know some rudimentary facts about it.[33] And after five years of war in that country, you should have some clues as to who's on which side. But, just like George W. Bush, John McCain shows a startling ignorance of even the most basic facts about Iraq.

Eight weeks before he gave the order to invade Iraq—after a rhetorical and propaganda buildup that had gone on for months—President Bush invited Iraqi exile Kanan Makiya to the White House to watch the Super Bowl. It was to be an all-American photo op before the American troops were sent to liberate Makiya's country. Makiya was among the staunchest critics of Saddam Hussein's dictatorship. His 1989 book, *Republic of Fear,* was a neocon favorite because even before Saddam invaded Kuwait, Makiya sounded the alarm about his brutality. (Of course, in those days Saddam was an American ally; Ronald Reagan famously sent Donald Rumsfeld to give him golden spurs and a wink and a nod after Saddam had used chemical weapons.) According to David L. Phillips, a former senior policy adviser to Bush, "Bush was apparently unaware of the animosity between Iraqi factions . . . Kanan was invited to watch the [2003] Super Bowl at the White House; he told me later that he had to explain to the president of the United States the differences between Arab Shi'a, Arab Sunnis and Kurds."[34]

Think about that. Just weeks before launching an invasion that has cost tens of thousands of lives—an unprovoked, unjust, unwise, unwarranted war that has left hundreds of thousands wounded and cost trillions of dollars—the president of the United States didn't even know that the country he was about to invade had three principal factions whose differences and rivalries dominated life in that country. Appalling, isn't it? I'll bet you think that could never happen again. I'll bet you think we could never again have a president so willfully ignorant, so bullheaded, so headstrong, so infused with that rare combination of ignorance and arrogance.

Meet the new boss. Same as the old boss.

In a radio interview in March 2008, McCain stated that al Qaeda was being trained by Iran.[35] Of course this completely ignores the fact that Iran is a Shiite country, al Qaeda is a Sunni-based terrorist group, and these two parties have been enemies for centuries.

I have to admit that at first I thought, what the heck. McCain is such a commanding presence, he's got such a legendary military pedigree that he must have simply misspoken. Everyone makes mistakes, and I hate the culture of gaffes that hamstrings public figures. So I cut him some slack. I did not pounce on McCain. Even I thought he couldn't be as bad as Bush. But I was wrong.

He kept on repeating his mistake throughout the interview. I'm a former congressional staffer, and McCain has an excellent staff. So I knew that following the interview they would take the old sailor to the woodshed, remind him which side was which in the Iraqi civil war, and why it was somewhere between unlikely and impossible that the Shiite Iranians would be training the Sunni al Qaeda terrorists. But then he did it again. McCain again confused Shiite and Sunni while on a foreign policy trip to Iraq's and Iran's neighbor, Jordan, that was supposed to highlight his "expertise."[36] His buddy Joe Lieberman had to whisper in his ear and correct his mistake while the entire press corps and the world were watching.[37]

Later, McCain the military expert got his facts wrong about troop levels. Again, everyone makes mistakes, but you'd think the author of the "McCain Surge," the man who boasts about his expertise in military affairs and denigrates all who disagree with him, would know how many troops we have in Iraq.[38] In May 2008, McCain was campaigning in the Milwaukee suburb of Greenvale, Wisconsin, when a woman asked about our policy in Iraq. "I can look you in the eye and tell you it's succeeding, we have drawn down to pre-surge levels," he said, adding that the Iraqi cities of Basra, Mosul, and Sadr City are now "quiet."[39]

Huh? What? Did he really say that? First of all, whether or not the surge is working is highly debatable. Its purpose, to give the Iraqis breathing room to form a functioning governing coalition, has certainly not materialized. It is true that as American troop strength has gone up, violence has decreased. But after stating his dubious opinion, McCain went on to assert a falsity as if it had been fact: "We have drawn down to pre-surge levels." We have *not.* Before the surge we had about 135,000 troops in Iraq. When McCain said we were down to pre-surge levels, we in fact had 155,000 troops in Iraq.[40] That's not even close. And by the way, even after the so-called surge brigades are brought home, we'll still have 140,000 troops in Iraq—more than we had before the surge began.

Senator Barack Obama pounced on McCain's misstatement. "This is the guy who says I need more knowledge," said Obama. "He's wrong. That's not true and anyone running for commander in chief should know better. As the saying goes, you're entitled to your own view, but not your own facts."[41]

McCain's additional comments about Basra, Mosul, and Sadr City being "quiet" were also unfortunate—and reminiscent of similar comments from George W. Bush. Just days after Mosul was declared "quiet," thirteen people, some of them children, were killed in a suicide car bombing at the city's main police headquarters. Forty-three more were wounded.[42] Also within days of McCain's proclamation of Basra as "quiet," an Iraqi cameraman was seriously injured when a musical instruments store was bombed.[43] And in the Shaar neighborhood next to Sadr City, more than a dozen civilians were killed when a rocket-loaded truck exploded as insurgents were preparing to attack an American military base in Baghdad.[44]

Point for Obama. McCain would have none of it. Instead of manning up and admitting he'd made a mistake, McCain doubled down on his flub. He and his supporters accused Obama of "nit-picking," prompting Obama to retort that he hardly views tens of thousands of troops as nitpicks.[45]

The mistake is less important, less illuminating, less instructive than the unwillingness to admit it. We have had eight long years of a president who knows too little and bullies too much. And John S. McCain and George W. Bush are cut from the same cloth.

McCAIN WANTS TO BE PRESIDENT OF FANTASY ISLAND, JUST LIKE BUSH

One of the most annoying things about President Bush—and there are so many—is his willful, frightening, maddening ability to deny reality. Before he launched his invasion, Bush told Reverend Pat Robertson he did not believe there would be heavy casualties in the war. Robertson says he tried to tell Bush that in fact casualties would be high, and that he urged the president to prepare the country for them. Bush persisted in his fantasy that this would be a relatively bloodless war.[46] When Pat Robertson is more in touch with reality than you are, you are seriously off in La-La Land. But that's where Bush prefers to live. He overstated the threat posed by Saddam Hussein while understating the risks and costs of occupying a large and bitterly divided nation.

Here again, you want to think McCain will be different. After all, he has seen the horrors of war firsthand—flying dangerous missions while Bush was downing tequila shots. But despite his combat experience, McCain has shown a talent for denying reality that is downright Bushian.

Before the war, McCain said the Iraqi people would "greet us as liberators."[47] Before the invasion, he said, "We will win this conflict. We will win it easily."[48] Five years and thousands of American lives later, in a town hall meeting in Houston, McCain said, "In fact we are succeeding in Iraq. . . . We are succeeding militarily and we are succeeding, uh, politically."[49] A month later, General David Petraeus said, "No one feels that there has been sufficient progress by any means in the area of national reconciliation."[50] With all due respect, General, someone does. Someone dangerously out of touch: John McCain.

Perhaps the most famous example of McCain being on Fantasy Island instead of terra firma was when, in 2007, he said that there "are neighborhoods in Baghdad where you and I could walk through those neighborhoods, today."[51] Right, Senator. You and what army? Oh, wait a minute. You did have an army with you while you strolled through that Baghdad neighborhood. Or didn't you notice?

In late 2007, as the Bush-McCain economy careened toward a recession, President Bush kept telling us, "The fundamentals of our economy are strong."[52] Ever the dutiful Bush acolyte (at least 91 percent of the time), McCain parroted his hero a few months later, telling Americans who are hurting, "I think our fundamentals are strong."[53]

But then McCain out-Bushed Bush. During a town hall meeting in West Palm Beach, Florida, in January 2008, McCain said about the economy, "A lot of this is psychological. A lot of it's psychological. Because I believe the fundamentals of our economy are still strong."[54]

Actually, our problems are not in our heads. But I'm beginning to wonder what's in Senator McCain's head.

MY WAY OR THE HIGHWAY, JUST LIKE BUSH

To call George W. Bush stubborn would be like calling Paris Hilton fun-loving. The description hardly does justice to the obscene, grotesque reality. Bush sees the world in black and white, heroes and villains, sinners and saints. He's a simple man, Lord knows, with a simple worldview: You're either for him, or you're against him.

McCain's apologists sound a lot like the Bush suck-ups did when he was first running for president. John is so deeply principled, they say. He's so gosh-darned committed to Truth, Justice, and the American Way. He doesn't suffer fools gladly. When you strip away the spin, the reality is that McCain is as pigheaded as Bush. (By the way, is "pigheaded" better or worse than "bullheaded"? I come from cattle country in Texas, so I don't know anything about pigs.)

According to *Newsweek,* McCain sees issues the same way Bush does. He "can be pragmatic in the pursuit of [issues], but seems to see them in largely black and white terms, not unlike George Bush, and rejects too much of the gray."[55]

Oh, great. The last thing we need is a president who gets all caught up in . . . nuance or complexity or, God forbid, reality.

A House Republican leadership aide said McCain has been "my-way-or-the-highway" in the Senate. When asked about McCain's address to the House Republican Conference, the Republican aide asked pointedly, "Will he sound like the 'my-way-or-the-highway' McCain that's graced the Senate for ten years?"[56]

When the Bush *Republicans* think you're too stubborn, man, you are definitely stubborn. Douglas Johnson, the legislative director of the National Right to Life Committee, which lobbies against the right to legal abortions, called McCain "the biggest bully in the Senate."[57] And McCain opposes legal abortions in nearly every circumstance. He wants to overturn *Roe v. Wade*, amend the Constitution, whatever it takes.[58] And yet the lobbying group that shares McCain's position most passionately still thinks he's the biggest bully in the Senate.

When you disagree with President Bush, he often reacts by questioning your motives. Not your ideas, your motives. He'll suggest you're not a real patriot if you don't want to give him a free pass to wiretap any American without a court order. He'll say you don't support the troops if you want to end the war. He'll say you want the terrorists to win if you oppose his dangerous and deranged foreign policy. John McCain shares that quality. Again, the National Right to Life Committee's Doug Johnson has been both observant and candid. "When someone disagrees with him, he immediately attacks their motives," he said. "[McCain thinks] anyone who disagrees with him is driven by selfish motives and perhaps even stupidity."[59]

AGAINST ACCOUNTABILITY, JUST LIKE BUSH

One of the hallmarks of the Bush presidency has been its penchant for secrecy. It is harder to pry information out of the Bush administration than to get buckshot out of Dick Cheney's hunting buddies. John McCain, on the other hand, has a reputation for openness, born of his endless bull sessions with sycophantic reporters on his campaign bus. But when it comes to more important forms of accountability than rolling, fawning press encounters, McCain can be as dark and secretive as Dick Cheney in a bunker.

John McCain voted against making Bush submit a report to Congress on the prewar intelligence.[60] He voted against creating an independent commission to study prewar intelligence.[61] He voted against requiring Bush to report on his plans for postconflict strategies in Iraq.[62] He voted against Bush having to report on what was going on with the detainee program.[63] McCain voted against making government open and accountable and transparent. And George Bush couldn't have been happier.

LET HIM EAT CAKE WHILE NEW ORLEANS FLOODS, JUST LIKE BUSH

Jim Watson/AFP/Getty Images

Why are these guys smiling?

This photograph was taken on Monday, August 29, 2005. Hurricane Katrina had already struck the American Gulf Coast.[64] The levees in New Orleans had already been breached. The city was flooded; American citizens were calling for help while John McCain and George W. Bush shared a birthday cake in Arizona to celebrate McCain's sixty-ninth birthday.

Let me repeat that: John McCain and George W. Bush took time out to share a birthday cake *while New Orleans was flooding after the levees broke.*[65]

Think John McCain is more caring and compassionate than George W. Bush? Think he's more competent or clued in? Think again. Look at that picture again. Bush and McCain posed for pictures and ate cake as the residents of New Orleans scrambled to their rooftops to avoid the rising waters.

Somewhere, Maria Antonia Josepha Joanna von Osterreich-Lothringen, better known as Marie Antoinette, is laughing. But no one in New Orleans is.

John McCain's actions following Hurricane Katrina mirrored the bumbling and incompetence we have come to expect from the Bush administration. A time line of McCain's "actions" during these tragic weeks demonstrates once more how he represents a third term of George W. Bush.

SATURDAY, AUGUST 27

- **A federal emergency is declared.** DHS and FEMA are given full authority to respond to Katrina.[66]

SUNDAY, AUGUST 28

- **Katrina is upgraded to a Category 5 hurricane.**[67]
- **Thousands of evacuees gather at the Superdome with roughly thirty-six hours' worth of food.**[68]
- **John McCain appears on CBS's *Face the Nation* to claim progress in the war in Iraq.** As thousands of Americans flee their homes in terror, John McCain pokes his head out of his vacation home (one of the nine homes he owns) for some good old-fashioned war cheerleading. McCain says of the war in Iraq, "I think it's clear that a premature withdrawal would be catastrophic in its consequences . . . we've made progress in many areas of Iraq."[69]

MONDAY, AUGUST 29

- **Several levees are breached throughout New Orleans; pumping stations go down.**[70]
- **On the morning Katrina strikes New Orleans, and hours *after* the levee breach, *McCain enjoys birthday cake with President Bush.*** The White House website posts a notice: "President George W. Bush joins Arizona Senator John McCain in a small celebration

of McCain's 69th birthday Monday, Aug. 29, 2005, after the President's arrival at Luke Air Force Base near Phoenix."

- **Later that night McCain appears on *Late Night with Conan O'Brien.*** With his stomach still full of delicious baked goods, and his party with George W. Bush still lifting his spirits, John McCain makes time to appear on *Late Night with Conan O'Brien* along with actress Amber Tamblyn and the band Alkaline Trio. (Perhaps McCain enjoyed their 1999 album, *I Lied My Face Off.*)[71]

TUESDAY, AUGUST 30

- **With 80 percent of the city flooded, there is mass looting throughout New Orleans; rescue efforts are still under way.**[72]

WEDNESDAY, AUGUST 31

- **Sixteen thousand people are still stranded in the Superdome; almost five hundred are taken away by helicopter for medical emergencies.**[73]

THURSDAY, SEPTEMBER 1

- **"A crumbling city and dead bodies."** Here is how CNN's Adaora Udoji described the scene: "The city's mayor is at his wits' end. Today, he issued a desperate SOS, saying, 'Currently, the convention center is unsanitary and unsafe, and we are running out of supplies for fifteen thousand to twenty thousand people. We are now allowing people to march.' They are marching in search of food, water, and relief. They're surrounded by a crumbling city and dead bodies. Infants have no formula, the children no food, nothing for adults, no medical help. They're burning with frustration, and sure they have been forgotten."[74]
- **McCain's Senate office releases its first paper statement on Katrina.** That's right, it is now five days after a federal emergency

> was declared and this is the first "action" McCain has taken. And yes, that "action" is having his office put out a meaningless piece of paper.[75]

McCain's statement said, "U.S. Senator John McCain (R-AZ) today extends his condolences to the victims of Hurricane Katrina who are dealing with a natural disaster of epic proportions. I urge Arizonans and all Americans to reach out to those affected by this tragedy. American citizens have proven time and again how generous and selfless a people we are, and now we have an opportunity to come to the aid of those in need. Our thoughts and prayers are with our fellow Americans as they struggle to cope with this emergency."[76] George W. Bush himself could not have issued a more vapid or useless press release.

CNN's Anderson Cooper could take no more. He raked Louisiana senator Mary Landrieu over the coals, saying, "Excuse me, Senator, I'm sorry for interrupting . . . for the last four days, I've been seeing dead bodies in the streets here in Mississippi. And to listen to politicians thanking each other and complimenting each other, you know, I got to tell you, there are a lot of people here who are very upset, and very angry, and very frustrated. And when they hear politicians slap—you know, thanking one another, it just, you know, it kind of cuts them the wrong way right now, because literally there was a body on the streets of this town yesterday being eaten by rats because this woman had been laying in the street for forty-eight hours. And there's not enough facilities to take her up. Do you get the anger that is out here?"[77] Anderson was speaking for most Americans. Senator Landrieu, at least, was trying to do her job. Trying to get federal funds. Trying to prod the Bush administration into action. After all, her family had lost its home, too. But John McCain wasn't even trying. He was eating cake with President Bush, talking up the war with Bob Schieffer, and cracking jokes with Conan O'Brien. His actions—and lack thereof—made George W. Bush look engaged.

REVISIONIST HISTORY, JUST LIKE BUSH

In Texas we say, "Don't pee on my boot and tell me it's raining." When it came to Katrina, George W. Bush and John McCain were praying that the American people didn't realize they were peeing all over our boots. Right after Katrina, McCain spouted rhetoric about how the American people wanted oversight and accountability. He said, "There's clearly a mood for aggressive oversight on this issue, because people are demanding it. It's a national catastrophe . . . I don't know if it affects the general mood of Congress on every issue, but there's a strong desire . . . to find out what went wrong and what went right."[78]

But a week later, like the Bush suck-up he is, he voted against creating a Katrina Commission to investigate how the federal government had failed.[79] And he repeated his vote against creating a Katrina Commission again the following year.[80] He also voted against investigating waste, fraud, and abuse in the reconstruction.[81]

McCain wanted to make sure that no one found out how badly his pal Bush had bungled Katrina. He still could have voted in favor of measures to help the people of New Orleans. But he didn't. Instead, he voted against them.

CALL FOR HELP FOR KATRINA VICTIMS, THEN VOTE AGAINST IT, JUST LIKE BUSH

In his press release, McCain called on the American people to aid the victims of Katrina, but back in the Senate, McCain consistently voted against sending help to the Gulf Coast. Like the Bush Republican he is, McCain voted to leave the victims on their own. Just two weeks after Hurricane Katrina devastated the Gulf Coast, McCain voted against allowing up to fifty-two weeks of unemployment benefits for individuals under the Disaster Unemployment Assistance Program.[82] Later in 2005, McCain voted against granting access to Medicaid for up to five months for victims of Hurricane Katrina. The amendment would have also provided full federal funding for Medicaid in Louisiana, Mississippi, and Alabama for up to one year and given $800 million to compensate providers caring for Katrina evacuees.[83]

CURING HIS RECORD ON KATRINA WITH A PHOTO OP, JUST LIKE BUSH

George W. Bush's father liked to quote the Woody Allen line "Ninety percent of life is just showing up." But John McCain just couldn't find the time to show up in New Orleans. The man who boasts of his many trips to Iraq did not even bother to visit the devastation in his own country for months. In fact, thirty-nine senators went to New Orleans before McCain finally went there in March of 2006[84]—seven months after Katrina.

And even then, McCain went to Louisiana only after he was criticized in the press for not going. On March 8, 2006, the *Hill* wrote, "Not visiting the sites of one of the nation's worst natural disasters could prove to be a political liability." The paper added that McCain was among six senators who were considering running for president who had "found time to visit Iowa, New Hampshire or South Carolina—key states in the 2008 primary races" but not New Orleans. Two days after being criticized in the press in 2008—and like the typical Washington politician that he is—John McCain flew down to New Orleans in the hope that it would help his presidential campaign. Just like George W. Bush, John McCain decided to have a photo op.[85]

It began smoothly enough, with McCain playing the Bush role of compassionate conservative. McCain gave a meaningless speech that sounded pretty good. He said, "There must be no forgotten places in America, whether they have been ignored for long years by the sins of indifference and injustice, or have been left behind as the world grew smaller and more economically interdependent."[86]

But then McCain showed his true colors.

Once McCain was safely back on his comfy, air-conditioned bus, surrounded by toadies—I mean journalists—he "told reporters he was not sure if he would rebuild the Lower 9th Ward as president. 'That is why we need to go back to have a conversation about what to do—rebuild it, tear it down, you know, whatever it is,' he said."[87]

Like Bush, McCain wants to rebuild Iraq. He wants to build roads and bridges and housing and hospitals for that war-torn country. But he does not know if we should rebuild one of the great cities in our own country? How very Bushian.

SUCK UP TO RIGHT-WING, NUTCASE PREACHERS, JUST LIKE BUSH

Pastor John Hagee is a San Antonio–based preacher with some . . . shall we say . . . eccentric ideas. He's the leader of the so-called Christian Zionist movement, which has, laudably, rallied millions of fundamentalist Christians to support the State of Israel.[88] No one supports Israel more strongly than I do, so when I heard that, I thought, *Good for him.* I support Israel because it is our most important ally in the Middle East, the only true democracy in that region, a bulwark of freedom, a stalwart ally against terrorism, and for a thousand other historical, geopolitical, and cultural reasons. Pastor Hagee, on the other hand, supports Israel because he believes the creation of the State of Israel is a necessary precursor to the Rapture, wherein believing Christians will be bodily assumed into heaven.[89] And those Jews in Israel, whom Pastor Hagee so strongly supports today? Well, they'll be busy fighting the Battle of Armageddon, and being tossed into a fiery pit, and all manner of unpleasantness.

But who cares about his crackpot motives, right? At least Pastor Hagee supports our most important ally, so the friend of my friend is . . . a lunatic, as it happens. Hagee has suggested that the Catholic Church—my beloved Holy Mother Church—is the "great whore" and an "apostate church."[90] (Hagee later apologized for those remarks.) Hagee has insulted African-Americans, Muslims, women, gays, and the victims of Hurricane Katrina, saying, "All hurricanes are acts of God because God controls the heavens. I believe that New Orleans had a level of sin that was offensive to God and they were recipients of the judgment of God for that."[91]

Despite all of those deeply disturbing views, Pastor Hagee is a favorite of George W. Bush. When Hagee organized a pro-Israel rally in 2006, President Bush sent a message praising Hagee for "spreading the hope of God's love and the universal gift of freedom."[92] Former Bush press secretary Scott McClellan described Hagee as someone who was "able to quickly get someone on the phone at the White House."[93] Imagine that, a phone call straight from the nuthouse to the White House.

Hagee, of course, is just one of many right-wing preacher-demagogues who have had easy access to the Bush White House. The late Jerry Falwell was a Bush stalwart. Reverend Pat Robertson, who defeated Bush's father in the Iowa caucuses in 1988, has met privately with Bush. But surely this is one area in which McCain represents a major change from Bush, right?

Wrong.

Back in the 2000 GOP primaries, Bush defeated McCain in part by rallying the most conservative wing of his party. Bush even spoke at Bob Jones University, a cuckoo's nest of right-wing crackpottery rife with homophobia, anti-Catholicism, and a stunning history of racism. With the support of the haters, Bush trounced McCain in South Carolina.

Stung, McCain lashed out. He went to Virginia Beach, the home of Reverend Pat Robertson, and gave a blistering speech decrying Robertson and Falwell by name, calling them "agents of intolerance." "We are," he said, "the party of Abraham Lincoln, not Bob Jones."[94]

Phew. We finally found that 9 percent of issues on which McCain disagees with Bush. McCain hates the haters whom Bush loves.

Not so fast. When he began his campaign for the 2008 GOP nomination, one of the first things McCain did was make nice with Reverend Falwell. He had a private dinner with Falwell in Washington. Afterwards, Falwell invited McCain to be the commencement speaker at Liberty University. McCain accepted. So chummy had the two become that Falwell said, "My intent was to say that John McCain and I are friends, that I respect him and that there are no problems with yesterday."[95]

I'll bet George W. Bush could not have been prouder of his tormentor-turned-disciple.

All of McCain's pandering to the religious right paid off when he traveled down to my home state of Texas to pick up Hagee's support. McCain said, "All I can tell you is I'm very proud to have Pastor Hagee's support."[96] Later, when the fertilizer hit the ventilator over Pastor Hagee's comment that perhaps Hitler was part of God's plan, McCain renounced him. But the evidence is clear: John McCain will slither into bed with the slimiest, most hateful, most divisive people in America if it suits his political ambitions.

Just like Bush.

3

NEWS STORIES FROM THE McCAIN PRESIDENCY

History is odd. I will be long gone before the true history of the Bush administration is written.

—*George W. Bush*[1]

Q: Is there any executive power the Bush administration has claimed or exercised that you think is unconstitutional? Anything you think is simply a bad idea?

A: McCain declined to answer this question.[2]

What would a McCain presidency look like? As a public service, here are what I think some of the news clippings from a McCain presidency might be: some tragic, some comic, some farcical.

McCain Stuns Congress in His Last State of the Union Address, Calls for Iraq to Be 51st State

WASHINGTON, February 2, 2011—President John McCain told a stunned Congress he will support a petition from Iraq to join the United States of America as the 51st state.

"Our brothers and sisters in Iraq want to be a part of America," McCain said. "And I support them in their dream. My friends, we have more troops in Iraq than any other state. And they will be there for at least another ninety-two years. We spend more on infrastructure in Iraq than any other state. The United States federal government has built more schools, more roads, more hospitals, more water and electrical systems for Iraq than for any other state.

"This chamber," the president continued, "is about five thousand miles from Honolulu, and a little more than six thousand miles from Baghdad. Hawaii was once an independent nation, as was Texas."

White House Communications Director Roger Ailes told reporters the Iraqi Statehood Petition seeks admission as a territory for ten years, then full statehood. "They're planning on finishing the job of Americanizing the place," said Ailes. "The state will be named Bushland, and the capital city will be Cheney."

Gas Hits $10 a Gallon; Energy Secretary Cheney Announces, "Mission Accomplished"

WASHINGTON, May 25, 2009—The price of gasoline hit the $10 a gallon mark, causing panic before the Memorial Day weekend holiday. Consumer groups and citizens expressed anger, but the McCain administration saw good news.

"This is a mission accomplished," said Energy Secretary Dick Cheney. "If American consumers want to reduce the price of gas, they should support drilling in the Alaskan wilderness and off the coast of Florida. Until then, they can all go f#%& themselves."

McCAIN TELLS NEW LEAGUE OF DEMOCRACIES TO EXPECT "WAR AND MORE WAR"; "AXIS OF I-COUNTRIES" TARGETED

BAGHDAD, January 23, 2010—President John McCain today told the first meeting of the League of Democracies to expect "war and more war." Meeting in the heavily fortified Bush Zone, in the new $1 billion Donald Rumsfeld Embassy and Freedom Gallery, McCain told representatives of the world's democracies, "War might not be the only way to confront those who disagree with us. But it's a damned effective way."

Creation of the League was a key McCain campaign pledge, and McCain used its first meeting to sound a clarion call for military action. Surrounded by 175,000 U.S. troops, with helicopter gunships, AWACS communications planes, and Unmanned Aerial Vehicles patrolling overhead and Navy SEALs in and around the Tigris River, McCain called combating radical Islamic terrorists "the transcendent cause of our time.

"Fighting those cowards whom George W. Bush famously labeled as evildoers transcends all other matters," he said. "We are fighting them here in Iraq. We are fighting them in Iran. Soon we will fight them in Indonesia and India, and then we will root them out of Italy, Ireland, Iceland, and Israel. Why they seem drawn to the I-countries I do not know. But, my friends, we are willing to fight them in Iowa and Indiana and Illinois and Idaho as well."

McCain expressed anger over a congressional resolution calling for talks before further invasions. "How the hell are we going to talk with them, my friends?" he asked. "We don't even speak their damn language. Besides, they can't be trusted. One day they're Shiites, the next day they're Sunnis."

New Orleans 9th Ward Razed; FEMA Follows Through on McCain Campaign Pledge

NEW ORLEANS, August 28, 2009—As shocked residents looked on in horror, bulldozers from the Army Corps of Engineers destroyed every remaining structure in the Lower Ninth Ward of New Orleans.

FEMA director L. Paul Bremer III said the destruction would save money and was in keeping with a campaign pledge President McCain made in 2008. "I'm not the one who said we need to 'have a conversation about what to do—rebuild it, tear it down, you know, whatever it is.'[3] That was John McCain."

President McCain said Bremer and FEMA had "overinterpreted" his comments but urged residents to "get a life. Those homes are gone and they aren't coming back."

Fiorina Praises Outsourcing; Calls Practice "Exporting Freedom"

BANGALORE, INDIA, May 12, 2011—National Economic Council Chair Carly Fiorina today praised the outsourcing of American jobs, calling the practice "exporting freedom."

Fiorina, who famously laid off eighteen thousand employees during her tenure as CEO of Hewlett-Packard, made the remarks during a meeting with American business executives. American jobs have migrated overseas at a record pace during the McCain administration.

Fiorina said she understood how laid-off American workers felt. "Look, I was laid off by the Hewlett-Packard board," she said. "I was left with nothing but the millions of dollars they paid me to lay off tens of thousands of Americans. That and the $42 million golden parachute.[4] As I often say, 'There is no job that is America's God-given right anymore.'"[5]

Economists say the American economy is changing in fundamental ways. President McCain has, if anything, accelerated the Bush economic policies he inherited: celebrating layoffs, extending special tax privileges for the wealthiest Americans, declaring that outsourced jobs will never return.

McCAIN TAPS FORMER EXXON CEO TO HEAD EPA; PLEDGES TO "STUDY GLOBAL WARMING TILL HELL FREEZES OVER . . . OR THE ARCTIC SEA BOILS"

SEDONA, ARIZONA, December 12, 2008—President-elect John McCain today stunned environmentalists by nominating former ExxonMobil CEO Lee Raymond to lead the Environmental Protection Agency. "Lee Raymond knows the environment from the ground up. Actually from 30,000 feet below the ground."

Raymond, who holds a Ph.D. in chemical engineering, led the world's largest oil company from 1993 until 2005. But standing with the president-elect in front of the arresting vista of his Arizona ranch, Raymond stressed other aspects of his background. "I helped fund millions of dollars of research on alleged climate change," he said. "And at EPA I will study global warming until hell freezes over . . . or the Arctic Sea boils, or whatever is supposed to happen."

Environmentalists were outraged. "It's bad enough to appoint an oilman to run EPA," said Gene Karpinski of the League of Conservation Voters. "But to pretend that you are taking action on climate change by funding millions of dollars of phony research designed to deny the reality of global warming is really dishonest."

Sources close to McCain said the former ExxonMobil CEO came to the president-elect's attention through a stable of current and former ExxonMobil lobbyists who helped elect McCain. Raymond is also the former chairman of the American Petroleum Institute, the chief oil industry lobbying group.

Roe v. Wade Overturned on a 5-4 Vote; Decision Written by Justice Ken Starr

WASHINGTON, January 22, 2010—In a landmark ruling that reversed 37 years of precedent, the Supreme Court today overturned *Roe v. Wade*, paving the way for states to outlaw abortion. The majority opinion, written by the newest member of the Court, Associate Justice Ken Starr, was a ringing rejection of *Roe*. "Roe was wrongly decided and should be overruled," Starr wrote, quoting from a brief written in 1991 by his then-deputy solicitor general, John Roberts. "The Court's conclusion in *Roe* that there is a fundamental right to an abortion . . . finds no support in the text, structure, or history of the Constitution."[6]

Starr, appointed by President McCain last year to replace Justice John Paul Stevens, provided the crucial fifth vote to allow states to outlaw abortion. President McCain was quick to praise the ruling, repeating his long-held position that *Roe* was wrongly decided. McCain told reporters, "Finally, the rights of the unborn are as important as the rights of the born."[7]

In citing a brief from nineteen years ago, written by the man President George W. Bush made chief justice, legal scholars said the high court tried to situate its sweeping, revolutionary ruling in decades of conservative opposition to *Roe*.

The four dissenters—Justices Ginsburg, Breyer, Souter, and Kennedy—strongly disagreed. "For this Court to overthrow thirty-seven years of constitutional jurisprudence is nothing less than radical," wrote Justice Ginsburg in a passionate defense. "I fear for other constitutional protections. Apparently nothing is safe from this majority—not desegregation, voting rights, affirmative action or environmental protections."

Ginsburg's stinging dissent brought a vigorous rejoinder from Justice Antonin Scalia. Long a critic of *Roe*, Scalia wrote, "The dissent worries about overturning thirty-seven years of precedent, but *Roe* itself upended 184 years of precedent. Just as this nation turned away from the wrongly decided case of *Dred Scott v. Sanford*, today this Court turns away from *Roe v. Wade*."

Budget Deficit Hits Another Record High; McCain Calls for Cuts in Health Care, Education, Environmental Protection to Pay for Wars and Tax Cuts

WASHINGTON, September 27, 2010—The federal budget deficit has set a new record, with red ink reaching $780 billion when the costs of the continuing wars in Iraq and Afghanistan are counted.

The deficit had been projected to be significantly lower, budget analysts said, but President McCain's insistence on making the Bush tax cuts permanent, as well as his open-ended commitment to a massive troop presence in Iraq, combined to send the deficit over the three-quarter-trillion mark.

"We need to take drastic steps," President McCain said today. "And so I am ordering George Steinbrenner, the director of the Office of Management and Budget, to outline hundreds of billions of dollars in cuts."

White House officials, who requested anonymity because they were not authorized to disclose the cuts, said the priorities are simple: "President McCain wants to cut everything except war funding," said a senior administration official. "Well, 'wants' is perhaps the wrong word. He needs to. In order to fight two wars, and perhaps more, while cutting taxes for the wealthiest 1 percent of Americans, we will need to cut health care, education, environmental protection, National Parks, the Border Patrol, everything."

TENSIONS RISE WITH RUSSIA AS McCAIN ACCIDENTALLY FALLS ASLEEP ON NUCLEAR BUTTON

MOSCOW, November 23, 2009—The Kremlin went into panic mode briefly today as Russian military leaders thought the United States was launching an all-out thermonuclear attack. But it turned out to be a false alarm: President John McCain had simply fallen asleep on the nuclear button.

"We have trained for such a scenario," said Yuri Andrupovich, chief of staff of the Russian General Staff. "This happened with some frequency when Bush was president. I guess you Americans like to take naps at your desks."

The McCain administration downplayed the event. Arms Control and Disarmament chief Paul Wolfowitz told reporters, "There was never any danger. The so-called nuclear button is not a launch trigger. The president pushing that button without inputting the launch codes has no effect."

McCain Administration Prepares for Military Draft; Defense Secretary Lieberman Calls Move "Prudent"

WASHINGTON, June 5, 2009—The McCain administration today ordered the Selective Service System to prepare to call able-bodied Americans between the ages of eighteen and twenty-five to serve in the military.

Citing what he called "emergency powers under the Selective Service Act," Defense Secretary Joe Lieberman issued the order. "This does not mean we are going to draft everyone between the ages of eighteen and twenty-five," Lieberman said. "It just means that we are being prudent. Our armed forces need to be prepared for any eventuality. By that I mean anything from more bad intelligence briefings to a day when the president is in one of his grumpy moods."

Congressional Democrats were quick to denounce the move. "He has no authority to begin a draft," said House Speaker Nancy Pelosi. The Speaker has ordered the House Government and Oversight Committee to hold hearings on what she called "a clear abuse of power." Committee sources, however, said they are already stretched thin, given ongoing investigations into alleged influence peddling throughout the McCain administration.

President McCain reacted forcefully, telling reporters gathered on the South Lawn of the White House, "She can send the Capitol police over here. I'll meet them with the 82nd Airborne. We'll see who has the g&$#d d%$# power. Now I have to go. It's three-thirty, time for dinner."

Secretary Lieberman excoriated his fellow Democrats, lecturing them to "stop fighting partisan political wars and help this president fight more real wars."

Some Pentagon officials said they regretted the step, which they fear will further dilute the quality of the personnel in the armed forces. Speaking anonymously because he was not authorized to comment, one high-ranking military commander said, "This stinks, but we have no choice. We've been losing our best troops—to death, wounds, and retirement—we've been taking dropouts, drug dealers and the mentally ill. We have to take radical steps to restore the military."

White House spokesman Sean Hannity defended the move, telling reporters, "Some of the finest men killed in Vietnam were draftees. They would never have been able to die for our country if there hadn't been a draft."

NATIONAL PRESS CLUB NAMES BUILDING FOR MCCAIN

WASHINGTON, January 30, 2009—The National Press Club announced today it is naming its D.C. headquarters after the newly inaugurated president. The John McCain Press Building will be officially renamed in a ceremony honoring the forty-fourth president next week.

"We in the media believe in full disclosure," said one Press Club official. "And the truth is we love John McCain. We love, love, love him. He has promised to cook us his famous barbecue on the South Lawn. He's going to let us take turns riding in the presidential limousine the way we rode with him on his bus."

Some critics have suggested the move reveals a deep media bias in favor of McCain. "Nonsense," said the Press Club official. "There's nothing biased about the truth. And the truth is John McCain is just so cool. If he ever did something bad, I'm sure we'd cover that too. As if."

White House Easter Egg Roll Canceled After McCain Yells at Kids: "Get Off My Damn Lawn!"

WASHINGTON, April 24, 2011—The White House canceled the annual Easter egg roll after President McCain stormed out on the South Lawn in his bathrobe and shouted, "Hey, you kids! Get off my damn lawn!"

An embarrassed First Lady Cindy McCain tried to reassure the children, many of whom were crying at the sight of the commander in chief, who was red-faced and wearing boxer shorts and a sleeveless undershirt under his bathrobe, which, untied, flapped softly in the spring breeze.

White House social secretary Ann Coulter tried to play down the outburst, telling reporters, "That's nothing. You should have seen him when we tried to set up the annual T-ball game."

McCain Vetoes Affordable Health-Care Bill

WASHINGTON, August 13, 2010—President McCain today vetoed Democratic-sponsored legislation that would have extended health-care coverage to all Americans. Speaking at a White House press conference, where he was joined by Health and Human Services secretary Newt Gingrich, McCain said the bill "extends health insurance to people who don't want it or need it." The president went on to say, "I don't know anyone who lacks health insurance. Hell, I'm a four-time cancer patient and I have health insurance. People ought to just do what I did: get elected president and enjoy the best government-guaranteed health care money can buy."

Democrats vowed to attempt to override the veto, but with former insurance industry lobbyists dominating the McCain White House and current insurance lobbyists working the halls of Congress, Democratic hopes appeared dim. "We will fight to override," said Senate Majority Leader Harry Reid (D-NV). "But the fact is President McCain's veto pen has more clout than all fifty-nine Democratic senators put together."

The legislation, cosponsored by Senators Barack Obama (D-IL) and Hillary Clinton (D-NY), has three essential components: affordability, availability, and portability. Affordability, its sponsors said, came from providing tax credits to working families to help cover costs. Availability was guaranteed by outlawing the insurance companies' right to refuse coverage to anyone with a preexisting condition. And portability was assured by allowing Americans to keep their coverage even if they lost their job or changed jobs.

McCain Spends Thanksgiving in Iraq; Tells Troops "Only 94 Years to Go"

BAGHDAD, NOVEMBER 26, 2009—President John McCain surprised troops in Baghdad with an unannounced Thanksgiving visit. "Your service and sacrifice are appreciated by a grateful nation," the former war hero told the soldiers. "We only have ninety-four years to go."

White House aides traveling with the president insisted he was only joking, but McCain told journalists in the heavily fortified Bush Zone he was deadly serious.

McCain Names Limbaugh to Run FDA; Cites Talk Show Host's "Vast Experience With Both Food and Drugs"

WASHINGTON, January 23, 2009—President John McCain announced today he will nominate radio talk show host Rush Limbaugh to head the Food and Drug Administration. "My friends, if there are any two things Rush is an expert on, they're food and drugs," McCain said.

Limbaugh, standing with President McCain in the Rose Garden, appeared deeply moved by the nomination. "It has long been my dream," he said, "to immerse myself deeply, wholly, completely in food and drugs. Thank you, President McCain, for letting me live that dream. I will not let you down."

Senate Democrats expressed dismay. "He doesn't even have a medical degree," said Tom Harkin (D-IA), a member of the Senate Health, Education, Labor and Pensions Committee. "But I can't wait to get him under oath about his vast and voracious experience with food and drugs."

President Has Annual Physical; Doctors Mum on Results

BETHESDA, MARYLAND, August 31, 2012—President John McCain had his annual physical at Bethesda Naval Medical Center today, but doctors refused to discuss the results with reporters.

"In the interest of patient privacy we respectfully decline to address your questions," said U.S. Surgeon General Bill Frist, who participated in the president's physical. "I know it's setting the bar low, but he has a better heart than Dick Cheney and a better mind than George W. Bush."

President McCain has had cancer four times. He is the first president to come to office after having had the disease. Other presidents, most recently Ronald Reagan, have battled the disease while in office, but they had been cancer-free before assuming the presidency.

At age seventy-two when he was inaugurated, McCain became the oldest first-term president in history. He turned seventy-six this week. As a candidate, McCain allowed reporters a three-hour glimpse of his medical records, but even that limited disclosure ended when McCain assumed the presidency.

★ ★ ★

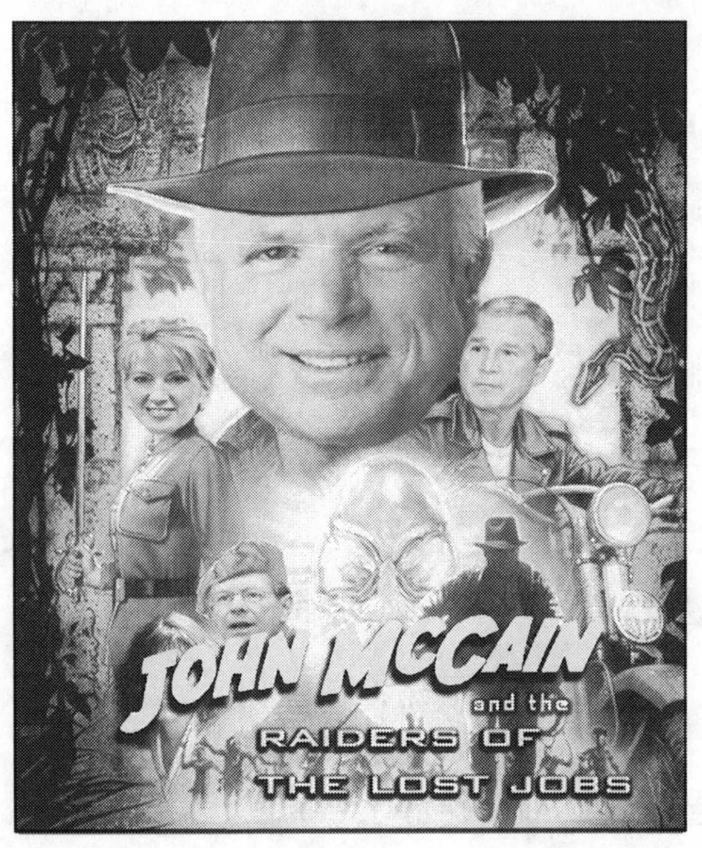
JOHN McCAIN
and the
RAIDERS OF
THE LOST JOBS

★ ★ ★

4

ECONOMY: McWORSE THAN BUSH

I believe the fundamentals of our economy are still strong.

—*John McCain*[1]

The fundamentals of our economy are strong.

—*George W. Bush*[2]

George W. Bush and John McCain are close on a lot of issues, but on economic issues they are thisclose. Inseparable, really. If John McCain embraced Bush's economic policies any more closely, they could get married in Massachusetts.

FUNDAMENTALISTS

When it comes to the economy, both George W. Bush and John McCain are self-described fundamentalists. They repeat the nostrum that "the fundamentals of the economy are strong" without really delving into what those fundamentals are. Watching these two economic illiterates, I want to scream, "Are you crazy?

What fundamentals are you looking at that are so doggone strong?" When I hear George W. Bush or John McCain blathering on about how the economic fundamentals are strong, I feel like Jack Nicholson in *Five Easy Pieces* when he hissed, "You keep on talking about the good life, Elton, 'cause it makes me puke."

At the risk of giving you gastrointestinal distress, let's take a look at those fabled fundamentals:

Jobs: Under the Bush-McCain economic policies, the American economy has created a little over five million jobs.[3] By contrast, the Clinton-Democratic policies brought twenty-three million new jobs.[4] As the Princeton economist and *New York Times* columnist Paul Krugman wrote, "If there's one thing that stands out above all over the economic record of the past sixteen years, it's the contrast between stellar employment performance under Clinton and dismal performance under Bush."[5] The difference is even greater when you look at the type of jobs each president created. Clinton produced full-time jobs, the kind that offer benefits like health insurance. In the Bush economy, by contrast, job creation has generated more part-time jobs, leaving families without benefits or health care.

Unemployment: In May 2008, the unemployment rate jumped to 5.5 percent—the largest monthly increase in twenty-three years.[6] The unemployment rate is up 1.3 percent since President Bush took office. The Clinton economy, on the other hand, was a very different story. According to the congressional Joint Economic Committee, "When President Clinton left office the unemployment rate was 4.2 percent—3.1 percentage points lower than it was when he took office."[7]

Income: The bottom line of any economic policy is ultimately the question Ronald Reagan asked: "Are you better off today than you were four years ago?" In this case it's eight years, but there's a reason the Gipper's question still resonates. Real median household income has fallen $1,273 under the Bush-McCain economic policies. Under the Clinton-Democratic policies, on the other hand, household income rose $5,825. That's a hell of a swing—from a nearly $6,000 pay raise to a $1,200 pay cut.[8]

Poverty: 5.4 million Americans who were in the middle class when George W. Bush was installed as president are in poverty today. By contrast, President Clinton's economic policies lifted 6.4 million people out of poverty. In percentage terms, the poverty rate increased 1.3 percent under Bush and declined 3.5 percent under Clinton.[9]

Consumer confidence: Consumer confidence has collapsed. As of June 2008, the Conference Board's measure of consumer confidence has fallen to a sixteen-year low. That is to say, it hasn't been this low since the last Bush recession. Another measure, compiled by Reuters and the University of Michigan, is, if possible, even gloomier. Its measure of consumer confidence is the lowest it's been since 1980—a twenty-eight-year low.[10] Under Bill Clinton consumer confidence soared 52 percent.[11]

Stock market: The Standard & Poor's 500 Index is up around 8 percent over the course of the Bush presidency. It rose 207 percent under Clinton.[12]

Federal deficit and national debt: The federal budget deficit, by the Bush administration's own projections, is estimated at $410 billion in 2008.[13] In eight years of the Bush-McCain economic program, the Republicans will have added about $4 trillion to the national debt.[14] The Clinton-Democratic economic plan eliminated the federal deficit entirely, left Mr. Bush with a large and growing surplus, and put our country on a glide path to zero national debt.[15] But instead of nearing zero, the national debt when George W. Bush leaves office will top $10 trillion.[16]

Fundamentally, the Bush-McCain economy sucks.

PETE AND REPEAT

As the Bush economic policies left millions of Americans struggling, both Bush and McCain claimed that the economy was doing just fine. The most either would say was that the economy was in a "slowdown" or a "rough patch." Frighteningly, John McCain has taken to parroting George W. Bush on the economy—word for word. Look at this:

- **"The fundamentals."** While speaking about recent economic troubles in Kansas City, President Bush said, "The **fundamentals are strong.** We're just in a rough patch."[17] In a report on CNN, McCain said, "I still believe the **fundamental underpinnings of our economy are strong,** but it's obvious that we are facing challenges, which will require actions such as the Federal Reserve took today."[18] Just a mild setback, according to Bush and McCain.

- **No recession.** According to CBS News, President Bush said, "**I don't think we're headed to a recession**, but no question we're in a slowdown."[19] While speaking at a Fox News Republican debate, McCain said, "**I don't believe we're headed into a recession.** I believe the fundamentals of this economy are strong, and I believe they will remain strong."[20]

- **"Just in a rough patch."** According to the *Los Angeles Times*, Bush said, "The fundamentals are strong. **We're just in a rough patch**, as witnessed by the employment figures today. And I'm confident we can get through this rough patch."[21] While speaking at a Fox News Republican debate, McCain said, "I believe the fundamentals of this economy are strong, and I believe they will remain strong. **This is a rough patch**, but I think America's greatness lies ahead of us."[22]

While Bush and McCain were whistling past the economic graveyard, a chorus of economic experts was contradicting their claims. The former chair of the Federal Reserve, Alan Greenspan, said there was a "50 percent or better" possibility that the United States would enter a recession in January 2008.[23] By April 2008, Greenspan said that he believed the U.S. economy was in a recession.[24] Another former chair of the Federal Reserve, Paul Volcker, described the present U.S. economic situation as not only a recession but "the mother of all crises."[25] Former treasury secretary Larry Summers chimed in, in typical

Harvard-speak, to say that it was "overwhelmingly likely" the U.S. economy was in recession. Summers also said, very clearly, that "from the perspective of Main Street and the real economy, there is a very large amount of pain left to be felt."[26] Warren Buffett, the Oracle of Omaha, joined the consensus in March, saying that, "by any commonsense definition, we are in a recession."[27]

The American public also believes the U.S. economy is in a recession: in April, a Gallup poll showed that three-quarters of Americans (76 percent) agreed that the United States is in a recession.[28] As I noted above, consumer confidence is at its lowest levels in decades.

Amazingly, Bush and McCain continued pushing for more tax cuts for the rich and more spending in Iraq, and they religiously denied that the U.S. economy was in shambles. After the economic devastation of the last eight years, John McCain's calling for continuation of the Bush economic policies is like the captain of the *Titanic* calling for more icebergs.

It wasn't until April 14, 2008, that John McCain even acknowledged the recession. During remarks at the Associated Press annual meeting he was asked if we are in recession. He said, "I certainly think so, but let me just add to that comment, America—it's really kind of a technical term used by people who are economists and make these kinds of judgment."[29]

Sure, Senator, it's a technical term. I guess it is if you, technically, are worth an estimated $100 million, and you technically own nine homes, and you technically have the best health care that American taxpayers can provide.[30] If that's the case, then I suppose a recession is really just a technical thing. How out of touch can you get?

PAGING DR. MELFI

Somewhere in America right now a man is walking into a psychiatrist's office. Let's call him Tony. Tony sits down on the psychiatrist's couch, looking pretty uncomfortable. The good doctor clears her throat and asks, "What brings you here today?" Tony reaches into his pocket and pulls out a bunch of bills. He says, "Well, Doc, I don't think you can help me with this, but John McCain said that my economic problems are psychological."

While economists and families acknowledged our economic woes, John McCain was saying things are great and our problems were psychological. At a town hall meeting in West Palm Beach, Florida, on January 24, 2008, John McCain looked his fellow Americans in the eye and said, "A lot of this is psychological. A lot of it's psychological. Because I believe the fundamentals of our economy is still strong."[31]

Set aside the contorted verb tense ("the fundamentals . . . is strong"), which in and of itself is eerily reminiscent of George W. Bush. The notion that job losses, unemployment, soaring gas prices, out-of-control health-care costs, the mortgage meltdown—all of that—is just psychological is crazy. Maybe McCain needs what my friend Kinky Friedman calls "a checkup from the neck up."

A shrink can't fix Americans' economic problems, and John McCain can't fix the U.S. economy. During a November 2006 appearance on ABC's *This Week*, John McCain said, "I think we have a very strong economy and the Bush administration and the Republican Congress deserves great credit for it."[32] On NBC's *Meet the Press*, in 2004, Tim Russert asked McCain if President Bush had "bet his presidency" on the Iraq war. McCain said, "No, I think he's bet it on the economy, which is becoming very strong and going to be very helpful to him."[33] McCain's predictions on the economy have not proven any more accurate than his prediction about Iraq, where, he said, we would be "greeted as liberators."[34]

It was not psychology that caused Bush and McCain to support policies that kept shipping our jobs overseas. The Economic Policy Institute found that from 2001 to 2006 the United States lost a *net* of 1,763,000 jobs because of growing trade deficits with China.[35] And that's just China.

DON'T KNOW MUCH ABOUT ECONOMICS

One of the reasons there are so many McCain toadies in the media is that the guy really does make great copy—like when he admits he doesn't know anything about the economy. In 2000, Jonathan Chait of the *New Republic* conducted an interview with John McCain in which McCain admitted not paying attention to economic issues. When asked about his sudden shift in economic policy, McCain said, "In the interest of full disclosure, I didn't pay nearly the attention to those issues in the past. I was probably a 'supply-sider' based on the fact that I really didn't jump into the issue."[36]

When Tim Russert confronted McCain with his self-confessed lack of economic knowledge, McCain falsely denied saying any such thing, telling Russert, "Actually, I don't know where you got that quote from. I'm very well versed in economics." Russert, who was not one to be challenged, noted that McCain had said just that—twice: "*Wall Street Journal*, November twenty-sixth, 2005. You repeated it to the *Boston Globe* in December of '07. You said it."[37]

He also confessed his ignorance to conservative columnist Cal Thomas. In an op-ed appearing in the *New York Sun,* Thomas explored McCain's lack of knowledge on economic and domestic policy. "McCain said that while he has a good handle on foreign policy, he intends to learn more on domestic issues, including economics, tax policy, and health care, saying, 'I'm going to have to be smarter on some issues than I am now.' "[38] According to a *Washington Post* op-ed, "Those who know McCain report a general lack of interest in domestic policy compared with his engagement in foreign affairs. 'It's sometimes unfairly argued that Bush is intellectually uncurious,' says one former member of Congress, 'but on domestic issues that is really true of McCain.'

McCain's foresight on Iraq has carried him far. But eventually he will need to engage Democrats on issues from health care to education to poverty. And being right on the war will not be enough."[39] During an appearance on ABC's *This Week*, McCain seemed unaware that Ben Bernanke's term as chairman of the Federal Reserve would expire during the next president's tenure. When asked if he would reappoint Bernanke, McCain said, "Oh I think . . . um, those terms of office . . . er . . ." George Stephanopoulos then told McCain that Bernanke's term expires in 2010.[40] One of McCain's Senate colleagues, whom I quote only in the strictest secrecy, once said to me, "You know, John just views the U.S. economy as a funding mechanism for his army."

But have no fear, McCain is hitting the books. Or at least one book. "The issue of economics is not something I've understood as well as I should," McCain said. "I've got Greenspan's book."[41] Greenspan is an admirable man and a dedicated public servant. But saying you're going to learn how to manage the American economy by reading Alan Greenspan's book is like me allowing my teenage son to drive because he's watched *Smokey and the Bandit.* It shows a—dare I say it?—Bushian ignorance of economics.

More and more Americans are working two jobs just to make ends meet—and John McCain thinks that's how it should be. In fact, when he finally, belatedly addressed the housing crisis in March 2008, McCain told homeowners who were struggling as a result of the housing crisis that they should be "working a second job" and "skipping a vacation."[42] This guy is Clueless Joe Jackson.

"I DON'T CARE HOW MANY JOBS YOU OUTSOURCE"

Perhaps because, like Bush, he's a multi-multi-millionaire, McCain just doesn't feel Americans' pain during this Bush-McCain recession. He has a callous and cavalier attitude that has been all too familiar to those of us who have watched George W. Bush these past eight years. In fact, McCain went to Michigan and told folks who'd lost their jobs, "There are some jobs that aren't coming back to Michigan."[43] McCain followed that up later with "I don't care how many American jobs you outsource."[44] There are millions of Americans who care a lot.

Of course, McCain's not hurting. In 2001, he was only worth "at least $14 million."[45] He now owns nine homes and has an estimated worth of $100 million.[46] No wonder he says that "Americans overall are better off" now than eight years ago[47] and "there's been great progress economically."[48] But while McCain is insulated, most Americans are not.

The public feels the economic crisis, and they're worried. In March 2008, more than three-quarters of Americans said that the U.S. economy was in a recession.[49] April brought a record number of Americans who said they were worried they would not be able to maintain their standard of living (55 percent).[50] In June 2008, a majority of Americans—55 percent—reported that they were worse off financially than they had been a year ago.[51]

But like a degenerate gambler who doesn't know how to quit when he's behind, John McCain wants to double down on Bush's economic policy.

McSAME ON THE ECONOMY

Like Bush, McCain is an economic reductionist. He believes that most—if not all—economic problems are cured by tax cuts. And tax cuts for—do I really need to say it at this point?—people making over $250,000, powerful corporations, and CEOs. Bush said, "Our message is this: We need a Republican president and a Republican Congress to prevent the Democrats from raising your taxes. We need to make the tax cuts permanent."[52] On the campaign trail in Massachusetts, McCain used almost exactly the same language. He said, "The first thing we want to do is not raise your taxes. So the tax cuts have to be permanent. We can't raise your taxes in a time of economic difficulty in America. We need to make—as I said, we need to make those tax cuts permanent."[53]

Like Bush, McCain has tried to make domestic spending the scapegoat for Bush's budget deficit, overlooking the trillions we're spending in Iraq. He rails against investing in America, but we don't hear a peep from Senator McCain about the astonishing corruption, waste, sweetheart deals, and no-bid contracts for corporations like Dick Cheney's Halliburton that have abounded in Iraq.

Pretending to be a fiscal conservative, McCain warned, "As president, I will also order a prompt and thorough review of the budgets of every federal program, department, and agency. While that top-to-bottom review is underway, we will institute a one-year pause in discretionary spending increases with the necessary exemption of military spending and veterans benefits."[54] If McCain's policy sounds familiar, that's because Bush proposed the same thing. According to the *Washington Post*, McCain's threat "mirrors the freeze in discretionary spending that Bush has had in place the past several years."[55]

The key word here is "discretionary." McCain exempts the Pentagon budget from his freeze. He exempts the massive waste and fraud in Iraq from his freeze. That means he's only freezing what budget nerds call "non-defense discretionary." That would mean deep and painful cuts in law enforcement, homeland security, food safety, consumer protection, national parks, you name it.

Given McCain's stunning—and admitted—ignorance of economics, it is more important than usual to take a hard look at who is advising McCain on economics. It's not a pretty sight.

CARLY FIORINA, OUTSOURCING QUEEN

McCain's highest-profile economic adviser is Carly Fiorina, the notorious former CEO of Hewlett-Packard. Ms. Fiorina also runs the Republican National Committee's Victory Fund.[56] Ms.

Fiorina is the Katherine Harris of Corporate America—a villain so over the top that if you didn't know the truth you'd think she was the figment of some screenwriter's drug-addled brain. McCain has called Fiorina his "role model" and said she's "very smart."[57] The *Washington Post* described her as the "face of McCain's economic team."[58]

The McCain campaign has been sticking Carly Fiorina on television as often as possible. I could not be happier. I want to see Ms. Fiorina on TV every day. She is the face of everything that's wrong with Republican economics, a poster child for corporate avarice, incompetence, and outsourcing. If she does for the McCain campaign what she did for Hewlett-Packard, McCain will be lucky to carry Utah.

Carly Fiorina's tenure as CEO of HP was described as "disastrous."[59] Jeffrey A. Sonnenfeld, the respected corporate management expert at the Yale School of Management, puts it this way: "You couldn't pick a worse, non-imprisoned CEO to be your standard-bearer."[60]

Ms. Fiorina may be best known for her catastrophic $24 billion merger with Compaq in 2003. She argued that the merger and its attendant job cuts would increase efficiency and reduce costs for HP. She forced the deal through HP, resulting in allegations of coercion and a lawsuit.[61] Between the merger and her "restructuring," she cut 18,000 jobs at HP in 2003 alone in the name of cost reduction.[62] That's 18,000 pink slips to 18,000 hardworking Americans. Eighteen thousand folks who had to walk into their homes and explain to the families they loved—the spouses and kids who were counting on them—that there would be no more paychecks.

Meanwhile Ms. Fiorina still managed to scrape together $13.5 million for lobbying fees and related expenses. She used twelve lobbying firms in addition to keeping lobbyists on staff. Laying off working people while loading up on Washington lobbyists—you don't get more Republican than that.

Two years after Fiorina's merger with Compaq, share prices were plummeting and HP was no longer the top personalcomputer company.[63] From 2000 to 2005, while Fiorina led HP, its stock decreased in value by two-thirds.[64]

When the board finally ousted Fiorina in February 2005, the former board director George Keyworth said, "She was a better saleswoman than a manager."[65] Sounds a lot like Bush and McCain. Walter Hewlett, son of cofounder William Hewlett, was less kind. He said Fiorina tried to use "a big, splashy" merger "to distract people from the fact that she wasn't really able to get her job done."[66]

Fiorina also proclaimed, à la Marie Antoinette, "there is no job that is America's God-given right anymore."[67] No, Ms. Fiorina. Not while you're shipping them overseas by the thousands. Outraged HP workers suggested she forfeit her own job in favor of a Chinese or Russian executive who would work for one-fourth of her massive salary.

Getting herself fired might have been the best thing Ms. Fiorina ever did for HP stock: after news of her exit broke, the stock price rose 11 percent.[68] But how's this for arrogant? She cited the fact that the company did better after firing her as evidence that she did a good job. I am not making this up. With an ego that would make even George W. Bush blush, she told the *New York Times,* "Well, see, the good news about business is, results count. And the results have been very clear. The results have been crystal clear. From the day I was fired, every quarter, even before they had a new CEO, has been record after record. That doesn't happen unless the foundation's been built."[69] Did you follow that? Let me reiterate it, because it is a flight of megalomania that makes the Flying Wallendas look like Cub Scout hikers: the fact that the company did better after firing her is evidence that she did a good job. Staggering, stunning conceit.

CARLY FIORINA: CORPORATE BENEDICT ARNOLD

When she wasn't laying off Americans, shipping jobs overseas, or tanking her company's stock price, Ms. Fiorina was betraying her country. As the *Washington Post* reported, "By the end of its 2003 fiscal year, Hewlett-Packard Co. had 'indefinitely' deferred taxation on $14.4 billion of foreign earnings, according to SEC filings, a move that helped lower its effective tax rate from the statutory corporate income tax rate of 35 percent to 12 percent."[70]

But parking billions overseas to avoid supporting the country that gave her the opportunity to get filthy rich is nothing compared to the help Fiorina's HP gave to the terrorist-supporting lunatics who run Iran. According to *Forbes* magazine, HP was "among many other U.S. companies" that kept offices in Dubai and were linked to Iranian traders there. As *Forbes* noted, "If you want to get around export controls, just sell the product to a front company in Dubai. The middlemen will take it from there." Why was there such demand for HP computers in Iran, which is run by ayatollahs who are, let's face it, some of the finest minds of the twelfth century? According to a leader of the Iranian Business Council, there was strong demand for "anything high-tech for military or oil services."[71] The CEO of Hewlett-Packard at the time was none other than Carly Fiorina. In fact, Ms. Fiorina bragged about Hewlett-Packard's success in the Middle East during a 2003 corporate earnings call, saying, "The [company's] strongest performance was in Europe, Middle East and Africa, where revenue was up more than six percent from the previous quarter."[72]

JOHN McCAIN, ECONOMIC HYPOCRITE

The fact that John McCain would turn to Carly Fiorina for economic advice and leadership says a lot about him, none of it good. While McCain is a man of honor, as he demonstrated in the suffering he endured for our country, Ms. Fiorina has hurt Americans and aided a terrorist state.

After all that—after laying off 18,000 people, after sowing bitterness and dissension on the HP board, after losing market share, declining stock price, public embarrassment, selling computers to the terrorist-loving ayatollahs in Iran—after all that, Carly Fiorina walked away with a $42 million golden parachute.[73] And the man she flacks for, John McCain, hypocritically feigns outrage about golden parachutes, saying, "Americans are also right to be offended when the extravagant salaries and severance deals of CEOs—in some cases, the very same CEOs who helped to bring on these market troubles—bear no relation to the success of the company or the wishes of shareholders."[74] I doubt Ms. Fiorina wrote that paragraph for Sen. McCain's economic speech.

As for trading with the enemy, there is no doubt HP's willingness to subvert American-led sanctions on the terrorist regime in Tehran hurt America and helped Iran help terrorists. If you're supporting the military and oil sectors of the Iranian regime, you're supporting two critical levers of power the ayatollahs use to subjugate the Iranian people. In a speech to the American Israel Public Affairs Committee, McCain spoke out forcefully in favor of sanctions against Iran, saying, "Years ago, the moral clarity and conviction of civilized nations came together in a divestment campaign against South Africa, helping to rid that nation of the evil of apartheid. In our day, we must use that same power and moral conviction against the regime in Iran, and help to safeguard the people of Israel and the peace of the world."[75]

Why, then, does John McCain fail to summon that moral clarity when it comes to one of his own top economic advisers?

PHIL GRAMM

The other hands on the McCain economic rudder are no better. Former Texas senator Phil Gramm is McCain's campaign cochair, as well as being the driving force behind his economic policy. CNN described Gramm as "McCain's chief economic adviser."[76] *Fortune* magazine dubbed McCain's economic policies as "vintage Gramm."[77] There's even talk of Gramm becoming treasury secretary under McCain.[78]

The idea of Phil Gramm at the helm of U.S. economic policy is outright terrifying. Gramm isn't just guilty of inaction in the housing crisis; he is partially responsible for causing it. As chairman of the Senate Banking Committee, Gramm drove through deregulation of the banking and financial services industries.[79] University of Texas economist James K. Galbraith said Gramm was "the most aggressive advocate of every predatory and rapacious element that the financial sector has" and that "he's a sorcerer's apprentice of instability and disaster in the financial system."[80]

As a rule, Gramm protects lenders at the expense of American homeowners. In 1999 he helped kill anti–predatory lending legislation in the Senate, phrasing his opposition as interest in making sure that "people with moderate income and limited credit ratings" had "the opportunity to borrow money."[81] He instructed banks to continue predatory practices, saying they "should not bow to the pressure to change practices."[82]

Ten days before Christmas 2000—only hours before the Senate's winter break began—then senator Phil Gramm tacked on an amendment to a government reauthorization bill in a move that would be described as "a stunning departure from normal legislative practice."[83] Gramm's cryptically named Commodity Futures Modernization Act amounted to a large-scale deregulation of commodities investment. In an impassioned speech, Gramm promised his amendment would serve as "a framework that will position our financial services industry to be world leaders into the new century."[84] Rarely has a speech, even a Senate speech, been so far off the mark.

Gramm's amendment became law. In essence, it stripped away years of legislation meant to protect Americans from Wall Street greed and it helped usher in an economic crisis. In 2003, the ever-prescient Warren Buffett described the investment options opened by Gramm's sweeping deregulation as "financial weapons of mass destruction."[85] We know what happened next: the housing crisis.

In 2001, as chairman of the Senate Banking Committee, Gramm flat-out refused to schedule hearings with victims of predatory lenders. He claimed that predatory lending hadn't been defined,[86] and that no action was necessary to address the issue.[87] Sounds a lot like plugging your ears and humming to me. Humming to the tune of the predatory lenders, that is. It wasn't until Paul Sarbanes, a Democrat, took over in June 2001 that the committee finally heard from these folks.[88]

Gramm has consistently blamed borrowers, not predatory lenders, for the housing crisis. He said that "the buzzword today is predatory lending, but there are predatory borrowers."[89] Tell that to the thousands of Americans who were deceived by predatory lenders who aggressively targeted the elderly and uneducated. He recently told reporters that we have become "a nation of whiners," and that we're in a "mental recession."

Since leaving the Senate, Gramm has continued his mission of serving big financial interests—but more openly as a lobbyist and executive. Two years after he pushed through an amendment that might as well have been written by the banks, he joined the giant Swiss-based bank UBS as a vice chairman. By 2005, Gramm was trading on his Washington connections as a lobbyist for UBS—lobbying Congress, the Federal Reserve, and the Treasury Department about banking and mortgages.[90]

According to federal lobbying registrations, Gramm was being paid to lobby Congress on the mortgage crisis at the same time he was advising John McCain on economic policy.[91] That's what I call killing two birds with one stone: lobbying senators on the mortgage crisis for a giant Swiss bank while "advising" Senator McCain on economic issues. Can you say "conflict of interest"? Apparently Senator McCain cannot.

McCAIN ECONOMIC OPPORTUNISM: THE HOUSING CRISIS

Just like Bush, McCain favors corporations over Americans. The housing crisis is a good example. He has a long record of voting against borrowers and homeowners—and voting for banks and lenders. In 2001, he voted to kill an amendment that would protect borrowers from lenders who misrepresented the terms of a loan or agreement.[92] As of spring 2008, the McCain campaign included fifteen lobbyists with ties to the housing and lending industry.

When McCain first addressed the mortgage crisis in March 2008, he offered no hope or comfort to Americans. In fact, he blamed them. He said, "I have always been committed to the principle that it is not the duty of government to bail out and reward those who act irresponsibly, whether they are big banks or small borrowers."[93] (Keep in mind that on the same day he said he supported the Federal Reserve's bailout of Bear Stearns.[94]) McCain economic adviser Douglas Holtz-Eakin was quoted as saying that foreclosure for homeowners "may be the appropriate outcome in some cases."[95]

In the same March speech in which he told homeowners to drop dead, McCain promised not to "play election-year politics with the housing crisis"—but that's just what he did.[96] After facing a tide of criticism over his plan, he reversed himself on housing, abandoning a long history of opposing protections for homeowners to adopt a more homeowner-friendly plan. It was an election-year conversion at best.

From saying he's "always been committed" to not having government "bail out and reward" irresponsible homeowners, he began edging toward a more supportive response to the housing crisis. A few days after his initial housing speech provoked harsh criticism, he said, "I think there is some tough love here, but I think there's got to be some love as well."[97] He also said he "would be more than happy to work out ways" to help homeowners.[98] He promised to offer "every deserving American family or homeowner the opportunity to trade a burdensome mortgage for a manageable loan that reflects the market value of their home."[99]

The *Washington Post* didn't mince words. It linked McCain's shift to the sharp criticism his initial plan received, reporting that "two weeks after drawing criticism for saying he favored only a limited federal role to help deal with the home mortgage crisis, Republican presidential candidate John McCain sought to assure Americans he is prepared to use the government where necessary."[100] The *New York Times* wrote that McCain had "pivoted" and that his new approach represented "a departure."[101] Even the *Wall Street Journal* pointed out McCain's inconsistency on housing, calling it a "major shift," commenting, "McCain called for an aggressive federal government role aimed at stabilizing the housing market, rejecting a largely hands-off approach he outlined two weeks ago."[102]

★ ★ ★

AS THE MORTGAGE CRISIS BECAME A POLITICAL ISSUE

"Unlike Rivals, McCain Rejects Broad U.S. Aid on Mortgages" [*New York Times*, 3/26/08]

"McCain 'Mean-Spirited and Economically Naïve' " [*New York Times*, 3/27/08]

CBS/*NYT* Poll Shows Housing Crisis Is Top Economic Issue. A CBS/*New York Times* poll released on April 3 revealed that 14 percent of Americans "named housing and the home mortgage crises" as the most important economic problem facing the country. [CBS News, 4/3/08]

Gallup Poll Shows Majority of Americans Favor Federal Help for Mortgage Crisis. A Gallup poll released on April 3 showed "that 6 in 10 Americans oppose the federal government taking steps to help prevent major Wall Street investment companies from failing," but that "in sharp contrast to their opposition to helping Wall Street investment companies, Americans—by a margin of 56% to 42%—support having the federal government take steps to help prevent people from losing their homes because they can't pay their mortgages." [Gallup, 4/3/08]

After all of his pivoting, dodging, hedging, and spinning on housing, McCain ended up pretty far from where he's been for most of his career. After consistently blaming homeowners, he started promising, "To help our workers and our economy, we must also act in the here and now." He said "our government will offer these Americans direct and immediate help."[103] During a political campaign, McCain may try to run from his long record of hammering homeowners and helping big banks, but as Joe Louis said about Billy Conn, "He can run but he can't hide."

JOHN McCAIN FLIP-FLOPPED ON THE MORTGAGE CRISIS

"McCain's New Housing Approach Represents a Major Shift" [*Wall Street Journal*, 4/11/08]

"McCain Reverses Himself on Mortgage Position" [*New York Times*, 4/11/08]

"McCain's Views on the Housing Crisis Appear to Be Evolving Quickly" [*American Banker*, 4/10/08]

"Conservatives Attack McCain for Shift" [*Atlantic*, 4/10/08]

"A Shift in Tone From McCain's Admonition Two Weeks Ago" [*Los Angeles Times*, 4/11/08]

THE MCCAIN ECONOMIC PLAN: MAKE BUSH'S PLAN PERMANENT

Given McCain's relationship to Bush and his cast of advisers, it's no surprise that his policies are out of touch. But McCain's economic plan isn't just out of touch. It's pure fantasy. Like Bush, he operates outside the realm of math and fact. A fact-check of McCain's economic plan shows it's well outside the bounds of fiscal reality.[104] No one can expect the presidential candidates to have perfect math, but McCain's figures are "out of whack by orders of magnitude beyond those of either Democratic candidate,"[105] said Dr. Jared Bernstein, the founder of the Economic Policy Institute.

Even as he rails against spending, McCain wants to make Bush's massive tax breaks for the very wealthy and big corporations permanent—while doing little for middle-class Americans.

McCain is offering more of the same economic policies that drove the U.S. economy into recession under Bush. Yet McCain has claimed, again and again, that he's different—that the Bush administration's economic woes are a result of wasteful spending. He's right about one thing: Bush is the king of wasteful spending. But McCain is wrong when he claims his economic plan would have a different effect. In fact, when it comes to the economy, McCain isn't just like Bush—he's worse than Bush. The Brookings Institution's Tax Policy Center found McCain would decrease federal revenues by 25 percent over ten years, the equivalent of leaping backward sixty years. The Center for Budget and Policy Priorities labeled McCain's economic plan "one of the most fiscally irresponsible plans we've seen by a presidential candidate in a long time."[106]

McCAIN WANTS TO MAKE PERMANENT TAX CUTS HE DIDN'T EVEN THINK SHOULD BE TEMPORARY

That's like marrying a girl you didn't want to date. It is not merely inconsistent; it's incoherent. If temporary tax cuts that are skewed to the wealthy are bad, then permanent tax cuts that are skewed to the wealthy are worse. But not in McCain-land.

We can look to McCain himself, circa 2001, for testimony that Bush's tax breaks helped the wealthy against the interests of the middle class—and that Bush's tax plan would hurt the United States economically and make the budget deficit worse. Back then, he opposed Bush's tax policies, saying, "I cannot in good conscience support a tax cut in which so many of the benefits go to the most fortunate among us at the expense of middle-class Americans who need tax relief."[107]

McCain even played the war hero card. He argued in 2004, "Throughout our history, wartime has been a time of sacrifice. . . . What have we sacrificed?" He continued, "Nothing tops my confusion for cutting taxes during wartime. I don't remember ever in the history of warfare when we cut taxes."[108]

In fact, "pre-hug" McCain was so concerned about Bush's tax breaks that he wrote the president a letter warning him that his plan would make the deficit worse and limit economic growth. In 2003, McCain wrote, "Deficits constrain our ability to respond effectively to unanticipated fiscal events. If we do not reduce them, projected long-term deficits will reach dangerous levels, lowering the national income and standards of living for future American generations."[109] McCain was right. The deficit has become a danger to Americans' economic well-being.

In the same letter, McCain wrote, "I would still be open, at some point, to proposals to stimulate the economy with tax cuts. But not now. We should, Mr. President, take a pause in our efforts to increase spending on non-defense needs and to reduce taxes."[110]

Then McCain hugged Bush. The fiscal situation has only deteriorated over the past five years, yet now McCain advocates making permanent the tax cuts he said would endanger Americans and their children for generations. On NBC's *Meet the Press*, McCain said, "We've got to make these tax cuts permanent. We have to, otherwise I think it'll have a negative impact on our economy."[111]

McCain's creepy, cozy relationship with Bush just keeps getting closer. In 2001, 2002, and 2003, McCain voted against accelerating the repeal of the estate tax.[112] As recently as 2006, McCain argued that repealing the estate tax would expand the deficit "too much."[113] Then later in 2006, McCain fell in line with Bush and the Republican Party, voting to move forward with the permanent repeal of the estate tax.[114] As Paul Krugman of the *New York Times* explained, McCain believes that "increasing the wealth of people who are already in line to inherit millions or tens of millions is more important than taking care of fellow citizens who need a helping hand."[115]

Worse than hugging Bush, McCain hugged a long record of crazy right-wing economic theory. McCain became a born-again supply-sider. During his very public conversion, McCain started telling everyone who would listen how cutting taxes increases revenues. In 2007, he claimed, "Tax cuts, starting with Kennedy, as we all know, increase revenues."[116] The *New York Times* reported that while campaigning in South Carolina in January, McCain told supporters, "Every time in history we have raised taxes it has cut revenues. And is there anybody here that needs to have their taxes increased?"[117] That's a pivot for the Panderers' Hall of Fame.

It's also—how do I say this delicately?—a load of crap. A bunch of bull. A pile of steaming horse-hockey. Bullfeathers. Balderdash. Hogwash. Buncombe. Caca.

As the nonpartisan watchdogs at FactCheck.org have written: "The Congressional Budget Office, the Treasury Department, the Joint Committee on Taxation, the White House's Council of Economic Advisers and a former Bush administration economist all say that tax cuts lead to revenues that are lower than they otherwise would have been. . . . "[118] Alan D. Viard, who worked as an economist in the Bush White House and also did a stint at the Treasury Department's Office of Tax Analysis, told FactCheck.org, "Federal revenue is lower today than it would have been without the tax cuts. . . . Among economists, there's no dispute."[119] Viard is no apostate. He works now at the conservative American Enterprise Institute. But he says, "I found Senator McCain's statement rather disappointing on this matter."[120]

Of course, a few of McCain's bad tax policies predate Bush—like his opposition to the Earned Income Tax Credit (EITC), which helps struggling American families who choose work over welfare. It is a pro-work, pro-family, anti-welfare tax cut first championed by Milton Friedman. Ronald Reagan called it "the best anti-poverty, the best pro-family, the best job creation measure to come out of Congress."[121]

In 1993, McCain voted against expanding the EITC.[122] Then in 1995, he voted for the 1996 Republican budget, which would cut the EITC—by $43.2 billion.[123] He also voted for an additional amendment to reduce spending on the EITC by $32 billion.[124] When another senator offered an amendment that gave

McCain the choice between cutting the EITC and repealing tax preferences for corporations, McCain voted to kill the amendment.[125] That is to say he would rather cut taxes for wealthy and powerful corporations than for struggling families who choose work over welfare. He took another shot at the EITC in 2004 by voting against an amendment that would protect the EITC from $14 billion in cuts.[126] Keep in mind, this is one of Ronald Reagan's favorite tax cuts that McCain is opposing—and no one ever accused Ronald Reagan of being overly generous to the poor.

TAX BREAKS FOR CORPORATIONS, BUT NO RELIEF FOR AMERICANS

McCain loves his language of personal responsibility when it comes to individuals, but he'll bend over backward to make life easier for corporations. He says homeowners caught in the housing crisis are responsible for their situation, and that Americans should be working a second job and skipping vacations. But what about ExxonMobil? If you want a welfare queen, look no further. Even as he does nothing to address American families' economic struggles, McCain calls for billions in taxpayer subsidies—that is, corporate welfare—for the polluters and profiteers at ExxonMobil, as well as every other big corporation in America.

He would cut the corporate income tax from 35 percent to 25 percent. According to the Center for American Progress Action Fund, McCain's plan would give corporations $170 billion in tax cuts. The five largest American oil companies would get breaks worth $3.8 billion a year. The top ten American insurance companies would rake in $1.9 billion a year.[127] Over a ten-year period, McCain's proposal would transfer $995 billion from the American people to big corporations.[128]

McCain also came up with some less obvious ways to slip perks to corporate interests. He would allow corporations to immediately expense investments in equipment and technology. I call it the Mother of All Loopholes. Over ten years, McCain's plan for corporate expensing would cost the American people at least $745 billion, according to the Center for American Progress Action Fund.[129] The true cost may be much higher. An estimate from the U.S. Department of the Treasury for a less generous proposal, to allow corporations to write off only 35 percent of investments, projected the cost at $1.3 trillion over ten years.[130]

The total cost of McCain's new proposed tax policies, between corporate tax breaks and allowing corporations to expense investments, would be at least $1.74 trillion over ten years.[131] That's almost too much to imagine. $1.74 *trillion*. Not millions. Not billions. *Trillions.* All of it coming from hardworking, taxpaying American families. And all of it going to large, heartless, avaricious, powerful corporations.

McCAIN CAN'T PAY FOR HIS TAX CUTS

Senator McCain likes to say he is against "earmarks"—congressionally directed spending. But the truth is that while he opposes congressional action to actually help the American people—by building hospitals, schools, bridges, and roads, for example—he is all for tax breaks that amount to earmarks for corporations or lobbyists.

McCain blames earmarks and pork-barrel spending for America's economic strain, but he somehow overlooks the $12 billion a month the Bush administration sends to Afghanistan and Iraq and Bush's extravagant tax breaks for corporations and the wealthy. Spending on defense and homeland security grew from 3.6 to 5.6 percent as a share of GDP under Bush, while domestic spending shrank from 3.1 to 2.8 percent.[132] Bush's tax cuts cost $3.7 trillion over ten years.[133] To compare the cost of these tax cuts with the social spending McCain claims is the biggest drain on the economy, the cost of Bush's tax cuts *each year* is eight times as much as the United States spends on K–12 and vocational education, and ten times our spending on hospital and medical care for veterans.[134]

In addition to making Bush's tax breaks permanent, McCain's plan would cut taxes by an additional $300 billion. All said, his plan would give $650 billion in tax breaks for corporations and the wealthy. Like the rest of his economic policies, McCain's tax cuts are fantastic—in the sense of fantasy, unicorns, and griffins, not in the "terrific" or "full-speed ahead" meaning of the word.

McCain says he can save $100 billion in earmarks, but he's full of beans. The most generous estimates place earmarks at only $18 billion in 2008.[135] According to the *Wall Street Journal*, all earmarks from 2008 totaled only $16.8 billion—a number that comes from the Office of Management and Budget.[136] Taxpayers for Common Sense estimated 2008 earmarks at $14.8 billion, while the *Washington Post*[137] and the *Economist* reported a total of $18 billion.[138] That's spit in the ocean compared to the money McCain wants to spend in Iraq, and the trillions he wants to lavish on big corporations and the megarich.

McCain has attempted to backtrack and widen his definition of earmarks, but that doesn't get him out of trouble. He sent out his director of Economic Policy, Douglas Holtz-Eakin, to explain that he would use the Congressional Research Service's definition of an earmark. The looser definition used by CRS would drive the estimate for earmarks up to $60 billion.[139] That's still $40 billion short of what McCain says he would save.

The *Wall Street Journal* stated simply, "Eliminating earmarks wouldn't restore revenue lost by Senator McCain's other propositions, including a litany of tax cuts. He plans to not raise taxes, but he also plans to increase the size of the military and institute health-care overhauls."[140] Even if McCain used CRS's liberal definition of an earmark, he would have to cut spending on social services and programs—like housing and cancer research—by at least 20 percent.[141]

The broadened definition of earmarks also leaves McCain

running to abandon his promise to eliminate all earmarks. He claimed, "The first earmarked bill that comes across my desk as president of the United States, I will veto it."[142] But throughout his presidential campaign, he has made a never-ending string of exceptions to his strict anti-earmark rule. For example, military housing is an earmark, as is aid to Israel,[143] our most important ally in the Middle East.[144]

No one seriously believes that John McCain, who has a perfect record of support for Israel over the twenty-five years he's been in Washington, would actually eliminate all aid to Israel. Which is why no one seriously believes his shell game on earmarks is anything other than pathetic grandstanding at best or purposeful mendacity at worst.

McCain also isn't as staunchly anti-earmark as he'd like us to believe.

- In the late 1980s, he helped pitch a request for $275.8 million to fund the Central Arizona Project, a water development initiative.[145]

- In 1990, he fought for $25 million for a space lab in Arizona.[146] According to Senator Dennis DeConcini, he "talked tough" to get the funding for Arizona. DeConcini also bragged about having interceded with then defense secretary Cheney to get the funding, saying, "Did we do anything wrong by interceding? Well, that's what I do for you, ladies and gentlemen. Maybe you didn't know it, but that's what I do. That's what I did for McDonnell-Douglas."[147] It's no surprise McCain lobbied for an earmark alongside a lobbyist-friendly colleague.

- In 1998, McCain fought for $4.2 million for a national mediation center in Tucson.[148]

- In 1999, McCain earmarked $56 million for a flood-control project in Arizona.[149] He even claimed this project in a press release in 1999 as "one of more than twenty initiatives either sponsored or cosponsored by Senator John McCain" during the 106th Congress.[150]

- In 2000, the *New York Times* reported on one of McCain's pet projects from 1991: a $3 million road in Arizona called the Turquoise Trail.[151] Lest he try to distance himself from his earmark, there's documentation tying him to it—in his own hand. He wrote a letter to Senator Frank Lautenberg advocating for the project, selling it as "a reliable and critically needed link between communities and employment centers."[152] In fact, the Turquoise Trail made the *Arizona Republic*'s list of "8 incidents that complicate" McCain's claim to being a maverick.[153]

It's not that these aren't worthy projects—it's that McCain claims he doesn't ask for earmarks when he has. If you ask me, earmarks are a smaller problem in Washington than hypocrisy.

WHAT McCAIN WOULD REALLY CUT

In order to fund the one-hundred-year war in Iraq and the $1.74 trillion in tax cuts for the hyper-rich and corporations, McCain would have to gut government services. Not trim earmarks, not crack down on waste, fraud, and abuse, not reduce pork. McCain hasn't said what he'd cut—but you can bet it won't be defense. According to an analysis of his economic proposals by FactCheck.org, "he hasn't said what he'd cut out of the discretionary budget. . . . He's even indicated that defense spending might increase."[154] Defense spending is likely to go up no matter who becomes president—if for no other reason than to rebuild our weakened army and Marine Corps after those heroes have borne the burden of the Bush-McCain Iraq policy for so many years.

All this means that McCain would have to cut domestic programs drastically to pay for his plans. The *Wall Street Journal* reported, "Most if not all of the cuts would have to come from domestic programs. The discretionary budget, which excludes entitlements such as Medicare or Social Security, covers areas such as medical research, federal prisons, border security, student loans, food inspections and much else."[155] They say his plan would mean "unprecedented spending cuts equal to one-third of federal spending on domestic programs."[156] The director of the Center on Budget and Policy Priorities, Bob Greenstein, said that "the cuts that would be needed to balance the books are 'inconceivable,' and 'wildly draconian.' "[157]

Jared Bernstein of the Economic Policy Institute agrees, saying that McCain's economic plan "clearly falls into the yo-yo camp." I'm with him there. Bernstein also debunks McCain's claim that he could pay for his policies with earmarks in unambiguous terms: "Earmarks don't even begin to scratch this itch. He can't get there with earmarks. The only way he can do that is by cutting the heck out of government spending, and it's not just discretionary spending stuff like training programs and child-care slots—it's entitlements. McCain's target, if he were telling the truth, is Social Security and Medicare. He can't possibly achieve what he wants to do without slicing government to the point where it would be unrecognizable and wouldn't provide the services that lots of people need."[158]

The McCain campaign denies that his economic policies would require spending reductions but Ronald Pearlman, Reagan's assistant secretary for tax policy, is calling McCain's bluff. Pearlman, who now teaches at Georgetown Law School, told the *Wall Street Journal* that the campaign's claim is "so intellectually dishonest it's outrageous." With no facts to turn to, a campaign spokesman replied only with, "Clearly there is a difference of opinion here."[159] Last I checked, addition and subtraction weren't a matter of opinion. If McCain wants to give trillions in tax breaks to the wealthy and corporations while boosting defense, he'll have to find the money somewhere. What he doesn't want to tell you is that he's going to find it in Social Security, Medicare, environmental protection, education, medical research, law enforcement, and other essential government services.

McCain has had Social Security and Medicare on the cutting block for a while. In the last fifteen years, McCain has rejected at least seventeen attempts to protect both programs.[160] He's chosen tax cuts over Social Security and Medicare before, and he's voted against protecting these programs for American seniors. McCain won't say whether he'll raise the eligibility age or cut benefits, but he's said they're on the table. I wouldn't bet on the health of either program with McCain in office.

McCain has a long and bad history on Social Security. Even before Bush took office, he was on the wrong side of seniors' issues. He has consistently opposed legislation to keep Social Security and Medicare surpluses from being spent elsewhere.[161] When he has had to choose between prioritizing tax cuts for the wealthy and the future of Social Security and Medicare, he has voted with the wealthy—and with Bush.[162]

For example, in 1999 he picked tax cuts over reserving the Social Security surplus for, well, Social Security. The same legislation would have directed funds to keeping Medicare solvent.[163] That same year he took another firm stand for his fellow millionaires, voting to protect $320 billion in tax breaks for the wealthy rather than direct the funds to Medicare or debt reduction.[164]

THE BUSH-McCAIN PLAN TO PRIVATIZE SOCIAL SECURITY

On March 3, 2008, the *Wall Street Journal* published one of the most remarkable interviews I have ever read. The paper wanted to talk to McCain about his economic priorities. Social Security, inevitably, came up. When he ran in 2000, he had proposed privatizing part of Social Security—the *Journal* called it "a centerpiece of McCain's 2000 presidential bid," and noted that he had been a strong supporter of President Bush's Social Security privatization plan. But in 2008, the paper noted, he had moved far away from that position, reporting that the official McCain website calls for private accounts *in addition to, not in place of,* guaranteed Social Security benefits. The difference is 180 degrees. Many Democrats support private accounts as an add-on to traditional guaranteed Social Security benefits, which is the position on McCain's website in 2008. The fight is over whether private accounts should *replace* part of the guarantee—a dream long held by George W. Bush and the position McCain supported before 2008.

The *Journal* asked him why he'd changed positions. I can't improve on the paper's account, so read it for yourself:

> Asked about the apparent change in position in the interview, Sen. McCain said he hadn't made one. "I'm totally in favor of personal savings accounts," he says. When reminded that his Web site says something different, he says he will change the Web site. (As of Sunday night, he hadn't.) "As part of Social Security reform, I believe that private savings accounts are a part of it—along the lines that President Bush proposed."[165]

It's a flip-flop-flip. He supported the Bush plan to privatize Social Security. Then he adopted the Democratic position of protecting Social Security. And then he switched again—even attacking his own campaign's position paper. How great is that? Most right-wing Republican politicians at least pretend they love Social Security while campaigning, then savage it when they get into office. McCain hates Social Security and supports the Bush-McCain plan to privatize it so strongly that he renounced his own campaign platform. I don't think I've ever seen that before.

But it's in keeping with McCain's long-standing, deeply held antipathy toward Social Security and Medicare. In 2005, the two amigos, Bush and McCain, teamed up to sell Bush's Social Security privatization scheme. While appearing with the president in Tucson, Arizona, in 2005, McCain wholeheartedly endorsed the Bush plan to replace part of the guaranteed Social Security benefit with risky so-called private accounts, saying, "Private savings accounts work. They have been proven to work not only in America but all over the world, and we ought to really strongly support it."[166]

The Associated Press described the 2005 Bush-McCain Social Security Privatization Tour as a "good-cop, bad-cop routine."[167] McCain gave an Oscar-worthy performance, backing up Bush with some creative fictions about Social Security. He claimed that in 2042, "We stop paying people Social Security." But, as the *St. Petersburg Times* pointed out, "McCain knows this isn't true." It's true that in 2041—not 2042—Social Security reserves would be exhausted, but benefits would shrink to 75 percent, not zero.[168]

McCain has also consistently voted against protecting Medicare. He's opposed efforts to extend its solvency at least nine times.[169] He has also voted twice to raise the eligibility age, making older Americans wait longer to get help paying for health care.[170] Between 1995 and 2008, he voted against funding for Medicare no fewer than 28 times.[171]

McCain economic adviser Douglas Holtz-Eakin used the same disarming—and distressing—bluntness his boss is known for when he said, "You can't keep promises made to retirees."[172] No, Doug. *You* can't keep promises to retirees because you're going to squander America's treasure on trillions in tax breaks for corporations and CEOs. But *we* can keep those promises—and we will—by electing Barack Obama president, keeping Nancy Pelosi as Speaker, and Harry Reid as Senate majority leader.

LIKE THE BUSH DEFICIT? YOU'LL LOVE THE McCAIN McDEFICIT

What happens when you spend endlessly in Iraq and lower taxes on corporations and the wealthy? The largest deficit in American history, that's what. That's a burden your children and grandchildren and great-grandchildren will bear for one hundred years. That is, once they return from duty in Iraq.

If McCain got his way on the economy, he would rack up the biggest budget deficit in a quarter of a century, and the largest debt since World War II.[173] The *Wall Street Journal* reported that McCain's plan would "explode" the deficit or force "unprecedented" cuts to discretionary spending.[174] The Center for American Progress Action Fund projected the full effect of McCain's tax breaks and stated, "After McCain's four years of Bush-style fiscal irresponsibility, tax breaks for corporations, and more tax cuts for the wealthy, America would have a $780 billion deficit (4.3 percent of GDP) and national debt of $8.5 trillion (47 percent of GDP). That's over $1.5 trillion more debt than would be accumulated under a continuation of current Bush policies."[175]

THE BOTTOM LINE

The bottom line on McCain and the economy is as clear as it is frightening. The man is a Bush clone. Like Bush, he doesn't know squat about the economy. Like Bush, he supports trillions of dollars in tax cuts for those who need it least—wealthy individuals and powerful corporations. Like Bush, he wants to cut Medicare and Medicaid, kill off Social Security, and wage war against the middle class.

A middle-class American who supports John McCain's economic policies is like a chicken voting for Col. Sanders.

5

IRAQ: BUSH ON STEROIDS

We've got to stay the course and we will stay the course.

—*George W. Bush, April 19, 2004*[1]

We've got to stay the course.

—*John McCain, October 24, 2004*[2]

When it comes to the war in Iraq, John McCain is George Bush on steroids. He wants more troops, more money, and more wars. McCain biographer Matt Welch wrote in the *Economist* that McCain "offers a more militaristic foreign policy than any U.S. president in a century."[3]

Like Bush, McCain is obsessed with the war in Iraq. But McCain goes further than Bush—he wants more boots on the ground right away, and he has said he is willing to keep U.S. troops in Iraq for one hundred years.[4] As he's told the American people several times, there are going to be more wars.[5] McCain has already started the drumbeat of war with Iran. Given the situation today—worldwide terrorism a constant threat, Osama

★ ★ ★

I'LL NEVER LET GO, GEORGE! I PROMISE.

★ ★ ★

bin Laden still on the loose, our military stretched to the breaking point,[6] taxpayers spending trillions in Iraq that we could use to transform our country—one has to question McCain's judgment when he talks about staying in Iraq one hundred years and waging more wars.

McCain's obsession with war has been a boon to George W. Bush. As Bush has played the ultimate cowboy on the world stage, bucking the world community, McCain has been his loyal sidekick: Gabby Hayes to Bush's Hopalong Cassidy. McCain was one of sixteen senators to cosponsor the Use of Forces Authorization that paved the way for Bush to invade Iraq,[7] and was among the Bush-Cheney administration's chief cheerleaders for war.

Echoing President Bush, McCain told the country that "Saddam Hussein continues to acquire, amass, and improve on his arsenal of weapons of mass destruction."[8] McCain also mimicked Dick Cheney, saying, "The Iraqi people will greet us as liberators."[9] He touted how quick and easy the war would be: "it will not be nearly as difficult as some allege";[10] "this conflict is still going to be relatively short."[11] Five years later, history has proved McCain wrong—again and again and again.

For someone who constantly boasts of his expertise in national security policy, McCain has been astoundingly off the mark on Iraq. In April 2003, McCain said, "The end is very much in sight."[12] During a *Meet the Press* appearance in 2003, McCain, talking about the war in Iraq, said, "We're going to prevail and we will win and it'll be one of the best things that's happened to America and the world in a long time."[13]

Even as more and more people in Washington and across America realized that Bush was digging a deeper hole in Iraq, McCain just kept on shoveling. Bush and McCain stayed relentlessly on their talking points, with McCain repeatedly saying, "We're on the right course"[14] and "stay the course."[15] McCain painted a rosy picture of Iraq, even when all evidence pointed to a very grim reality. When violence in Iraq was still at its peak in 2007, McCain praised the safe neighborhoods, claiming that there "are neighborhoods in Baghdad where you and I could walk through those neighborhoods, today."[16] That is, if, like McCain, you were wearing a flak jacket, surrounded by one hundred American soldiers, with three Black Hawk helicopters and two Apache gunships overhead.[17]

BUT DIDN'T McCAIN CALL FOR RUMSFELD TO BE FIRED?

One of McCain's great revisionist myths is that he was a consistent critic of Donald Rumsfeld's handling of the war. As so often is the case, the truth is more complicated. To be sure, McCain offered the occasional criticism of Rumsfeld, but even as Republican senators were calling for Rumsfeld's head, McCain never called for his ouster. At other times McCain praised Rumsfeld, saying he was an "admirer"[18] and that Rumsfeld had "done a good job."[19] Even in the wake of the Abu Ghraib scandal, McCain defended Rumsfeld. Appearing on the unintentional comedy show *Hannity & Colmes*, McCain was asked whether Rumsfeld could still be effective in his job. "Yes, today I do and I believe he's done a fine job,"[20] McCain responded. He continued, describing Rumsfeld as "an honorable man."[21] In 2006, McCain still refused to call for Rumsfeld to resign. McCain said, "I will continue to work with Secretary Rumsfeld as much as I can as long as he is secretary of defense. We have to, because we need to win this war."[22] In the end, not even McCain could save Rummy. But I'm sure Rummy is thankful he tried. America, on the other hand, is not.

THE "McCAIN SURGE" HAS FAILED

Today, we have McCain to thank for helping Bush continue the war. When it comes to the surge in Iraq, Bush has had no greater friend than McCain. Some people even called it the "McCain Surge."[23]

During an April 2008 speech to the Veterans of Foreign Wars, McCain said, "The American people deserve the truth from their leaders. They deserve a candid assessment of the progress." Mr. Straight Talk then proceeded to give us more Bush double-talk. McCain touted the success of the surge—"the dramatic reduction in violence"—and Iraq experiencing "a return to something approaching normal political and economic life." The very day McCain made those remarks, the *Los Angeles Times* ran a story with the headline "Officials Foresee No Ebb in Iraq Violence."[24] I do not know if Senator McCain's fervor for this godawful war has blinded him to the reality or if he is simply so out of touch as to be disconnected from reality. But at some level it does not matter. We have seen the cost—in blood and treasure—of having a commander in chief who will not deal with the real world.

The whole point of the so-called surge of U.S. troops was to create room for political progress in Iraq. Judging by that measure, the surge of which McCain is so proud has been a complete failure. When it comes to political progress, even General David Petraeus has admitted that "no one" in the U.S. and Iraqi governments "feels that there has been sufficient progress by any means in the area of national reconciliation."[25] Yet with continuing violence and little political progress, McCain still argues for the same strategy. It's as if McCain's Iraq policy had been written and directed by the producers of *Groundhog Day*. The same course, day after day, year after year, with no end in sight. *Groundhog Day*, of course, is a classic Bill Murray comedy. But nobody's laughing at the prospect of an endless Bush-McCain war in Iraq.

And when I say no end in sight, that's not an exaggeration. In May 2008, McCain gave a speech in which he said he hoped the troops would be home by 2013—which, conveniently, is the end of the next president's first term.[26] Hurray, the McCain suck-ups in the media cheered, McCain has finally committed to pulling troops out of Iraq. But, sadly, no. In his speech McCain didn't outline a plan to make that happen. He didn't set any benchmarks or timetables. Nothing. As the *New York Observer* wrote, "[John McCain] does not believe in timetables or deadlines, secret or otherwise."[27] He does, apparently, believe in endless war.

ONE HUNDRED YEARS OF SOLITUDE

While Campaign McCain "hopes" to have the troops home by 2013, future president McCain says he's "fine" if they're in Iraq for one hundred years. At a town hall in New Hampshire in January 2008, a questioner said, "President Bush is talking about our staying in Iraq for fifty years," at which point McCain interrupted and said, "Make it a hundred. We've been in South Korea, we've been in Japan for sixty years, we've been in South Korea for fifty years or so."[28] A few days later he took it further, saying, on *Face the Nation*, "And then I don't think Americans are concerned if we're there for one hundred years or one thousand years or ten thousand years."[29]

McCain compares leaving troops in Iraq to our long-term troop presence in South Korea and Japan and Germany. Small problem—Iraq is not South Korea or Japan or Germany. As Joe Klein of *Time* magazine wrote, "It may well be possible to station U.S. troops in small, peripheral kingdoms like Dubai or Kuwait, but Iraq is—and has always been—volatile, tenuous, centrally located and nearly as sensitive to the presence of infidels as Saudi Arabia. It is a terrible candidate for a long-term basing agreement."[30] Our troops always have been and always will be targets in Iraq, and the only way to keep them safe is to bring them home.

There's another big problem with McCain's one-hundred-year war. We don't have enough troops. The Bush/McCain Iraq strategy has stretched our military to the breaking point.[31] So what's the solution? Former Pentagon officials and military experts say the United States will need to reinstate the draft if we are going to have a long-term presence in Iraq.[32] Funny that I never hear Straight Talk McCain talk about the draft when he talks about a one-hundred-year presence in Iraq. Then again, honest talk has never been a part of the Bush/McCain Iraq strategy.

The McCain campaign has furiously tried to clean up his most extreme statements on the war, like that "one hundred years" business, claiming that anyone who brings them up is "distorting"[33] and "twisting" the truth. But there's no need to spin McCain's statements. McCain did say he is fine with leaving troops in Iraq for one hundred years—go watch him say it on YouTube. He also really did say, on multiple occasions, that there are going to be more wars. Why does he say these things? Maybe because he means them. Maybe because he actually wants troops in Iraq for one hundred years. Maybe because he believes more wars are inevitable. Maybe, just maybe, instead of making excuses and attacking those who quote him accurately, McCain defenders ought to concede the point that their man is saying exactly what he thinks.

For someone who claims to be a foreign policy expert, McCain's logic on this one shows a stunning lack of understanding about the situation in Iraq. (Of course, he can't even keep Sunni and Shiite straight[34]—that's what Joe Lieberman is for.)

"HE HASN'T SEEN A COUNTRY HE DOESN'T WANT TO BOMB OR INVADE"[35]

McCain's hawkish streak extends beyond Iraq. Bloomberg News summed it up by saying, "John McCain is at least as determined as George W. Bush to stay the course in Iraq and more confrontational than the president on foreign policy issues ranging from Russia and China to North Korea."[36]

Even as our commitment in Iraq is literally bleeding both the military and the treasury, Bush, McCain, and company have turned their sights to a new target—Iran. When it comes to Iran, McCain hasn't been content to be the backup singer to the Bush-Cheney duo. When a voter asked McCain about sending "an air mail message to Tehran," McCain answered by singing, "Bomb bomb bomb, bomb bomb Iran" to the tune of the Beach Boys' "Barbara Ann."[37] It's good to know that McCain remembers songs from the 1960s, but it's terrifying that he has such a cavalier attitude about war with Iran. I'm not the only one who's scared. Even Pat Buchanan is. "You get John McCain in the White House, and I do believe we will be at war with Iran," said Buchanan. "That's one of the things that makes me very nervous about him."[38] I was sitting with Pat one morning on the set of the *Today* show and he said McCain "will make Cheney look like Gandhi."[39]

The *Columbia Journalism Review* wrote about McCain's foreign policy, "More recently, he has said that North Korea should be threatened with 'extinction,' and has threatened to attack Iran. It's no exaggeration to say that, during this period, McCain has appeared considerably more willing to use military force than has Bush."[40]

More willing to use military force than Bush. Let that sink in. Bush was so willing, so eager to use military force that he conducted what his former press secretary called a campaign of "propaganda" to mislead the American people in supporting his war. And McCain would be **more** willing to use military force. Bush was so willing to use force that he alienated nations that had been our allies from the invasion of Normandy to the fall of the Iron Curtain. And McCain would be **more** willing to use military force. Bush was so willing to use force that he destroyed the credibility of Secretary of State Colin Powell, ignored the advice of his top army general, Eric Shinseki, dismissed the pleas of his father's national security adviser, even ignored the entreaties of the pope—and plunged this nation into an unwarranted, unwise, unjust war. *And John McCain is more willing to use force than George W. Bush.*

McCain has a long record of supporting military action in countries across the world. He supported military escalation in Bosnia, wanted to offer "defense assistance"[41] to Argentina and Brazil, and, in 2007, promised to overthrow the Libyan government. He's also taken a hard line on North Korea, wants to throw Russia out of the G8, and says we should create a League of Democracies to supplant the United Nations. Ivo Daalder, a former

National Security Council aide, said McCain "is a man who hasn't seen a country he doesn't want to bomb or invade."[42]

McCain has taken cowboy diplomacy to a whole new level. He's not a shoot first, talk later guy. He's a shoot first, talk never guy. Like Bush, McCain believes that talking with any of our enemies is appeasement. McCain says he will not talk to Iran, he will not talk to Syria, he will not talk to Cuba.

McCain's no-talk strategy flies in the face of American values—and history. Nixon talked to China, Reagan talked to the Soviet Union. Even Bush, despite his rhetoric, has held talks with North Korea, Iran, and Libya. And our strongest ally in the Middle East, Israel, has for more than a year conducted secret talks with the Syrians, using Turkey as an intermediary. A statement from Israeli prime minister Ehud Olmert said Israel and Syria are engaged in "serious and continuous" talks, "in order to achieve the goal of comprehensive peace."[43]

Talking with one's enemies is what serious world leaders—especially strong world leaders—do. As Churchill, no wimp, said, "To jaw-jaw is better than to war-war."[44]

Even McCain supporter James Baker, former secretary of state to President George H. W. Bush, disagrees with McCain. In a 2006 interview he said, "You don't just talk to your friends, you talk to your enemies as well. Diplomacy involves talking to your enemies. You don't reward your enemies necessarily by talking to them if you are tough and you know what you are doing. You don't appease them. Talking to an enemy is not in my view appeasement."[45] Instead of following the example of Baker or Nixon or Reagan or Kennedy, McCain is looking to Dubya as the model of his presidency—and taking his no-talk policy to a new level. We should all be afraid—very afraid.

THE NEOCONS' NEOCON

When you have a man like John McCain, who thinks the war in Iraq is one of the best things to happen to America, you sure hope he is surrounded by people who can pull him out of La-La Land. Unfortunately, that is not the case with McCain. His foreign policy advisers read like a who's who list of Washington neoconservatives.

McCain's top foreign policy aide, Randy Scheunemann, helped get us into Iraq, and now he's eyeing Iran. Salon.com reported that Scheunemann "was also a spokesman for the Committee to Liberate Iraq, the neoconservative outfit that promoted the overthrow of Saddam Hussein for years before it got its way in 2003—and that the committee, like most of the war's enthusiasts, insisted on the connection between al Qaeda and Baghdad,"[46] a connection that was almost wholly fictitious. Fast-forward to 2008, and Scheunemann is calling a National Intelligence Estimate that concluded that Iran stopped its nuclear weapons program "misleading."[47]

Next up is former UN ambassador John Bolton, who has advocated using force against Iran. He supports McCain in part because he believes he is more hawkish than Bush. And, dear God, he may be right. During an address to the ultra–right-wing Conservative Political Action Conference, Bolton said, "I think Senator McCain's statement here yesterday on how he would handle the Iranian program is stronger than the current Bush administration policy." He added, "I didn't think the policy the administration was pursuing was robust enough."[48]

McCain adviser Max Boot wants to invade Syria,[49] supporter Lawrence Eagleburger wants to "knock [Iran] around a bit,"[50] and informal adviser Niall Ferguson supports preemptive war with Iran.[51] McCain did not choose these men as advisers despite their aggressive, pro-war posture. He chose them because of it.

TROOPS DESERVE BETTER

McCain is an American hero, and I honor his service to our country. Hell, I never finished the Boy Scouts, so I deeply admire McCain's service in uniform. But many veterans believe he has failed as a senator to honor the service of today's men and women in uniform. Our military is stretched thin, and the men and women serving today are under immense stress. Yet McCain has voted against guaranteeing troops as much time at home as they served while deployed.[52] He won't even reimburse National Guardsmen and -women who lose their pay while they fight for our country.[53] He's also voted against body armor[54] and equipment for the troops abroad and opposed educational benefits for them at home.[55]

The GI Bill of 1944 allowed millions of veterans to get a college education and helped build the middle class, but it has failed to keep up with the skyrocketing cost of college. According to the *Hill* newspaper, "The most a veteran can receive now is approximately $9,600 per year for four years. Those who served combat tours with the National Guard or Reserves are eligible for even less—typically just $440 per month, or $5,280 a year. By contrast, the College Board reports that the average four-year public college costs more than $65,000, or about $16,250 a year, for an in-state student. A private university costs on average about $133,000 for four years."[56]

When Senators Jim Webb of Virginia and Chuck Hagel of Nebraska proposed the new 21st Century GI Bill—a bill that would make sure our veterans could afford college—McCain not only refused to cosponsor the bill but he also cosponsored a watered-down alternative bill[57] that would do far less for our veterans. Our troops have given our country 100 percent—they don't deserve less.

In May 2008, seventy-five senators from both sides of the aisle joined together to pass the Webb-Hagel 21st Century GI Bill.[58] Senator McCain was not among them. He skipped the vote. And he devoted his 2008 Memorial Day speech to a defensive denunciation of the GI Bill. He cited a study by the Congressional Budget Office, which said increasing benefits for veterans would create an incentive for troops to leave the military. And indeed, CBO projected a 16 percent decline in reenlistment if the GI Bill's generous education benefits became law.

McCain cited that 16 percent figure. Serious people nodded their heads seriously. No one wants to hurt reenlistment when we're fighting two wars. But what McCain did not tell his audience was that the very same CBO study projected a countervailing *increase* in recruitment—more young men and women would sign up due to the increased education benefits. And do you know how much those incentives would boost recruitment? That's right: 16 percent.[59]

By citing the 16 percent decline in reenlistment but failing to note the offsetting 16 percent increase in recruitment, McCain was employing a skill he no doubt acquired in his twenty-six years in politics: he was lying. Lying by omission, to be sure, but lying nonetheless. There is no conceivable way McCain could have known that the CBO study projected a 16 percent drop in reenlistment and not been aware the same study foresaw a countervailing 16 percent increase in recruitment.

Sadly, it's not just educational benefits McCain has voted against. Nearly thirty thousand troops have been injured in Iraq. McCain has voted against health care for veterans at least thirty times.[60]

Our men and women returning home from Iraq and Afghanistan have been under incredible strain. So have their families. And they have performed heroically under that strain. They've done everything our country has asked of them. But our government isn't holding up its end of the bargain. We don't have to do a favor for our veterans. Just repay one.

The scandal at Walter Reed exposed the deplorable conditions many veterans have faced. Funding for veterans' health care is woefully inadequate, yet time and time again McCain has voted against increasing funding.[61] He's voted against money for hospitals,[62] treatment,[63] and mental services.[64] McCain even voted against a bill that would have given more money to veterans' health care instead of extending tax cuts for millionaires.[65]

It doesn't end there. In addition to voting against health care for veterans, McCain has voted to gut, eliminate, or cut funding for other veterans' programs at least nine times.[66] He voted against funding the Department of Veterans Affairs. He voted against funds to make sure our National Guard members can retire with security.[67] He even voted against a cost of living adjustment for benefits,[68] which wouldn't even give vets more money, it would just make sure they could keep up.

And when McCain isn't actively voting against cutting aid to veterans, he's failing even to show up to vote on critical bills that would support them. For example, McCain failed to vote for an increase in benefits for the orphans and widows of veterans.[69]

McCain has no problem spending $12 billion a month in Iraq, but he has an issue with spending an extra $20 million to upgrade our veterans' health-care facilities.[70] Most Democrats hate the war but love the warriors. The respect and admiration all Americans have for our troops is impressive—and bipartisan. But when it comes to honoring our heroes with the health care, education, and support they need, John McCain's record does not match his rhetoric.

THE ONE PLACE McCAIN SUPPORTS PORK IS IN A COUNTRY WHERE THEY DON'T EAT PORK

John McCain claims to be a crusader against wasteful spending. He hates earmarks, he hates pork, he's a regular fiscal tightwad. Well, it turns out McCain's stance on pork is a bunch of bull.

While McCain considers money for things like highways, schools, and railroads in the United States "wasteful," he supports sending billions to Iraq for the same thing. "The American people, when it's explained what's at stake here, will support whatever is necessary,"[71] he said in 2003. Some of the projects McCain supports in Iraq are no doubt deserving, but so are many of the projects McCain opposes here at home. Here are just a few instances where McCain opposed infrastructure investment in America but supported billions in pork in Iraq:

Roads and Bridges: According to the Department of Defense, as of December 2004, the United States was working on the construction of sixty-six roads and fifty-eight railroad stations in Iraq.[72] McCain supported all of that spending without questions. A few specifics: nearly $1.5 million to build a seven-mile road connecting Showairrej, Taq Meka'ael, and Tak Harb,[73] and $147,560 to "construct six new municipal road segments in the town of Bartilla, in the Ninewa Governorate of Iraq."[74]

Even as he's supported projects in Iraq, he's opposed similar projects in America, including:

$410,000 for Bayfield County bridge projects in Wisconsin[75]

$1,000,000 for the Cameron Street Bridge in Shamokin/Coal Townships in Northumberland County, Pennsylvania[76]

$750,000 for the Tienken Road Bridge over the Paint Creek in Rochester Hills, Michigan[77]

$1,000,000 for U.S. Route 33 Corridor improvements at Winchester-Cemetery Road in Ohio[78]

$500,000 for improvements to U.S. Route 33 in Pendleton County, West Virginia[79]

$250,000 for the Blackford Bridge project in Kentucky[80]

Those six projects combined cost less than $4 million. That's "million," with an *m.* Or the cost of fifteen minutes of the war in Iraq. Keep that in mind if you're a voter in Wisconsin or Pennsylvania or Michigan or Ohio or West Virginia or Kentucky: McCain seems to care more about improving the infrastructure in Iraq than in your state. So when he comes to your state to campaign, you might want to tell him to hit the road.

Health Care for Iraqis, Not for Americans: The McCain record on health spending tracks his record on transportation: he votes against health-care facilities in America, then votes for them in Iraq. A few examples:

- According to the Department of Defense, as of December 2004, the United States was working on the construction of fourteen hospitals and forty-one public health clinics in Iraq.[81]
- As part of the reconstruction in Iraq, the United States built the Erbil Maternity and Pediatric Hospital, which was completed and turned over to the Iraqi government in May 2006.[82]
- The United States spent $1,986,462 to rehabilitate the Al Alwaiya Maternity Hospital in Baghdad.[83]
- The United States spent $579,284.70 to design and construct the Ibn Al Bitar Critical Care Unit in Baghdad after it was destroyed by looters after the initial invasion.[84]

Again, I hasten to add, these projects may well be worthwhile. But so were some of these American health-care projects McCain voted against in just one piece of legislation (the Fiscal Year 2004 Consolidated Appropriations Bill):

- $450,000 for pediatric diabetes research in Oklahoma[85]
- $1.2 million for a pediatric mobile unit in Tennessee[86]
- $167,000 for a pediatric brain tumor and neurological disease institute in Florida[87]
- $200,000 to renovate the maternity facility at Sinai Hospital in Baltimore, Maryland[88]
- $100,000 for pediatric center renovations and expansion at Cape Cod Hospital in Hyannis, Massachusetts[89]

Those health-care facilities in America cost a total of $2.1 million, roughly what we spent to refurbish one hospital in Baghdad—and less than ten seconds of the total cost of the war. To be fair, the bill had lots more in it than just the health-care spending I cited. McCain claimed it had contained $11 billion of what he called pork-barrel spending.[90] When he voted against spending that money in America—less than what we spend in just one month in Iraq—he issued a press release that said in part, "It appears that the big spenders in Washington have all but stolen the credit card numbers of every hardworking taxpayer in America and gone on a limitless spending spree for parochial, pork-barrel projects, leaving the taxpayers to pay and pay."[91]

But that tough talk on pork disappears when it comes to spending money in Iraq. This is what he said as he voted for billions in Iraq: "There will be amendments, there will be debate, there will be fiery rhetoric, and at the end of the day they will get the money because we have no choice."[92] We have no choice when it comes to limitless spending on an endless war. But John McCain suddenly has a choice when it comes to our roads, our bridges, our hospitals, our health care. He chooses to vote against investing in America.

Public Safety: McCain supported building seventeen police stations in Iraq,[93] a $70 million Baghdad police academy, a $15 million upgrade to the Nassiriyah prison, a $10 million police academy in Erbil, $2.5 million for new offices for the Iraqi highway patrol, a $2.2 million SWAT station in Hilla, and a $500,000 fire station in Nassiriyah.[94] But he opposed $200,000 for a SWAT team in Las Vegas, $122,000 for new police equipment in Georgia, $20,000 for anti-gang efforts in Ohio, $500,000 for police video surveillance equipment in Pittsburgh, and $500,000 for police equipment in Mississippi.[95]

Water Projects: McCain voted in favor of spending $227 million on the Nassiriyah water supply project,[96] another $5.7 million on water projects in Sadr City,[97] and $546,000 on the Talha reverse osmosis water unit in Basra.[98] But he voted against other, less expensive water projects here at home. He opposed $18.9

million in rural water assistance and groundwater protection, voted against $1 million for water infrastructure in Michigan, against $100,000 for the Georgia Water Planning and Policy Center, $500,000 to address problems caused by aging sewer infrastructure, $750,000 to complete a review of dioxin in the Ohio River, and against $500,000 to reduce lead-contaminated water in Hawaii.[99]

Schools: McCain supported spending $693,000 on the construction of the Sarawaran primary school in Kurdistan,[100] $601,000 to build the Binaslawa middle school, also in Kurdistan,[101] $460,000 to build the Sheile primary school in Dahuk,[102] and $86,000 to renovate the Al Escanddrona school.[103] But when it comes to investing in schools here at home, McCain does not exactly believe the children are our future. He opposed an amendment to invest $1.6 billion in construction and renovation of public schools in 2001,[104] voted to cut $1.3 billion in funding for school construction and modernization in 2000,[105] as well as voting against school repair and renovation funds in 1997,[106] 1998,[107] and 2003.[108]

Planes, Trains, and Automobiles: If you fly on a plane or ride a train, John McCain has voted to subsidize your travel. That is, if you're an Iraqi. If you're an American traveler, well, McCain says you're on your own. He voted in favor of spending $11.8 million to build a new power generator for the Baghdad airport,[109] and over $5 million to renovate the airport in Basra.[110] He also supported spending $5.9 million to rehabilitate the Baghdad railway station in the interests of health, safety, and "public convenience."[111] But McCain opposed investing $6.8 billion in improving homeland security, including new explosive detection devices at airports—perhaps because the money was to come from reducing the tax cuts for people making over $1 million a year.[112] And he opposed $200,000 to improve a railroad station in Illinois, $500,000 to renovate a train station in Topeka, $2 million to relocate the rail station in Orangeburg, South Carolina, $500,000 for a railroad bridge replacement in Galveston, Texas, and $1 million for the Reno-Stead railroad in Nevada.[113]

OVERSIGHT? WE DON'T NEED NO STINKING OVERSIGHT

I don't want to shock you, but it turns out that a whole lot of the money that McCain has spent in Iraq has been wasted. The *Washington Post* reported, "As little as twenty-seven cents of every dollar spent on Iraq's reconstruction has actually filtered down to projects benefiting Iraqis."[114] The military spending may not be any more efficient. According to an audit performed by the Pentagon's inspector general, the Defense Department can't account for as much as $15 billion of stuff. Fifteen billion dollars worth of purchases—ranging from Nissan trucks to rocket-propelled grenades, from bottled water to machine guns.[115]

We know about some of this waste because of the intrepid Henry Waxman. Waxman is a California Democrat whose district includes Beverly Hills, Malibu, Northridge, and West L.A. He is a lawyer and a career politician, rising from the State Assembly to chair the powerful U.S. House Committee on Oversight and Government Reform. Unlike John McCain, Waxman never served a day in uniform, but he is a hero in his own right. Because he has had the courage—as we say in Texas, the *cojones*—to fight to ensure that the money we are spending in Iraq actually helps the American troops we have sent to Iraq. That's his job. It's called oversight, and it's one of the most important ways Congress makes sure you're not getting ripped off by war profiteers.

Waxman is in the tradition of Harry Truman, who, when he was a senator during World War II, chaired an oversight committee on war spending that called 1,798 witnesses for 432 hearings and issued fifty-one reports. Truman took on major defense contractors, Pentagon bigwigs, and even the army's top brass. His work saved $15 billion—in 1940s dollars—and, more important, saved lives.[116]

John McCain is no Harry Truman. He's no Henry Waxman either. He has been remarkably quiescent in the fraud, waste, and rip-offs that have characterized the Bush-McCain era of contracting, especially in Iraq. Last year, the *New York Times* reported that the special inspector general for Iraq reconstruction found "that of 2,797 completed projects costing $5.8 billion, Iraq's national government had, by the spring of this year, accepted only 435 projects valued at $501 million."[117] In other words, the central government in Baghdad is so weak that it cannot even accept billions of dollars of free construction projects. And yet McCain wants to spend billions more.

U.S. taxpayers are paying for roads, schools, hospitals, and police stations in Iraq. We're paying for airports and filtered water systems. McCain says Iraq needs all of this, but he never explains why he thinks the United States doesn't. At home, we've got crumbling schools and overwhelmed hospitals. Our highways are in desperate need of modernization, and our first responders are woefully underfunded. What has McCain done about all this? He's voted against road improvements, against kids' health care,[118] and against public-school funding here in America.

Senator McCain, like President Bush, is obsessed with Iraq, and his obsession is standing in the way of helping the American people. As John Edwards said, "We don't need a surge in Baghdad, we need a surge in New Orleans."[119] For the trillions we'll end up spending in Iraq, we could guarantee everyone health care or fix our schools or fully equip our firefighters and policemen.

And when I say "trillions," that's not a typo. I mean it. Not millions or billions. The Bush-McCain war in Iraq is costing us trillions. Dr. Joseph Stiglitz is a Nobel Prize–winning economist who served on President Clinton's Council of Economic Advisers. He estimates the total cost of the war will exceed $3 trillion.[120] Three trillion dollars. That's not just a little pork, that's enough to buy—get this—every one of the one billion hogs on the entire planet Earth. And buy another billion hogs next year.

And another billion hogs the year after that. And to keep on buying a billion hogs a year for fifty years. Now *that's* what I call a lot of pork.[121]

And the $3 trillion figure certainly doesn't anticipate an endless American troop presence in Iraq. The current American troop presence in Iraq and Afghanistan costs roughly $12 billion a month.[122] That's $400 million a day, or $16,666,666 an hour, or $277,777 a second. Over a quarter of a million dollars per second. So, while you are reading this sentence, you're spending a million dollars in Iraq. Not on health care for Americans. Not on education for Americans. Not on protecting the American environment or cleaning up our streets. A quarter of a million dollars a second in Iraq.

And John McCain is only getting warmed up.

MAKING OUT LIKE A BANDIT IN BAGHDAD

While taxpayers have been hit hard by the war, defense companies have been raking in the war bucks. As the *Nation* reported, "According to the Institute for Policy Studies and financial reporter Michael Brush, CEOs at top defense contractors have seen annual pay raises of 200 to 688 percent since 9/11. The average annual salary for a CEO at a top defense contracting firm is now more than $12 million."[123]

McCain and his cronies haven't been doing so bad themselves. According to the Center for Responsive Politics, McCain has received more than half a million dollars in campaign contributions from defense companies.[124]

McCain senior adviser Charlie Black has successfully lobbied on behalf of defense contractors. Black's firm BKSH has lobbied for eight of the top sixty companies (or roughly 13 percent) receiving DOD contracts during 2007.[125] Black isn't the only McCain aide making money from defense contractors who are making money from the war. Four McCain aides—senior adviser Charlie Black and fund-raisers Eric Burgeson, James Courter, and Steve Phillips—have all lobbied for Lockheed Martin.[126] John Green, a top McCain aide and McCain's liaison to Congress, has been paid over $4 million since 1999 to lobby for a number of firms receiving and seeking defense and homeland security contracts.[127]

The self-appointed crusader against government waste has been strangely silent as bandits in Baghdad have looted the United States Treasury. Back in 2005 the special inspector general for Iraq reconstruction reported that an audit revealed that some $9 billion was unaccounted for.[128] Just gone. Vanished. Nine billion dollars is a lot of money. But it just vanished in the desert. To cite but one example from the audit, one ministry claimed to have 8,206 guards on the payroll, but only 602 actual guards could be found.[129] You would think that paying 7,604 guards who don't exist would ignite the famous temper of Senator Hothead. But no.

When you hear John McCain rail against what he calls pork-barrel spending, keep this in mind: what he's really talking about is investment in roads and schools and hospitals in your community, your town, your country. But when it comes to spending in Iraq, he makes drunken sailors look downright parsimonious. It is ironic but true: the only place John McCain wants pork is in a country where they don't even eat pork.

CONCLUSION

After eight years of Bush, Americans and the world are ready for a change. McCain, like Bush, is bent on waging endless war—war that doesn't make us safer and forgets the urgent crises facing American families here at home. More troops, more war, more occupation, more deployments, more spending, more no-bid contracts, more, more, more.

"Meet John 'Dubya' McCain; if you like George Bush's foreign policy, you'll love the GOP's current candidate," said the *Los Angeles Times*.[130] And the right-wing *National Review* concurs, saying, "If you liked the second Bush term . . . you will find much to admire in a Commander-in-Chief McCain."[131]

Bush & McCain: Which One Is the Ventriloquist and Which One Is the Dummy?

McSAME ON . . .	BUSH WHITE HOUSE	McCAIN
. . . Being Greeted as Liberators	While appearing on NBC's *Meet the Press*, Vice President Cheney said, "I really do believe that we will be **greeted as liberators**." [NBC, *Meet the Press*, 3/16/03; emphasis added]	While appearing on NBC's *Today* show, McCain said, "But I believe, Katie, that the Iraqi people will **greet us as liberators.**" [NBC, *Today*, 3/20/03; emphasis added]
. . . How to Pay for War	"We are dealing with a country that **can really finance its own reconstruction** and relatively soon." [Paul Wolfowitz, testimony before the Defense Subcommittee of the House Appropriations Committee, 3/27/03; emphasis added]	"Everybody now is talking of post–Saddam Hussein Iraq. I look on it with optimism and hope. As far as the cost is concerned, **Iraqis have vast oil reserves and they, I'm sure, would shoulder the cost of the transition.**" [*National Journal*, 2/15/03; emphasis added]

McSAME ON . . .	BUSH WHITE HOUSE	McCAIN
. . . ***Mission Accomplished***	While giving a speech aboard the USS *Abraham Lincoln* and standing under a giant **Mission Accomplished** banner, Bush announced, "Major combat operations in Iraq have ended." [Associated Press, 5/2/03]	During an interview on ABC News' *This Week*, McCain was asked about the capture of Saddam Hussein and the effect on U.S. forces. McCain said, "Their morale could not be higher. This is a **mission accomplished.**" [ABC, *This Week*, 12/14/03; emphasis added]
. . . ***Staying the Course***	**"We've got to stay the course and we will stay the course."** [*Newsweek*, 4/19/2004; emphasis added]	**"We've got to stay the course."** [*ABC News*, 10/24/04; emphasis added]
. . . ***Cutting and Running***	Iraqis "need to know two things: we're not going to **cut and run**; and two, we believe they have the capacity to run their own country." [*Washington Post*, 11/17/03; emphasis added]	"We can't **cut and run.**" [Associated Press, 9/22/05; emphasis added]

McSAME ON . . .	BUSH WHITE HOUSE	McCAIN
. . . Terrorists Following Us Home	"Unlike in Vietnam, if we withdraw before the job is done, this enemy will **follow us home.**" [The president's speech to the VFW convention, 8/22/07; emphasis added]	"I believe al Qaeda would trumpet to the world that they had defeated the United States of America, and I believe that therefore they would try to **follow us home.**" [*Atlantic Free Press*, 3/9/08; emphasis added]
. . . The Surge Is Working	"I strongly believe the **surge is working** and so do the Iraqis." [*CQ* Transcriptions, 3/11/08; emphasis added]	"The **surge is working.** If it weren't, we'd be in a different place right now, no question." [White House Bulletin, 1/14/08; emphasis added]
. . . Waving the White Flag of Surrender	"There's a group in the opposition party who are willing to retreat before the mission is done. They're willing to wave **the white flag of surrender.**" [*Los Angeles Times*, 7/2/06; emphasis added]	"I'm so proud of the jobs that the men and women in the military are doing there, and they don't want us to raise the **white flag of surrender** like Senator Clinton does." [Agence France-Presse, 1/25/08; emphasis added]

McSAME ON . . .	BUSH WHITE HOUSE	McCAIN
. . . al Qaeda	"Ladies and gentlemen, some may deny the surge is working, but among the terrorists there is no doubt. **Al Qaeda is on the run** in Iraq, and this enemy will be defeated." [2008 State of the Union address, 1/28/08; emphasis added]	"Please remember this, **Al Qaeda is on the run** but not defeated." [Town Hall in Exeter, New Hampshire, 3/1/08; emphasis added]

6

IF McCAIN'S A REFORMER, I'M A HASIDIC DIAMOND MERCHANT

Hypocrisy, my friends, is the most obvious of political sins—and the people will punish it.

—John McCain[1]

I'm a reformer with results.

—George W. Bush[2]

PAY NO ATTENTION TO THOSE LOBBYISTS BEHIND THE CURTAIN

John McCain is not a reformer, but he plays one on TV. Just as George W. Bush conned millions of Americans with his "reformer with results" claptrap in 2000, McCain is hoping that if he proclaims himself a reformer loudly enough and often enough, he can distract folks from the fact that he has spent twenty-five years hugging lobbyists and serving corporate interests in Washington.

From the moment he entered Congress a quarter century

ago, McCain has doled out favors to his corporate supporters and cemented close relationships with the lobbyists who represent them. McCain has 134 lobbyists on staff or raising money for his campaign.

Think about that: if you walked into McCain's campaign headquarters and yelled, "Hey, dirtbag!" 134 necks would jerk around. You'd need a chiropractor. And yet John McCain stands in front of God and everyone and proclaims himself a reformer. If McCain had 134 cannibals running his campaign, would he be credible as a vegetarian? If he had 134 hookers running his campaign, would he be credible with a message of abstinence?

Lobbyists are running McCain's campaign, raising money for him, and advising him—even on policy. Mind you, these lobbyists have made millions working to try to get McCain and his colleagues in Congress to listen to big oil companies, drug companies, insurance companies, and even foreign dictators.

In May 2008, McCain began taking heat for surrounding himself with the same special-interest lobbyists he denounces on the trail. The first crack in McCain's public image came when the news broke that two McCain aides, Doug Davenport and Doug Goodyear, had represented the military junta in Burma.[3] Let me give you an idea of how bad the two Dougs' client is. In the aftermath of the cyclone that devastated Burma, the government barred aid workers and impounded UN shipments of food. A representative of the Asia Society described the junta's refusal to allow humanitarian workers or aid into the country as "nothing less than murder of the Burmese people at the hands of the military leaders."[4]

McCain did his best to run away from the situation. In one of the phoniest moves I've ever seen, McCain pretended to be shocked, shocked that these lobbyists were in his campaign. In an election-year conversion, he ostentatiously ousted them. Not all 134 of them, mind you. Just four. That's not good government. That's not even pretty good government. That's phony, transparent, cynical, election-year politics.

Throughout his career, McCain has adopted a "do as I say, not as I do" attitude. From the Keating Five to today, he has preached reform but practiced politics as usual. When McCain was pushing to restrict campaign donations, he was quietly accepting hundreds of thousands of dollars of corporate money into a nonprofit group set up to avoid contribution limits.[5]

While McCain claims he's never used his office to benefit his benefactors, he conveniently forgets the numerous times he's acted to help enrich his campaign contributors. When McCain railed against special-interest influence during his 2000 campaign, what he didn't say was that his corporate friends were subsidizing his private jet travel around the country.

McCain has never been a reformer. He just puts on a good show. Take, for example, one of the pillars of McCain's claim to being a reformer, a bill he sponsored back in the 1990s that would have banned campaigns from hiring lobbyists. McCain didn't manage to get the bill passed into law—but if he had, right now he'd be breaking the law several times over.

The bill McCain sponsored in 1996 and again in 1997 "would ban a candidate or a candidate's authorized committee from paying registered lobbyists."[6] When he introduced it, McCain said his bill, the Lobbying Conflict of Interest Elimination Act, was necessary because "unfortunately, a loophole allows lobbyists to serve as fund-raisers for members of Congress, which could result in an increase in their influence."

McCain continued, "This practice must stop. Registered lobbyists who work for campaigns as fund-raisers clearly represent a conflict of interest. When a campaign employs an individual who also lobbies that member, the perception of undue and unfair influence is raised."[7] Later, when proposing new ethics reforms in 2006, McCain promised he was going to try to impose new restrictions on the ability of lobbyists to hold fund-raisers.[8]

It's a good thing for McCain that his bill never made it out of committee.

McCain wants it both ways. Even while he rails against the influence of lobbyists on the Senate floor and the campaign trail, he's been thick as thieves with half the bandits on K Street (the red-light district of corporate influence in Washington).

When the McCain campaign panicked in May and announced that they would begin to require all staff to disclose their lobbying ties, I laughed. All lobbyists already have to disclose their clients, and after a quarter century in Washington, McCain certainly knows who they are and what they do.

McCain's hypocrisy is so deep that the *Washington Post* reported, "The fact that lobbyists are essentially running his presidential campaign . . . seems to some people to be at odds with his anti-lobbying rhetoric."

FIFTEEN MILLION DOLLARS FROM THE SAUDIS: "I DO NOT FIND A CONFLICT OF INTEREST AT THIS TIME"

Exhibit A in the McCain-Lobbyist Dirtbag Hall of Fame is Tom Loeffler, the man McCain asked to cochair his presidential campaign. Loeffler is a former Republican congressman from Texas. My dear, departed friend Molly Ivins once described Loeffler as "smarter than a box of rocks." She noted that Loeffler bragged that as a youth he had played football with two broken wrists. "This caused uncharitable persons to question the man's good sense," Molly wrote, "so he explained he didn't know his wrists were broken at the time."[9]

No fool he, Loeffler took extra precautions to protect himself against AIDS. "Loeffler went to San Francisco during the campaign to make a speech," Molly reported. "While there, he wore shower caps on his feet while showering lest he get AIDS from the tile in the tub. He later denied that he had spent the entire trip in his hotel room. He said: 'I did walk around the hotel. I did see people who do have abnormal tendencies. I'd just as soon not be associated with abnormal people.' "[10]

Now that you have a sense of the man's intellect, here's what the nonpartisan Texans for Public Justice says about Loeffler's ethics as a congressman:

> Loeffler also topped a list of five members of Congress whose campaigns received illegal corporate money from Vernon Savings & Loan, which failed at a taxpayer cost of $1.3 billion. A Vernon officer told an '89 grand jury that Loeffler offered to set up a meeting with then Treasury Secretary James A. Baker III if they helped pay Loeffler's debt from a failed '86 gubernatorial bid. Four Vernon executives then moved $8,000 in laundered corporate money to Loeffler's campaign, this officer testified, just before federal regulators forced them to resign.[11]

After taking illegal money from a failing S&L when he was a dirtbag congressman, Loeffler found a second life as a dirtbag lobbyist and a dirtbag fund-raiser. He was ranked as the fourth biggest donor/fund-raiser for George W. Bush's political career. Ken Lay was No. 3.[12]

Loeffler's firm, cleverly called the Loeffler Group (where does he come up with these?), has received, since 2002, at least $15 million in lobbying fees from the Kingdom of Saudi Arabia.[13] The Kingdom of Saudi Arabia, for those unfamiliar with it, is a charitable institution based in Riyadh. Its principal purpose is to screw Americans by charging $140 for a barrel of oil. But in their spare time the Saudis use some of that oil money to spread anti-American and anti-Semitic hatred. Freedom House, the watchdog group founded in 1941 by Eleanor Roosevelt and Wendell Willkie, reports that the Saudis tell Muslims living in America "that it is a religious obligation for Muslims to hate Christians and Jews and warn against imitating, befriending, or helping them in any way. . . . The documents promote contempt for the United States because it is ruled by legislated civil law rather than by totalitarian Wahhabi-style Islamic law. They condemn democracy as un-Islamic."[14]

Freedom House found and published documents that the government of Saudi Arabia sends to Muslims living in America. "For example, a document in the collection for the 'Immigrant Muslim' bears the words 'Greetings from the Cultural Attache in Washington, D.C.' of the Embassy of Saudi Arabia, and is published by the government of Saudi Arabia. In an authoritative religious voice, it gives detailed instructions on how to 'hate' the Christian and Jew: Never greet them first. Never congratulate the infidel on his holiday. Never imitate the infidel. Do not become a naturalized citizen of the United States."[15]

This is what they are telling Muslims *living in America*. In their own country, of course, Mr. Loeffler's clients are famous for their treatment of women. Saudi apologists point out that women in their country in some ways have it better than men. "I use a sword to kill male criminals . . . and firearms, specifically pistols, to kill female criminals," said Sa'id bin Abdullah bin Mabrouk al-Bishi, a Saudi Arabian executioner. "I think firearms are used to spare the woman, as to be executed by sword would mean uncovering her head and exposing her neck and some of her back."[16] Women there cannot drive, cannot travel abroad without the permission of a male relative (usually her father or husband), and if they walk in public unaccompanied or with a man who is not their husband or relative, they can be arrested for suspicion of prostitution.[17]

The United States of America has, of necessity, a complicated relationship with the House of Saud. We buy their oil, they spread their hate. And yet there have been moments of real cooperation against al Qaeda, and there are plainly close economic ties and mutual interests that must be pursued. The Saudis deserve—indeed, require—representation in America. But if you're John McCain, of all the people whom you could ask to cochair your campaign, do you really have to turn to a lobbyist for the Saudi Arabian government?

Tom Loeffler's lobbying firm has collected nearly $15 million from Saudi Arabia since 2002 and millions more from other foreign and corporate interests.[18] Loeffler told *Newsweek*'s

Michael Isikoff, "At no time have I discussed my clients with John McCain." But, Isikoff reported, lobbying disclosure records prove that he did. On May 17, 2006, Loeffler disclosed that he had met with McCain and the Saudi Arabian ambassador to "discuss U.S.–Kingdom of Saudi Arabia relations."[19]

When Loeffler joined McCain's campaign, he boasted he would still carry on "all of the work" of his lobbying firm, whose clients include other foreign entities and corporations, like a French defense firm seeking business from the Defense Department.[20] Summoning the ethical compass that guided him to take illegal S&L money and raise a fortune for George W. Bush, Loeffler said, "I do not find a conflict of interest at this time."[21] Loeffler's dirtbag lobbying business benefited from his access to McCain, and McCain's presidential campaign benefited from Loeffler's fund-raising. No conflict there.

When the fertilizer hit the ventilator, McCain dumped Loeffler. But he hasn't given back the sacks full of special-interest money that Loeffler raised for his campaign.

CHARLIE BLACK

Tom Loeffler is just the tip of the lobbyist-filled iceberg that is the McCain campaign. McCain's senior political adviser, Charlie Black, headed the lobbying firm BKSH & Associates. (In the interest of full disclosure, it should be noted that BKSH & Associates is part of the firm Burson-Marsteller, whose CEO, Mark Penn, was Hillary Clinton's chief strategist.) Black's firm's client roster has included numerous foreign dictators and governments and defense contractors. In 1992 Black's firm had the distinction of earning an award from *Spy* magazine for representing the worst foreign leaders.[22] The same year the Center for Public Integrity noted that Black's firm was one of the top lobbying firms that won U.S. funding for countries that abuse human rights.[23]

Black helped Ahmed Chalabi and the Iraqi National Congress navigate Washington in the run-up to the Iraq War and even arranged a meeting in the Pentagon for Chalabi just days after 9/11.[24] Chalabi went on to help Bush build his dishonest case for the war in Iraq, and Chalabi's "right-hand man" was a paid consultant to Black's firm. Chalabi, of course, was central to the administration's sales job. A *New Yorker* profile of Chalabi called "The Manipulator" noted, "Diplomatic and intelligence officials accuse [Chalabi] of exaggerating the security threat that Iraq posed to the U.S.; supplying defectors who offered misleading or bogus testimony about Saddam's efforts to acquire nuclear, biological, and chemical weapons; promoting questionable stories connecting Saddam to Al Qaeda; and overestimating the ease with which Saddam could be replaced with a Western-style democracy."[25] Other than that, ol' Ahmed is a splendid fellow.

Black has said he wants to set up Iraq's first lobbying firm.[26] As they say in Baghdad, that takes *chutzpah.* And yet, it makes sense. Black has represented a cadre of defense contractors whose war profits have totaled billions of dollars.

None of Black's previous work or his current ties to the war in Iraq seem to bother McCain. Black has boasted about conducting business from the back of McCain's Straight Talk Express campaign bus.[27] And McCain has publicly praised Black, saying, "I'm proud of the record of many of my advisers."[28]

RICK DAVIS

Rick Davis is a longtime McCain political aide and lobbyist. Unlike Loeffler, who migrated from the lobbyist-laden Bush operation to the lobbyist-laden McCain operation, or Black, who has been with nearly every leading Republican since Ronald Reagan, Davis has been at John McCain's side through thick and thin. He's also a longtime lobbyist. But he's walked away from all that—for now—to manage McCain's campaign. He also ran McCain's 2000 campaign and led McCain's "Reform Institute." Davis founded the lobbying firm Davis, Manafort, which has raked in lobbying income of at least $2.8 million since 1998.[29]

McCain knew Davis's lobbying well—and even pitched in.

While McCain was chair of the Senate Commerce Committee, Davis earned $640,000 lobbying on behalf of Verizon.[30] In fact, McCain helped Davis woo clients. McCain met with a prospective client of Davis, a Russian tycoon who was such a stand-up guy that the U.S. government had revoked his visa.

It goes without saying that Davis escaped McCain's lame, cosmetic attempt to de-lobby his campaign high command. Far from being ejected for his corporate ties, Davis has been responsible for implementing the campaign's lobbyist policy. Ironic, isn't it? Or maybe just hypocritical.

"PAJAMA PARTIES WITH LOBBYISTS"

After the 2000 campaign, McCain set up what is called the Reform Institute. One of the charming things about McCain is his highly developed sense of irony, and perhaps that was at work when they named this vehicle for special-interest money the "Reform Institute." The Reform Institute looked a lot like McCain's campaign does today: pretending to stand for reform but actually dominated by lobbyists and corporate interests. In fact, Rick Davis, now McCain's campaign manager and then a corporate lobbyist, got an annual salary of $110,000 to run the Reform Institute. Far from promoting reform, the Reform Institute allowed corporate interests with business before the McCain-chaired Senate Commerce Committee to send him hundreds of thousands of dollars.[31]

Take Cablevision, for example. Cablevision twice donated $100,000 to the Reform Institute. Around that time, McCain took actions that benefited Cablevision. He allowed Cablevision executives to testify before the Senate Commerce Committee, then he sent a letter to the FCC supporting Cablevision's position on new regulations.[32] Eventually, McCain was forced to distance himself from the group, but the damage was done. A whopping 15 percent of the Reform Institute's money came from Cablevision alone.[33]

When confronted, McCain naturally declared that he'd

done nothing wrong—but immediately stepped down from the group in 2005, as did Rick Davis. If everything was aboveboard, then why did McCain and Davis jump overboard?[34]

The Reform Institute was just a corporate-funded extension of McCain's presidential campaign. Ken Silberstein of *Harper's* wrote that even after McCain left the group, "the nonprofit has continued to advance an agenda indistinguishable from his own." The group broadened its focus in 2006 at the same time McCain organized his presidential campaign to include issues beyond campaign finance "that just so happened to be the struts of McCain's political platform."[35] The director of the nonpartisan campaign finance watchdog group Political Money Line, Kent Cooper, said, "Senator McCain derives a clear benefit by using The Reform Institute to help the debate on campaign finance reform."

McCain even violated the spirit of his own campaign finance law. Cooper of Political Money Line pointed out, "His McCain-Feingold bill helped break the connection between members of Congress and large contributions. Here is an example of a large contribution going to the foundation connected with a member of Congress. I don't see a difference."[36]

McCain didn't limit his courtship of corporations to the "Reform Institute." He was also a member of the Main Street Partnership, a nonprofit group that traded tax-exempt donations from corporations for access to policy-makers. One Republican campaign finance lawyer described the Main Street Partnership as a group "that basically raises a variety of corporate funding and apparently pays for pajama parties with lobbyists."[37] I can just imagine McCain and his lobbyist friends painting one another's nails and giggling about the notes he was passing to his colleagues on the Senate floor.

"HIGHLY UNUSUAL"

Another notable episode in McCain's series of flings with corporate interests was his entanglement with Paxson Communications. Lowell W. Paxson lavished McCain with money and perks while McCain chaired the Senate Commerce Committee. And, for his part, he took actions that benefited Paxson, a move that even he said would "absolutely" look suspicious to voters.[38]

McCain and Paxson took care of one another. In 1998, Paxson and Sinclair Communications joined forces to raise about $17,000 for McCain.[39] Shortly thereafter McCain wrote a letter to the FCC, which scolded the commission for misinterpreting the 1996 Telecommunications Act.[40] Voters weren't the only ones who might have thought McCain's activity was suspicious—William Kennard, then chairman of the FCC, called McCain's intervention "highly unusual."[41] Yet McCain's relationship with Paxson continued. At the behest of Paxson lobbyist Vicki Iseman, McCain even wrote letters urging the FCC to act on a matter Paxson had before the commission.[42]

When the dust settled, McCain hadn't done too badly either. He took $20,000 in campaign contributions from executives at Paxson Communications—as well as four trips on Paxson's airplane during his 2000 presidential campaign.[43]

McCain wrote letters to the FCC urging the commission to allow one of Iseman's clients to control two television stations within the same market. He also introduced a bill in the Senate to create tax incentives for minority ownership of stations—when several of the businesses standing to benefit were represented by Ms. Iseman.[44]

Of course, Paxson wasn't McCain's only corporate interest. During his time on the Senate Commerce Committee:

- McCain suggested that the FCC allow BellSouth to enter the long-distance telephone market after it raised over $16,000 for his campaigns.
- McCain got $27,000 from Sprint, MCI, WorldCom, and AT&T executives before writing letters on their behalf to the FCC.
- McCain wrote two letters to the FCC on EchoStar's behalf to allow the satellite television company to broadcast local

stations; in the period between those two letters, EchoStar's chairman raised around $25,000 for McCain.

- McCain received $120,000 raised by executives of SBC Communications and Ameritech. Not long after that, McCain sent a letter to the FCC criticizing the commission for bias against the two companies, which were attempting to merge.[45]

"ONE WORD, ABRAMOFF"

When Jack Abramoff was caught channeling contributions and outright bribes from Indian tribes to dozens of lawmakers in 2006, McCain was chairman of the Senate Indian Affairs Committee. It was his job to lead one of the largest congressional corruption investigations in decades. He could have followed the facts without fear or favor, forcing accountability from everyone involved, including numerous colleagues in the House and Senate. It was the perfect opportunity to force reform in lobbying activity and campaign contributions, not to mention congressional ethics. McCain punted.

He gave lip service to reform. He argued that the scandal proved the need for reforms to bring greater transparency: "It's obvious why it's needed. One word, Abramoff."[46] McCain described the relationship between lobbyists, clients, and campaign contributions as "unfortunately, the ordinary way of doing business in this town."[47] But after all that windup, his pitch fell flat.

The final report delivered from McCain's committee's investigation into the scandal declared "no new or revised federal legislation needed." The report said, "Without doubt, the depth and breadth of [Abramoff's and associate Michael Scanlon's] misconduct was astonishing," but "the Committee concludes that existing federal criminal statutes are sufficient to deter and punish such misconduct."[48]

Worse yet, as the Associated Press reported, McCain covered for members of Congress who had received money from Abramoff.[49] His report included a section on recommendations for further investigations, but it omitted the activity of congressmen. Numerous congressmen were omitted from the report, but the most notable absences were powerful Republicans apparently caught up in the scandal, like House Speaker Dennis Hastert, GOP house whip Roy Blunt, and senators Conrad Burns, Thad Cochran, Trent Lott, Chuck Grassley, and John Ensign. Combined, those members received over $610,000 from Abramoff clients.[50] These members had written letters to the secretary of the interior seeking action on matters that would benefit tribes for whom Abramoff had lobbied.

BOTTOM LINE: A DEN OF LOBBYISTS

McCain has at least 134 lobbyists on staff or raising money for his campaign. His May feint at reforming his campaign only dropped the lobbyist total by four. McCain's attempts to rewrite the history of his campaign, like his attempts to airbrush out his history of ethical lapses, buckle under the weight of reality. Like Bush, he is a true Washington insider who is trying to brand himself as an outsider. But the "reformer" label just doesn't hold up.

A reformer doesn't accept money and trips from a campaign contributor and then try to use the power of the office to help the contributor at the expense of the American taxpayers. A reformer doesn't reward a campaign contributor with lucrative land deals at the expense of the government. A reformer doesn't deride corporate influence in politics, then set up an organization to accept donations from corporations with business before his committees. A reformer doesn't reward campaign contributions with official interventions and favors. A reformer doesn't punt when it's his duty to investigate a corruption scandal. A reformer doesn't surround himself with lobbyists.

McCain claimed he was a victim of the system, saying, "People give money to buy access. We're all tainted by this system . . . they have access, and therefore they have influence. It corrupts the system. And I'm a victim of it too."[51] But McCain is no victim—and he's sure not a reformer. For a list of lobbyists in McCain's campaign, see the Appendix.

GET OFF
MY
LAWN. . .

7

McNASTY

F—— you! I know more about this than anyone else in the room!

—John McCain to his Republican colleague, Sen. John Cornyn of Texas[1]

You f——ing son of a bitch. I saw what you wrote. We're not going to forget this.

—George W. Bush to journalist Al Hunt, in front of Hunt's wife, Judy Woodruff, and their then four-year-old son, in 1986[2]

I must confess I have a high tolerance for hot-tempered leaders. When I worked in the White House, I saw President Clinton angry more than once. When he was governor of Texas, George W. Bush once poked me in the chest and hissed expletives. I thought it was fine, even cool. But I'm weird that way. I don't mind a little anger, and I love, love, love cussing. My wife doesn't call me "Potty Mouth" for nothing. So I resisted the legion of stories about McCain's temper for years. Besides, it hasn't hurt him politically. McCain usually answers with a charming blend of self-criticism and self-aggrandizement. In his 2002 autobiography, tellingly titled *Worth the Fighting For*, McCain wrote, "I have a temper, to state the obvious, which I have tried to control with varying degrees of success because it does not always serve my interest or the public's."[3] That's the self-condemnation. Now, here's the turn. Watch carefully, because only a trained professional should attempt this maneuver, telling the *Washington Post*, "When I see corruption, . . . when I see people misbehaving badly, [voters] expect me to be angry."[4]

Wow. Did you follow that? On the one hand, the humble politician is very contrite about his bad temper. (He told students while campaigning at his old high school, "In all candor, as an adult I've been known to forget occasionally the discretion expected of a person of my many years and station when I believe I've been accorded a lack of respect I did not deserve."[5]) But then—get ready, here it comes again—the temper is actually a sign of how doggone virtuous McCain is. "If you wanted a programmed, subdued, always-on-message politician, he wasn't and will never be your guy," says a former McCain chief of staff.[6]

Because I love a well-executed pirouette as much as the next guy, here's one more example. Self-criticism: "My anger didn't help my [2000] campaign. It didn't help. People don't like angry candidates very much."[7] Gee, ain't he honest. And then (whammo!) rage = principle. "He may have a short fuse," says his colleague, Iowa GOP senator Chuck Grassley—who has been on the receiving end of a famous McCain explosion—but, he told the *Washington Post*, "I've come to the conclusion that his strong principles, sometimes backed up by considerable . . . not temper, but considerable conviction, is what a president ought to have."[8]

But even though I was not particularly frightened by the stories of McCain's temper—and even though I can curse with the best of them—I have come to a very different conclusion than Senator Grassley has. I think McCain's volcanic temper is at least worth exploring.

EARLY DAYS OF RAGE

John McCain's temper is nothing new. Then again, when you're almost seventy-two years old, nothing about you is very new, is it? He's always been the type of guy who behaved as if the rules didn't apply to him. First-year students at McCain's private high school, Episcopal, in Alexandria, Virginia, were known as "rats," and McCain earned the "distinction at the end of the year as 'worst rat.' " Of course, that's nothing compared to the nicknames he earned: "Punk" and "McNasty."[9]

At the Naval Academy, McCain racked up demerits as if they'd been going out of style. McCain was a consistent member of the "Century Club"—students who managed to get more than one hundred demerits.[10] In fact, it was only because McCain let a friend take the fall for a particularly grave infraction during his senior year that he managed to graduate. He and some friends were caught with a TV, which was prohibited on campus. The thirty demerits they earned would have gotten McNasty kicked out, but he let one of his buddies take the heat instead, so McCain graduated, albeit near the bottom of his class.[11]

McCain himself acknowledges he was a hothead as a student. He has said, "I would respond aggressively and sometimes irresponsibly to anyone whom I perceived to have questioned my sense of honor and self-respect."[12] It would have been one thing if McCain had grown out of his volatile temper, but he hasn't. And what was charming in a young midshipman can be alarming in a potential president. There are few people who have worked closely with John McCain who have not witnessed his bizarre behavior or outbursts.

SENATOR HOTHEAD: "HE IS ERRATIC. . . . HE LOSES HIS TEMPER AND HE WORRIES ME"

According to the *Los Angeles Times*, McCain's "temper has ranged far and wide, directed at other members of the Senate, congressional staffers, heads of government agencies, corporate chieftains, high-ranking military officers and teenage campaign volunteers."[13] McCain tries to say he just gets angry about issues. In *Worth the Fighting For*, he writes, "When public servants lose their capacity for outrage over practices injurious to the national interest, they have outlived their usefulness to the country."[14]

Oooh, I like that one. Yet another attempt to redefine rage as righteous indignation. Here's the problem with McCain's self-serving take on his temper: He often goes ballistic over petty, personal, and political matters—not policy. When John McCain doesn't get his way, he explodes, plain and simple. That's why he has consistently made *Washingtonian* magazine's ranking of Congress's "hottest tempers."[15]

His colleagues, including some of the most conservative and loyal Republicans in the Senate, have testified almost as one about McCain's temper. I find this remarkable. The Senate is filled with big egos and hot tempers, so to stand out as a hothead in that body takes some real doing. It's kind of like being singled out as especially nerdy at a *Star Trek* convention. Or like Amy Winehouse saying you're too wild. What I'm saying is, this guy must have one hell of a temper. But don't take my word for it. Listen to his colleagues:

- When asked if McCain's temper would be disabling or disqualifying in a potential president, Senator Thad Cochran responded, "I certainly know no other president since I've been here who's had a temperament like that."[16] Cochran also publicly said of McCain that "the thought of his being president sends a cold chill down my spine . . . he is erratic. He is hotheaded. He loses his temper and he worries me."[17]

- Republican senator Orrin Hatch of Utah said McCain "does have a temper and sometimes it's awful to be on the wrong side of it."[18]

- According to the *Boston Globe*, former senator Rick Santorum—the defeated Republican senator from Pennsylvania—has "personally witnessed problems with McCain's temperament, which he declined to detail. 'I don't know anybody in the Senate who hasn't,' Santorum said. 'Everybody has their McCain story.' "[19]

- Republican senator Bob Corker of Tennessee twice refused to agree that McCain has the temperament to be president when he was asked in an appearance on the show *Hannity & Colmes*. Corker said, "You know, his temperamental issues have been written about" and "Well, I think he is an American hero."[20] What Corker didn't say speaks louder than what he did.

And that's just what his *Republican* colleagues in the Senate say. To be sure, being disliked by one's Senate colleagues may be something of a badge of honor. Al Gore was not the most popular of senators, but he was America's best vice president—and would have been a great president had the five thieves in black robes who laughingly call themselves "justices" not intervened. But none of Gore's colleagues questioned his fitness for high office. None of them said the thought of Gore in the Oval Office sent chills down their spine.

"MY FRIEND . . ."

It's not just McCain's colleagues in the Senate.

The *Arizona Republic* has reported on McCain's temper quite a few times. A stand-out among these has to be the account of a 1996 meeting with the legislative director of the National Right to Life Committee, David Johnson, and the president of the National Committee for Adoption, Bill Pierce. Although the two men were trying to meet with McCain to talk about a bill he was sponsoring, " 'McCain didn't want to hear any of that . . . all he wanted to do is berate this man,' Johnson said, referring to Pierce."[21]

Even the chairman of the Arizona State Republican Party,

Randy Pullen, said of McCain's temper, "He's tough to deal with, there's no doubt about it."[22]

In his defense, McCain offers up this gem: "Do I insult anybody or fly off the handle or anything like that? No, I don't."[23] Oh, yes, you do, Senator. But I will let you, dear reader, be the judge. Herein are my Top Ten John McCain Blowups.

10: PICKING A FIGHT WITH A NINETY-TWO-YEAR-OLD

Being a hothead is one thing. Challenging a much older man to a fistfight is quite another. It is true that George W. Bush challenged his dear old dad to a fistfight one drunken night in 1972, (see chapter 2).[24]

But John McCain did him one better. He tried to pick a fistfight with Senator Strom Thurmond—when Strom was ninety-two.

McCain got into a "scuffle" with nonagenarian Thurmond back in 1995. McCain was giving a statement at the Senate Armed Services Committee, and he must have been running on a bit, because Thurmond asked, "Is the senator about through?" According to *Washingtonian* magazine, "McCain later confronted Thurmond on the Senate floor. A scuffle ensued, and the two didn't part friends." *Newsweek* reported that McCain was rumored to have shoved "one or two" senators, including Thurmond, who was in his nineties at the time of the alleged incident.[25]

9: THE BUMILLER BLOWUP

During a town hall meeting in Atlanta in March 2008, McCain was asked whether he might ask Senator John Kerry to join his ticket. "No. No," McCain said. "We have very vastly different philosophical fundamental political views. I respect those views. I respect them, I just totally disagree with them." McCain went on to note that he had been approached by the Kerry '04 campaign about possibly joining Kerry on the Democratic ticket.

"When I was approached," McCain said, "when we had that conversation back in 2004, I mean that's why I never even considered such a thing."

Later, on his campaign plane, the *New York Times* reporter Elisabeth Bumiller followed up. She reminded McCain that in 2004, he had denied any such meeting but now was confirming that he had had a conversation with Kerry, which would make St. John . . . well . . . a fibber. McCain blew a gasket. He interrupted Bumiller repeatedly. To fully appreciate it, you have to watch the tape (available on YouTube). But here's the transcript:

BUMILLER: I just went back and looked at our story, the *Times* story, and you told Sheryl Stolberg that you had never had a conversation with Kerry about being vice president—

McCAIN: Everybody knows that I had a private conversation. Everybody knows that. That I had a conversation. There's no living American in Washington—

BUMILLER: Okay.

McCAIN: —that knows that, there's no one.

BUMILLER: Okay.

McCAIN: And you know it too. You know it. You know it. So I don't even know why you ask.

BUMILLER: Well I ask because I just read—

McCAIN: You do know it. You do know it.

BUMILLER: Because I just read in the *Times* in May of '04 you said—

McCAIN: I don't know what you may have read or heard of, I don't know the circumstances. Maybe in May of '04 I hadn't had the conversation—

BUMILLER: But do you recall the conversation?

McCAIN: I don't know, but it's well known that I had the conversation. It is absolutely well known by everyone. So do you have a question on another issue?

BUMILLER: Well can I ask you when the conversation was?

McCAIN: No. Nope, because the issue is closed as far as I'm concerned. Everybody knows it. Everybody knows it in America.

BUMILLER: Can you describe the conversation?

McCAIN: Pardon me?

BUMILLER: Can you describe the conversation?

McCAIN: No, of course not. I don't describe private conversations.

BUMILLER: Okay. Can I ask you—

McCAIN: Why should I? Then there's no such thing as a private conversation. Is there [inaudible] if you have a private conversation with someone, and then they come and tell you, I don't know that that's a private conversation. I think that's a public conversation.

BUMILLER: Okay. Can I ask you about your [pause] Why you're so angry?[26]

8: THE F-BOMB

The *New York Post* reported, "Presidential hopeful John McCain—who has been dogged for years by questions about his volcanic temper—erupted in an angry, profanity-laced tirade at a fellow Republican senator. . . . In a heated dispute over immigration-law overhaul, McCain screamed, 'F—— you!' at Texas Sen. John Cornyn, who had been raising concerns about the legislation. 'This is chickens—— stuff,' McCain snapped at Cornyn, according to several people in the room off the Senate floor Thursday. 'You've always been against this bill, and you're just trying to derail it.' "[27]

Amazingly, McCain's F-Bomb strategy did not work, and the bill died in the Senate.

7: A**HOLE

According to *Newsweek*, "McCain [once] erupted out of the blue at the respected Budget Committee chairman, Pete Domenici, saying, 'Only an a——hole would put together a budget like this.' Offended, Domenici stood up and gave a dignified, restrained speech about how in all his years in the Senate, through many heated debates, no one had ever called him that. Another senator might have taken the moment to check his temper. But McCain went on: 'I wouldn't call you an a——hole unless you really were an a——hole.' A Republican senator who witnessed the scene had considered supporting McCain for president, but changed his mind. 'I decided,' the senator told *Newsweek*, 'I didn't want this guy anywhere near a trigger.' "[28]

6: "F——ING JERK": "I WAS SITTING THERE AND WAS ABOUT TO WITNESS A MURDER"

In 1992, McCain exploded at Iowa Republican senator Chuck Grassley, saying, "I thought your problem was that you don't listen. But that's not it at all. Your problem is that you're a f——ing jerk." One senator who witnessed the exchange said he was convinced McCain "was going to drive the top of his head into Grassley's nose. I was convinced that bone fragments were going to go into Chuck's brain, and I was sitting there and was about to witness a murder."[29]

McCain and Grassley had been debating how to deal with ex–U.S. Marine Bobby Garwood, a former POW who had been an accused defector, during a meeting of the Senate Special Committee on POW/MIA Affairs. McCain believed Garwood had been a "traitor," while Grassley believed Garwood had been wrongly accused.[30] It's an emotional issue, to say the least, and McCain was convinced that he and other POWs had been beaten because of Garwood. But to be so hostile as to cause a fellow senator to wonder if you're about to kill another senator is a little extreme.

5: BROWBEATING YOUNG CAMPAIGN VOLUNTEERS

According to the *Arizona Republic*, "It was election night 1986, and John McCain had just been elected to the U.S. Senate for the first time. Even so, he was not in a good mood. McCain was yelling at the top of his lungs and poking the chest of a young Republican volunteer who had set up a lectern that was too tall for the five foot nine politician to be seen to advantage, according to a witness to the outburst." Jon Hinz, then executive director of the Arizona Republican Party, noted, "You'd have to stick cotton in your ears not to hear it. He [McCain] was screaming at him, and he was red in the face. It wasn't right, and I was very upset at him."[31] This is not righteous indignation over a matter of public policy. This is a powerful man humiliating a powerless subordinate. It's the kind of behavior that earns you the nickname "Punk."

4: PRESSURING A COLLEAGUE TO FIRE A MID-LEVEL STAFFER

Judy Leiby was a veterans' affairs expert on the staff of McCain's Arizona colleague, Senator Dennis DeConcini. In a meeting with veterans in the late 1980s, Leiby believed McCain had misstated her boss's position on a veterans' issue, so she set the record straight. That kind of thing happens every day, in every line of work. And if you're the powerful senator, you let it go. Heck, she might have been right; after all, she was the expert on DeConcini's record. Instead, McCain went to DeConcini and repeatedly insisted that he fire Leiby. To his credit, DeConcini "politely told McCain to go to hell."[32]

Petty, vindictive—the words come up over and over again when people discuss McCain's temper. To use your power as a United States senator to try to deny someone their livelihood—on more than one occasion—is an abuse of power. And if someone abuses his office as senator to punish nearly defenseless staffers, do we really want to give him more power than anyone else on earth?

3: "YOU BETTER SUPPORT ME"

In 1985, Carl Kunasek felt the wrath of McNasty. McCain was in his first race for the Senate, and Kunasek refused to endorse him. Kunasek was a GOP state senator, hardly a kingmaker, but if you're the kind of guy who goes after secretaries and congressional staffers, Carl Kunasek was a big shot by comparison. Kunasek recalls McCain "standing on his feet and leaning over and telling me what would happen to me" if he did not endorse McCain. Kunasek has never specified the threat but says the blowup "was not pleasant, and I was surprised."[33]

At one level, this is perhaps not a very big deal. But I include it because it contradicts the notion that McCain reserves his flare-ups for policy disputes, rip-offs of taxpayers, or other lofty matters. This was straight politics—naked ambition—and it brought out McNasty's ugly side.

2: DENIGRATING THE SERVICE OF A NAVY VET—AND FELLOW SENATOR

Former senator Bob Smith, a New Hampshire Republican and a Navy veteran who also served in Vietnam, said that in an argument, McCain denigrated his service in Vietnam. "I was in the combat zone, off the Mekong River, for ten months," Smith said. "He [McCain] went on to insult me several times," Smith recalled. "I wasn't on the land; I guess that was his reasoning. . . . He suggested I was masquerading about my Vietnam service. It was very hurtful. He's gotten to a lot of people [that way]."

No fan of McCain, Smith expresses deep concern about a potential McCain presidency. "His temper would place this country at risk in international affairs, and the world perhaps in danger. In my mind, it should disqualify him." Smith went on to say, "It raises questions about stability. . . . It's more than just temper. It's this need of his to show you that he's above you—a sneering, condescending attitude. It's hurt his relationships in Congress. . . ."[34]

1: USING HIS POWER TO ENFORCE VENDETTAS AGAINST LOW-LEVEL PUBLIC SERVANTS

When power is used on behalf of the vulnerable, it can be a wonderful thing. Conversely, there is little uglier than a powerful politician seeking to crush a vulnerable person. Karen Johnson had been the secretary for the Republican governor of Arizona, Evan Mecham. Not secretary of state or secretary of transportation—just his secretary. When McCain launched into a tirade against the governor—who, no doubt, deserved it, being a crook and a kook and all—Ms. Johnson stood up for her boss. She dared to yell back at Senator Hothead. When McCain called Governor Meacham "an embarrassment to the party," Ms. Johnson stepped up and said, "How dare you? You're the embarrassment to the party."

Another politician might have been chastened, perhaps even impressed, with Ms. Johnson's moxie. Not John McCain. Years later—years, mind you—when Johnson applied to be an aide to the chairman of the Maricopa County Board of Supervisors, McCain dropped the hammer. He personally called the board chairman, Tom Freestone, and asked him not to hire Johnson. "Everyone in [Freestone's] office thought it was ridiculous . . . and petty," Johnson told the *Washington Post.* To his credit, Freestone hired Johnson anyway. And today Ms. Johnson is State Senator Johnson—described by the *Post* as "a devout Republican conservative."[35]

Few things are uglier than using great power to harm weaker people. But that is what John McCain has done more than once. McCain has "a bit of a vindictive streak." A former Pentagon official stated, "John has an enemies list longer than Nixon's. And unlike Nixon, McCain really does try to get you."[36]

I WISH I KNEW HOW TO QUIT YOU!

8

CRAZY BASE WORLD

JON STEWART: You're not freaking out on us? Are you freaking out on us? Because if you're freaking out and you're going into the crazy base world—are you going into crazy base world?

McCAIN: I'm afraid so.[1]

[John McCain is a] true conservative . . . his principles are sound and solid as far as I'm concerned.

—*President George W. Bush*[2]

THE MYTH OF THE MODERATE

In 2000, John McCain introduced his "straight talk" mantra. He traveled around the country blasting other Republicans for toeing the party line. In particular, McCain made decrying the hatred and intolerance of the extreme religious right a pillar of his campaign. In a speech to supporters in Virginia Beach, Virginia, McCain blasted Pat Robertson and Jerry Falwell as "agents of intolerance." McCain then said, "Neither party should be defined by pandering to the outer reaches of American politics and the agents of intolerance, whether they be Louis Farrakhan or Al Sharpton on the left, or Pat Robertson or Jerry Falwell on the right."[3]

Conservative Republicans, who form the base of the GOP, didn't much care for it. But the press loved it. Reporters fell in love with John McCain. The word *love* doesn't really do justice to their reaction. Think of the kind of love felt by a ninth-grade boy: red-faced, doe-eyed, I-go-to-sleep-thinking-of-you-and-wake-up-thinking-of-you, pubescent puppy love. I mean, the media love McCain.

Problem is, they don't know him. As McCain himself has said repeatedly, he is, has been, and ever will be a right-wing conservative. He was a right-wing conservative who, before he ran against George W. Bush in 2000, voted against honoring Dr. Martin Luther King, Jr., and he is a right-wing conservative who voted with George W. Bush 91 percent of the time after he ran against Bush.[4]

That brief period in 2000 when he was courting the press is the only time John McCain has ever even pretended to be a moderate. And he's been living off it ever since. The John McCain of 2008 has abandoned his 2000 flirtation with centrism and returned to the wholehearted embrace of the furthest fringes of the right wing that was the hallmark of McCain's pre-2000 political career.

Apparently McCain concluded he could not win the Republican presidential nomination without moving back to the right. And so, in 2008, McCain isn't just actively courting the most intolerant members of the far right but he is also openly campaigning with them and has said he is "proud" to have their support and endorsements.[5]

The ugly truth of the matter is that McCain has now spent nearly a decade wooing the radical right. After his bitter loss to President Bush in the Republican primaries, McCain went groveling to the "agents of intolerance" to try to salvage his political ambitions.[6] An honest look at McCain's actual record reveals that McCain is hardly the self-created maverick the press embraced in 2000. Instead, it reveals that McCain is not just a Republican but an extremist within the Republican Party when it comes to women's issues, civil rights, and social issues—not to mention the economy, health care, and the war in Iraq (which are dealt with in other chapters).

Don't take my word for it, just review some of McCain's positions and promises. Check out this record, and then try to pretend McCain is a moderate.

DISHONORING MARTIN LUTHER KING, JR., HIRING A RACIST, VOTING AGAINST CIVIL RIGHTS

On April 4, 2008, John McCain traveled to Memphis to commemorate the fortieth anniversary of the assassination of Dr. Martin Luther King, Jr. That rainy Friday, McCain stood in front of a largely black crowd to give a speech on his "evolution" on civil rights.

In 1983, McCain voted against honoring Dr. Martin Luther King, Jr., with a federal holiday.[7] Let me repeat that—McCain voted against honoring Dr. King. Four days after King was assassinated, the visionary congressman John Conyers of Michigan proposed a national holiday honoring King. Fifteen years later, Congressman Conyers's dream was on the verge of becoming law. President Ronald Reagan signaled that he would sign the King Holiday bill into law. The Senate bill, sponsored by the indomitable Teddy Kennedy, garnered seventy-eight votes. The House bill was cosponsored by Republican Jack Kemp and supported by 338 congressmen, including Newt Gingrich of Georgia. But one of the ninety congressmen to oppose the holiday was John McCain of Arizona.

But wait, it gets worse.

In 1987, McCain supported the decision of Arizona's Republican governor to rescind the holiday in Arizona.[8] Governor Evan Mecham had horrible relations with African Americans and had a regular and nasty habit of using racial slurs.[9] Yet McCain supported Mecham at the Arizona Teenage Republican Convention. "McCain said that he felt the governor was correct."[10] What a terrible lesson for those teenagers to learn—that some politicians will pander to the worst elements of human nature in order to gain votes.

In 1989, six years after Ronald Reagan signed the federal holiday into law, mind you, McCain grudgingly supported the state holiday, but was still bitching about the federal one. "I'm still opposed to another federal holiday," he said, "but I support the [Arizona] Martin Luther King holiday because of the enormous proportions this issue has taken on as far as the image of our state and our treatment towards not only blacks but all minorities."[11] So he was against honoring Dr. King in principle, but he understood that Arizona's continued opposition made the state look bad.

In 1992, to his credit, McCain endorsed Proposition 300, which would establish a paid state holiday honoring Dr. King in Arizona.[12] But just two years later, he was still trying to cripple the federal holiday, voting with Senator Jesse Helms (R-Confederacy) to bar funding for the Martin Luther King Jr. Federal Holiday Commission. The commission was established in 1984 "to encourage the observance of King's birthday."[13]

McCain also voted against the Civil Rights Act of 1990 four times.[14] The bill, which had bipartisan support, was designed to address employer discrimination after the Supreme Court overturned a 1971 ruling requiring businesses that discriminate to show a "business necessity" behind their hiring practice. Calling it a "quota bill," President George H. W. Bush vetoed it, and the Democratic Congress sought to override the veto. It all came down to one vote. As Sam Stein of the *Huffington Post* wrote, "The environment was so charged that white supremacist David Duke watched from one section of the Senate gallery while civil rights leader Jesse Jackson stood briefly at the chamber's other end. Ultimately, the vote fell one short: 66 to 34. Prominent Republican senators like John H. Chafee, John Danforth, Pete Domenici, and Arlen Specter all chose to override the veto. McCain—who had earlier voted for a watered-down version of the bill, one that didn't reverse the court's decision—backed the president."[15]

In 2000, McCain was claiming that he had "evolved" on the issue of race, but he was simultaneously relying on Richard Quinn, an overt racist, as one of his key strategists. Quinn described the Martin Luther King holiday as "vitriolic and profane."[16] In a 1983 column that appeared in *Southern Partisan*, Quinn wrote: "King Day should have been rejected because its purpose is vitriolic and profane. By celebrating King as the incarnation of all they admire, they [black leaders] have chosen to glorify the histrionic rather than the heroic and by inference they spurned the brightest and the best among their own race. Ignoring the real heroes in our nation's life, the blacks have chosen a man who represents not their emancipation, not their sacrifices and bravery in service to their country; rather, they have chosen a man whose role in history was to lead his people into a perpetual dependence on the welfare state, a terrible bondage of body and soul."[17]

Quinn openly advocated for the election of former Ku Klux Klan grand wizard David Duke as Louisiana's governor, writing, "What better way to reject politics as usual than to elect a maverick like David Duke? What better way to tweak the nose of the establishment?"[18] Quinn's magazine also sold T-shirts celebrating the assassination of Abraham Lincoln.[19] Yet John McCain didn't fire him. Even after evidence of Quinn's racist past was brought to McCain's attention, he praised Quinn as a "respected" and "fine man."[20]

On April 4, 2008, McCain went to Memphis to commemorate the fortieth anniversary of the assassination of Martin Luther King, Jr. Standing outside the Lorraine Hotel, where King had been shot, McCain said he had been wrong. "We can be slow as well to give greatness its due," he said, "a mistake I myself made long ago . . . when I voted against a federal holiday in memory of Dr. King. I was wrong, I was wrong."[21]

I do not doubt McCain's sincerity, but the apology, however

heartfelt, was incomplete. The senator did not explain why, even years after the holiday became law, he still refused to support it, why he tried to de-fund and undermine it. He did not explain why, having served honorably alongside sailors of every race, he could have hired a racist. He did not explain why, when employment discrimination was the issue, he voted four times against the Civil Rights Act of 1990. He did not explain those actions because, I suspect, he cannot.

McCain was loudly and openly booed by the assembled crowd. It's no wonder. McCain has a long and disturbing record on civil rights. It also probably didn't help that as McCain stood there giving his speech, he left it to an African American man to hold an umbrella over him, an image no American who saw the speech will be able to forget.[22]

EQUAL PAY? NO WAY

According to the National Women's Law Center, "Women in the United States are still paid only 77 cents for every dollar earned by men. For women of color, the numbers are even worse—African-American women earn 63 cents and Latinas earn 52 cents for every dollar paid to white men."[23] Oftentimes when a woman is the victim of wage discrimination it takes some time to uncover it. It's not like folks wander the halls of their office declaring their salaries. But when Lilly Ledbetter found out she was the victim of wage discrimination, she set out to fight for her rights.

Ms. Ledbetter worked for Goodyear in Gadsden, Alabama. She made $3,727 a month, and when she found out that all the men with comparable jobs were consistently given higher raises than she was—and were all making between $4,286 and $5,236 a month—she sued and won. But the Supreme Court, led by Bush-appointed Justice Samuel Alito and Chief Justice John Roberts, overturned Ledbetter's victory on a technicality. The Bush Court ruled that the 1964 Civil Rights Act, which Ledbetter had used to sue, required her to file a claim for wage discrimination within one hundred and eighty days of the first incidence of discrimination—even though at the time the raises had been doled out, she'd had no way of knowing she'd been discriminated against.[24]

Justice Ruth Bader Ginsburg—the Thurgood Marshall of women's rights litigation—took the unusual step of reading her dissent from the bench in order to highlight how strongly she felt about the Court's decision. Speaking for herself and Justices Stevens, Souter, and Breyer (the same brave four who dissented in *Bush v. Gore*), Ginsburg said, "In our view, the Court does not comprehend, or is indifferent to, the insidious way in which women can be victims of pay discrimination." She called on Congress to fix the Court's interpretation of the law and make equal pay the law of the land.[25]

You'd think this would be a fairly straightforward case, especially for a conservative legislator who opposes courts rewriting laws from the bench. This is a case in which the Supreme Court twisted the plain meaning of Congress's legislation to restrict the rights of American citizens. A true jurisprudential conservative would, one might think, want to reassert Congress's primacy here.

But not John McCain. John McCain missed the vote but issued a statement saying he opposed the Lilly Ledbetter Fair Pay Act, claiming it would only encourage more lawsuits.[26] That's like opposing a crime bill on the grounds that it will only cause more arrests. It will only cause more lawsuits if employers keep violating the law and denying women equal pay. During a campaign event in Michigan, McCain was asked by a fourteen-year-old girl about his opposition to equal pay laws. McCain showed no mercy, saying, "I don't believe that this would do anything to help the rights of women, except maybe help trial lawyers and others in that profession."[27]

If that fourteen-year-old girl wants to live in a country in which women earn as much as men for the same work, she better pray the grown-ups all vote for Barack Obama.

JUDGES

One of George W. Bush's most enduring and damaging legacies is his appointments to the federal judiciary. John McCain hopes to extend George W. Bush's conservative stranglehold on the Supreme Court and the rest of the judicial branch of government.

In May 2008, McCain gave a major speech on the federal judiciary in North Carolina. It amounted to nothing less than a big wet kiss to the radical right wing of the Republican Party. When you read it, the one thought that comes to mind is, *Get a room.*

In his speech, John McCain promised the right wing of his party that he would continue the Bush policy of appointing judges from the far right, judges in the mold of Chief Justice John Roberts, Jr., and Associate Justice Samuel Alito, Jr., who are today two of the most conservative members of the Supreme Court.[28]

Let's break down McCain's speech. His exact words were, "I have my own standards of judicial ability, experience, philosophy, and temperament. Justice Roberts and Justice Alito meet those standards in every respect. They would serve as the model for my own nominees."[29] Allow me to translate. McCain used George W. Bush's judicial code words to assure the far right: "I have the same right-wing standards as Bush, and I'll appoint judges just like Roberts and Alito." Like Bush, McCain would pack the courts with judges set on dismantling Americans' rights—civil rights, consumers' rights, women's rights, and individuals' rights—in favor of the government and businesses. Among Roberts's and Alito's handiwork has been a gutting of federal laws that protect our water[30] and the denial of equal pay to a female factory worker who had been paid less than men for doing the same job.[31] In the words of Simon Lazarus of the National Senior Citizens Law Center, the Court is "repealing the twentieth century . . . merrily revoking a century of legislation protecting citizens, consumers, workers, and minorities against business."[32]

In his speech to the kook right, McCain said, "I will look for accomplished men and women with a proven record of excellence in law and a proven commitment to judicial restraint."[33] This right-wing notion of "restraint" is a crock of caca. In the whole history of American jurisprudence, there has never been a case of more outrageous judicial overreach than *Bush v. Gore.* That stinking pile of judicial crap is a monument to the hypocrisy of the Bush-McCain claptrap about "restraint." If the Supreme Court—or, more precisely, five thieves in black robes appointed by Reagan and Bush's daddy—can stop the lawful counting of legal votes, then the judiciary has no restraint. But when it comes to protecting consumers against corporations, when it comes to protecting citizens against the Bush government's heavy hand, when it comes to protecting women and minorities and gays, the elderly and the disabled—well, then we need a little restraint.

What McCain really means when he says he will appoint judges who will practice "restraint" is that he will appoint right-wing Bush-approved judges who oppose laws that protect hard-working Americans but will bend, break, and contort the law to protect the powerful and the privileged. Like Bush, McCain is set on appointing judges who will look the other way when giant corporations take advantage of average Americans.

McCain has promised, "I pledge to appoint strict constructionist judges."[34] What he means is he will support judges who will want to rewind the clock and take us back to the eighteenth century. These judges will pretend no Court case has been argued since the Constitution was written.

A sample of the judges Bush tried to appoint to the federal bench with McCain cheering him on will send chills down your spine. Keep in mind that George W. Bush nominated all of these people—and John McCain supported them all:

Priscilla Owen

On the Texas Supreme Court, Owen consistently threw out jury verdicts for workers and consumers.[35] She regularly dismissed suits brought by workers for job-related injuries, discrimination, and unfair employment practices.[36] The *Minneapolis Star Tribune* noted that "even her court colleagues have commented on her habit of twisting the law to fit her hyperconservative political views."[37] Papers in Texas agreed that Owen "is less interested in impartially interpreting the law than in pushing an agenda."[38] Owen also has a nasty and regular habit of inserting her personal anti-choice beliefs into her judicial opinions.[39] Priscilla Owen has the kind of record only a corporate tycoon could love. Because of George W. Bush and John McCain, Priscilla Owen enjoys a lifetime appointment to the powerful Fifth Circuit Court of Appeals.[40]

William Pryor

President Bush nominated William Pryor, Jr., to the Eleventh Circuit Court of Appeals in 2003. The *Washington Post* and the *Atlanta Journal-Constitution* immediately declared that Pryor was "unfit to judge."[41] During Pryor's tenure as attorney general of Alabama, he was the only attorney general to join a suit asking the Supreme Court to strike down the Violence Against Women Act.[42] (Thirty-six attorneys general took the other side, asking the Court to preserve the Violence Against Women Act.) He also asked the Court to give its blessing to Texas cops who broke into a man's home, caught him in bed with another man, and prosecuted him. Even the right-wing Reagan-Bush court refused to go along with that.[43]

Pryor has also consistently shown hostility to laws that protect working people. In a letter to the Senate Judiciary Committee, the AFL-CIO said Pryor "has authored or joined numerous legal briefs challenging the constitutionality of a host of federal employment protections, including the Family and Medical Leave Act, the Americans with Disabilities Act, the Age

Discrimination in Employment Act, and the Fair Labor Standards Act."[44]

From the bench, Pryor actively sought to gut the Family Medical Leave Act, the Americans with Disabilities Act, the Clean Water Act, and the Voting Rights Act.[45] He is known for his knee-jerk hostility to civil rights and for calling *Roe v. Wade* the "worst abomination of constitutional law in our history."[46] Yet John McCain voted to give him a lifetime appointment to the federal bench.[47]

Janice Rogers Brown

Janice Rogers Brown is a proud right-wing radical. She has compared government with slavery, declared that no government should try to protect individual rights, and called the New Deal a triumph of a socialist revolution.[48] When she was nominated to the California Supreme Court in 1996, the California Judicial Commission gave Rogers Brown a "not qualified" rating. The Judicial Commission noted her tendency to "interject her political and philosophical views into her opinions," and said that she was "insensitive to established legal precedent and lacked compassion and intellectual tolerance for opposing views."[49] George W. Bush nominated Brown for the prestigious and powerful Appeals Court for the District of Columbia Circuit. John McCain voted to confirm her—for life.[50]

Brett Kavanaugh

Mr. Kavanaugh is a poster child for the Bush administration's appointees. Unqualified, partisan, less than honest . . . and appointed to a powerful job nonetheless.[51] At the time of his nomination to the U.S. Court of Appeals for the D.C. Circuit, Kavanaugh had been a lawyer for only thirteen years, half the time of a typical nominee. He also had almost no courtroom or litigation experience.[52] Kavanaugh's sole qualification appears to have been his partisan loyalty to President Bush. That and writing pornography. Kavanaugh was a deputy in the Starr Chamber, and in service to Starr was the primary author of the *Starr Report,* which was lurid and gratuitous and vicious.

Oh, yeah. Kavanaugh might have lied under oath. (Ironic coming from a Starr acolyte, isn't it?) In the Senate Judiciary Committee hearing on Kavanaugh's confirmation to the U.S. Court of Appeals for the D.C. Circuit, Senator Dick Durbin (D-IL) asked Kavanaugh if he'd played any role in the legal analysis and debate over enemy combatants. Kavanaugh categorically denied it. But according to National Public Radio's Ari Shapiro, "Multiple sources have confirmed that Kavanaugh, who denied any prior or current involvement in 'rules governing detention of combatants' at his confirmation hearing, did in fact meet with a group of top White House lawyers about enemy combatants in 2002."[53] The diplomatic Durbin was understated, saying he was "perilously close to being lied to. I will just say that . . . [Kavanaugh] had to know he was misleading me and the committee."[54]

This amateur pornographer and part-time truth-twister now sits on the powerful D.C. Circuit Court for life—because of George W. Bush and John McCain.[55]

McCain's support for ultra–right-wing judges is nothing new. Back in the Reagan administration, he supported the nomination of Robert Bork to the Supreme Court. He said, "I believe Robert Bork is well qualified in all four respects and observed Judge Bork in his capacity as solicitor general and federal court of appeals judge." He criticized what he called "the tactics of distortion, hysteria, and politicized paranoia that many of the special interests have used and exploited to oppose this man."[56]

"CRAZY PREACHERS FOR $1,000, ALEX"

Oceans of ink have splashed across acres of trees documenting the kooky comments of Reverend Jeremiah Wright. But when it comes to being involved with truly nutty, scary, crazy preachers, John McCain's buddies make Jeremiah Wright look like Billy Graham. Here are just a few.

Jerry Falwell

It is one of the most remarkable turnarounds since Saul of Tarsus was struck down on the road to Damascus. The first time John McCain ran for president, he called Reverend Jerry Falwell an "agent of intolerance," who exerted an "evil influence" on the Republican Party.[57] But by the time he was gearing up for his second presidential campaign, he said, "I believe that the Christ—quote 'Christian right' has a major role to play in the Republican Party," and reasoned that Falwell was no longer intolerant. When asked if he still believed his 2000 statement to be true, he answered, "No, I don't."[58]

Reverend Falwell is no longer with us, of course. But he lived long enough to welcome John McCain to the ranks of the kook right. In 2006, the *Lynchburg News & Advance* reported that McCain "will be Liberty University's graduation speaker. 'I was in Washington with him about three months ago,' Falwell said. 'We dealt with every difference we have. There are no deal breakers now.' Falwell, Liberty University's chancellor, said McCain, an Arizona Republican, is among the presidential candidates he could support in 2008."[59]

Rod Parsley

Perhaps I have a soft spot for the late Reverend Falwell because I interviewed him so many times on *Crossfire.* But some of Senator McCain's other right-wing friends make Jerry Falwell look like a bleeding heart. Take Rod Parsley, please.

While appearing together in Cincinnati, Ohio, John McCain and Rod Parsley traded compliments in front of a large crowd. McCain called Parsley his "spiritual mentor" and "moral compass."[60] Parsley said McCain was a "strong, true, consistent conservative."[61] The only problem with that is . . . how do I say this delicately? . . . Pastor Rod Parsley is a whack-job. In his book *Silent No More*, Parsley wrote, "The fact is that America was founded, in part, with the intention of seeing this false religion [Islam] destroyed, and I believe September 11, 2001, was a generational call to arms that we can no longer ignore."[62]

In Parsley's view, America was created not to "form a more perfect Union," as the Constitution says. Not to declare that "all men are created equal," as the Declaration of Independence says. Not so that "government of the people, by the people, and for the people shall not perish from the earth," as Lincoln said at Gettysburg. No, according to Hot Rod Parsley, America was created to destroy Islam. Research into the type of guidance Parsley gives people yields disturbing facts. Parsley has consistently advocated for a modern holy war against Islam, much like the Crusades.[63] He has asserted that the United States was founded to destroy Islam.[64] He has accused liberals of advocating racism, genocide, and segregation.[65] Parsley also advocated criminal punishment for adultery, which would put about half of the GOP—or, for that matter, the Democratic Party—in prison.[66]

John McCain called Pastor Rod Parsley his "spiritual mentor" and "moral compass."[67]

Parsley is a key leader in a group calling itself the Patriot Pastors, a collection of apocalyptic evangelical preachers who are aiming to "transform" America by applying the resources of their churches to political campaigns. The Patriot Pastors are a church-based campaign that has referred to political opponents and church leaders who oppose their radical agenda as "secular jihadists," the "forces of darkness," and the "hordes of hell."[68] My, that sounds like a unifying force in America, doesn't it? These lunatics support politicians who adhere to their radical agenda of gutting social services for the poor (because Jesus really hated the poor, didn't he?), vicious opposition to gay rights, and other hard-line right-wing positions. They are different from other conservative religious organizations in their advocacy not just on social issues but also a wide range of economic issues. These Patriot Pastors support more tax cuts for the superwealthy and gutting the minimum wage.[69]

Again, John McCain called Pastor Rod Parsley his "spiritual mentor" and "moral compass."

Maybe Pastor Rod and Senator McCain are right. In a little-quoted part of the Sermon on the Mount, Christ said, "Blessed are the investment bankers, for they shall be called Children of the Trust Fund. Blessed are the CEOs, for their parachutes are golden. Blessed are those with capital gains, because if you can't walk on water, you ought to have a yacht."

I would also point out in the Patriot Pastors' defense that Jesus never once spoke out in support of Social Security (all that "honor thy father and thy mother" stuff is so Old Testament), nor did he ever call for increased funding for the school lunch program. So, you have to admit, Pastor Parsley and his disciples George W. Bush and John McCain are on pretty sound theological ground here.

During the 2006 congressional midterm elections, Parsley was a busy man. He traveled around Ohio advocating for the election of radical right-wing Republican Ken Blackwell as governor. Blackwell is a charming guy; I've interviewed him any number of times. But he's also a charming guy who, as secretary of state of Ohio and a Bush-Cheney campaign cochair, helped swing the state of Ohio to Bush by putting too few voting machines in predominantly Democratic neighborhoods.[70]

Parsley didn't tell his flock to vote for Blackwell because of economic or even political reasons. Instead, he used radical biblical and religious terms to tell his followers, "Let the Reformation begin! Shout it like you're going to carry the blood-stained banner of the cross of Christ the length and breadth of the Buckeye State!"[71] I've read the Bible. I've studied the Bible. I've tried to live my life by its eternal Truth, as God gives me the light. So I'm pretty sure that nothing in the Bible requires me to carry the blood-stained banner of Christ for any politician, least of all Ken Blackwell.

Parsley's propensity to stir crowds with violent imagery has surfaced at other times as well. During a speech to the "War on Christians and Values Voters Conference," Rod Parsley said, "So my admonishment to you this morning is this: Sound an alarm! A spiritual invasion is taking place." He added, "Man your battle stations! Ready your weapons! They say, 'His rhetoric is so inciting.' I came to incite a riot! I came to effect a divine disturbance in the heart and soul of the church. Man your battle stations, ready your weapons, lock and load!"[72]

Did I mention that John McCain called Pastor Parsley his "spiritual mentor" and "moral compass"? Because he did.

Now, imagine if the leading Democratic candidate for president were associated with a pastor who advocated for the complete obliteration of a major world religion and called for a new holy war, led by the United States, to retake the Holy Land. Imagine that candidate had called that pastor his "spiritual mentor," his "moral compass." Would he (or she) be getting the free ride that John McCain has enjoyed for his association with Rod Parsley?

John Hagee

Pastor John Hagee is one of the most controversial right-wing extremists John McCain has courted. McCain spent an entire year wooing this right-wing hatemonger,[73] following the playbook written by George Bush and Karl Rove. After all, Hagee is a big supporter of George W. Bush.[74]

Hagee is a bigoted right-wing pastor who has called the Catholic Church the "great whore"[75] and who once asserted that Hitler was doing God's work through the Holocaust.[76] During a televised sermon, Pastor Hagee said, "When Adolf Hitler came to power he said, 'I'm not going to do anything in my lifetime that hasn't been done by the Roman Church for the past eight hundred years, I'm only going to do it on a greater scale and more efficiently.'"[77]

At a press event in Texas in late February 2008, John McCain accepted Hagee's endorsement. He said, "Pastor John Hagee, who has supported and endorsed my candidacy, supports what I stand for and believe in."[78] McCain also said, "A lot of people are coming in our direction."

For his part, Hagee said that McCain had his "vigorous enthusiastic and personal support for his solid pro-life record for the past twenty-four years."[79]

Not only did McCain accept Hagee's endorsement but his

campaign also said he "speaks regularly" with Hagee.[80] After McCain sealed Hagee's endorsement, Catholic groups on the left and the right became outraged and denounced Hagee.

In discussing what he sees as the history of the Catholic Church, Hagee said, "This false cult system that was born in the Genesis 10 and progressed through Israel and became Baal worship."[81] Pointing to an icon representing the Catholic Church, Hagee said, "This is the Great Whore of Revelations 17. This is the Anti-Christ system. This is the Apostate Church."[82] He has also said, "While the church is in heaven, this false religious system is going to be totally devoured by the anti-Christ."[83]

Real nice, Pastor Hagee. We Catholics love you, too.

You would think that when John McCain learned of Hagee's virulent anti-Catholicism (as if he didn't already know about it), he would denounce such hatred. And you would be wrong. McCain stood by Hagee, just as his role model, George W. Bush, stood by the anti-Catholic bigots of Bob Jones University. "I will say that he said that his words were taken out of context, he defends his position," McCain told Bill Bennett's *Morning in America* radio audience. "I hope that maybe you'd give him a chance to respond. He says he has never been anti-Catholic, but I repudiate the words that create that impression."[84]

Under pressure from Catholic activists, Hagee issued an "apology." Right, Pastor. A long history of hate disavowed in one press release. It reminded me of Emily Litella, the Gilda Radner character on *Saturday Night Live* who would go off on a long tangent, then, when told she had misunderstood the issue, would say, "Never mind."

Women aren't spared from Hagee's hatred either. Hagee is the author of *What Every Man Wants in a Woman,* and if there is anything he knows, it's what men want. Hagee suggested that women naturally have a desire to lead through "feminine manipulation," and that every man had the God-given role to be the loving leader of the home.[85] "The feminist movement today is throwing off authority in rebellion against God's pattern for the family," he said.[86]

If he ever gets tired of spreading hatred, Hagee could do open mic at the Laff Lounge. "Do you know the difference between a woman with PMS and a snarling Doberman pinscher?" Hagee asks. "The answer is lipstick. Do you know the difference between a terrorist and a woman with PMS? You can negotiate with a terrorist."[87] Ha ha ha. Oh, stop, Pastor! You're killing me!

Unsatisfied with attacking Catholics and women, Hagee has also explicitly said that Hurricane Katrina was God's revenge on the city of New Orleans. "I believe that New Orleans had a level of sin that was offensive to God," he said. "And they are—and they are—were the recipients of the judgment of God for that."[88] Hagee thinks New Orleans is inherently more sinful than other American cities.[89] As recently as April 2008, Hagee has said that he continues to believe that not all natural disasters are wrought because of sin, but that New Orleans was a special case because it was a city planning sinful conduct.[90] He did not explain why the rest of the Gulf Coast was also savaged by Katrina. Mississippi was hit as hard as Louisiana was, and it is overwhelmingly Republican and Christian. But I think I've already thought this through more rigorously than Pastor Hagee did.

But Hagee crossed the Rubicon with his comments about Hitler. A leader in the Christian Zionist movement, Hagee was long seen as a stalwart friend of Israel—if for some rather controversial theological reasons. But when Hagee said Hitler was part of God's plan . . . well, that went a little too far. "Now how is God going to bring them [Jews] back to the land [Israel]?" Hagee asked. "The answer is fishers and hunters . . . behold, I will send for many fishers and after will I send for many hunters. And they the hunters shall hunt them from every mountain and from every hill and from out of the holes of the rocks. If that doesn't describe what Hitler did in the Holocaust . . . you can't see that . . . then God sent a hunter. A hunter is someone who comes with a gun and he forces you. Hitler was a hunter."[91] The message is pretty unmistakable. According to Hagee, God sent Hitler to Earth to round up and exterminate the Jews who did not return to Israel.

John McCain stuck by Hagee for weeks even as Catholics from both parties made clear they were troubled by McCain's acceptance of support from one of the most prominent anti-Catholic figures in America. The furthest McCain would go was to "repudiate" the anti-Catholic statements Hagee had made. It took weeks of constant revelations of Hagee's anti-Catholic, anti-Semitic, and sexist remarks before McCain finally backed away.[92]

After spending so much time courting these right-wing figures, McCain no doubt knew—at least generally—about their past comments. After all, these are the hatemongers whom McCain had called "agents of intolerance" in 2000. These "spiritual advisers" are only some of the many inheritances from George W. Bush that John McCain has embraced.

ABORTION RIGHTS—FLIP-FLOP-FLIP; CONTRACEPTION—NOPE, NOPE, NOPE

Abortion is one of the most difficult and divisive issues in America. John McCain has been on both sides of it. "Certainly in the short term, or even the long term, I would not support repeal of *Roe v. Wade,*" he said in 1999, "which would then force X number of women in America to [undergo] illegal and dangerous operations."[93] That same year, McCain said he wanted to revise the party platform to make it clear "to young women in this country who may have a disagreement with us on the issue of abortion" that "there's room for all of us in our party."[94] Back then McCain said he wanted to return to the 1980 GOP platform, which he said recognized divergent views on abortion within the Republican ranks. He even went so far as to say he would consider a pro-choice running mate.[95]

But before and after that brief interlude, McCain was strongly pro-life. He brags about having a zero lifetime rating from NARAL,[96] whose president, Nancy Keenan, said, "He voted against family planning, he voted against the freedom of access to clinic entrances—that was about violence against women in clinics." She added, "He voted against funding for teen pregnancy-prevention programs, and making sure that abstinence only was medically accurate. This is very, very extreme."[97]

So McCain was pro-life before he was pro-choice, then pro-choice before he was pro-life again. That's a flip-flop-flip that should insult and concern every American, no matter where they stand on abortion.

Although he's been all over the map on abortion, McCain is, oddly, more consistent in his opposition to contraception, family planning, AIDS education, and sex education. In 2003, McCain voted against an amendment that would allow states to expand the States' Children's Health Insurance Program to include low-income pregnant women. It also would have authorized $10 million for a program to educate public health organizations, providers, and the public about the availability and effectiveness of emergency contraceptives; allowed state public health agencies to apply for grants for further programs; required private health plans to cover prescription contraceptives and related medical services; and required hospitals to make emergency contraceptives and information about them available to rape victims.[98]

In 1998, McCain voted for a State Department authorization bill that included language barring any U.S. contributions for contraceptive and reproductive health programs to international family planning programs that used their own separate funds to lobby or speak out on abortion.[99]

I have no idea whether John McCain "saved" himself for marriage, but he sure is interested in telling other people that they should. Back in 1996, McCain voted to siphon funds from the Maternal and Child Health Care Block Grant to an abstinence education program.[100] And in 2003, McCain voted to require that 33 percent of the money designated for AIDS prevention in the Global AIDS Relief package be devoted to abstinence education,[101] a pet cause of the right wing despite the fact that, as the *New York Times* has reported, "the most comprehensive study of abstinence education found no sign that it delayed a teenager's sexual debut."[102] Think about that. People are dying of AIDS all around the world, and John McCain, not exactly a medical specialist, is dictating that one-third of the AIDS prevention funds be spent on a crackpot theory of the right wing.

When asked about these issues aboard his campaign bus, McCain launched into what at first seemed to be a comedy routine. Then observers realized it wasn't comedy, it was tragedy. Here's the exchange:

REPORTER: Should U.S. taxpayer money go to places like Africa to fund contraception to prevent AIDS?

MR. McCAIN: Well I think it's a combination. The guy I really respect on this is Dr. Coburn. [Note: that would be Tom Coburn, Republican senator from Oklahoma, who supports the death penalty for abortionists.[103]] He believes—and I was just reading the thing he wrote—that you should do what you can to encourage abstinence where there is going to be sexual activity. Where that doesn't succeed, then he thinks that we should employ contraceptives as well. But I agree with him that the first priority is on abstinence. I look to people like Dr. Coburn. I'm not very wise on it.

(Mr. McCain turns to take a question on Iraq, but a moment later looks back to the reporter who asked him about AIDS.)

MR. McCAIN: I haven't thought about it. Before I give you an answer, let me think about. Let me think about it a little bit because I never got a question about it before. I don't know if I would use taxpayers' money for it.

REPORTER: What about grants for sex education in the United States? Should they include instructions about using contraceptives? Or should it be Bush's policy, which is just abstinence?

MR. McCAIN: (long pause) Ahhh. I think I support the president's policy.

REPORTER: So no contraception, no counseling on contraception. Just abstinence. Do you think contraceptives help stop the spread of HIV?

MR. McCAIN: (long pause) You've stumped me.

REPORTER: I mean, I think you'd probably agree it probably does help stop it?

MR. McCAIN: (laughs) Are we on the Straight Talk Express? I'm not informed enough on it. Let me find out. You know, I'm sure I've taken a position on it in the past. I have to find out what my position was. Brian [press secretary Brian Jones], would you find out what my position is on contraception—I'm sure I'm opposed to government spending on it, I'm sure I support the president's policies on it.

REPORTER: But you would agree that condoms do stop the spread of sexually transmitted diseases. Would you say "No, we're not going to distribute them," knowing that?

MR. McCAIN: (twelve-second pause) Get me Coburn's thing, ask [adviser John] Weaver to get me Coburn's paper that he just gave me in the last couple of days. I've never gotten into these issues before.[104]

The Straight Talk Express had, indeed, taken a hard right turn, straight into the dank, rotting hell that is Crazy Base World.

★ SOME AMERICANS ARE MORE EQUAL THAN OTHERS ★

Like George W. Bush, McCain has a poor record on gay rights. McCain opposes protecting Americans from job discrimination on the basis of sexual orientation.[1] That is, he thinks it's okay for someone to have the power to fire you based on whom you date, dance with, or do whatever with. He even voted against updating hate crimes legislation to extend to gender and sexual orientation—three times.[2]

It's interesting. People who know Bush and McCain say in private they say all the right things about gays. Bush, for example, has by all accounts been perfectly comfortable with close aides and advisers who are gay. When then Arizona congressman Jim Kolbe was coming out of the closet, he said McCain's response was "I know what this is about, and it doesn't matter."[3]

And yet each man has been just as comfortable appealing to the worst, most base, most homophobic tendencies of the right wing. In his 2005 State of the Union address, Bush said, "For the good of families, children and society, I support a constitutional amendment to protect the institution of marriage."[4] Meanwhile McCain appeared in a particularly vicious anti-gay ad in Arizona to support Proposition 107, a ban on gay marriage. It's up on YouTube, like most things these days.

In the McCain-approved ad, a speaker warns that "marriage is the foundation of our society" as images of gay couples cross the screen to gloomy, the-end-is-coming music. Then a family portrait—man, woman, and child—pops onto the screen to an uplifting, light melody. That's about as subtle as a brick to the head. The last face on the screen is McCain's, as he urges Arizonans to vote with him and against gay Americans.[5]

Of course, McCain wants it both ways on same-sex marriage.

In fact, he once took both sides of the issue on either side of a commercial break. Appearing on MSNBC's *Hardball* in 2006, McCain was asked by host Chris Matthews a very simple question: "Should gay marriage be allowed?" McCain replied, "I think that gay marriage should be allowed, if there's a ceremony kind of thing, if you want to call it that. I don't have any problem with that, but I do believe in preserving the sanctity of the union between man and woman."[6]

That, to me, is an endorsement of gay marriage. Sure, he yapped about "the sanctity of the union between man and woman," but he didn't speak of the exclusivity of heterosexual marriage.

Then, during a commercial break, McCain's aide John Weaver whispered in his boss's ear. After the commercial, McCain interrupted himself while answering a question about the farm bill. And he said this: "Could I just mention one other thing? On the issue of the gay marriage, I believe that people want to have private ceremonies, that's fine. I do not believe that gay marriages should be legal."[7]

The audience at Iowa State University booed, but perhaps they should have cheered. Not many seventy-year-olds have the dexterity to execute a complete flip-flop over the span of one commercial break. According to *Vanity Fair*, McCain later was heard barking at Weaver, "Did I fix it? Did I fix it?"[8]

While trying to establish his right-wing bona fides by opposing gay marriage, McCain is also against a federal marriage amendment. He wants to punt the issue to the state legislatures. That hasn't kept McCain from flirting with a federal ban to stay cozy with the far right. In 2006, when McCain was courting Reverend Jerry Falwell, McCain apparently told Falwell what he wanted to hear. Falwell declared that "McCain has expressed a willingness to support a federal marriage amendment."[9] Then McCain still voted against the marriage amendment.[10] Voting against a federal ban while keeping up his vocal opposition to same-sex marriage was a savvy, low-cost move to shore up his maverick image.

On gay rights, McCain is anything but moderate. He sought and coveted the endorsements of bigots. While being interviewed by Ellen DeGeneres, McCain said, "I know that we have a respectful disagreement on that issue."[11] Yet McCain accepted the support of Reverends Rod Parsley and John Hagee. Parsley is a man who said that he opposed hate-crimes legislation because "we cannot allow . . . a radical homosexual lobby to dictate what we say." Parsley's second reason for opposing hate-crimes legislation was even worse: if hate-crimes legislation passed, Parsley said, "the next person charged with a crime could be me."[12]

McCain's buddy Pastor Hagee is, if possible, worse. In his book *What Every Man Wants in a Woman*, Hagee wrote, "There is no justification or acceptance of homosexuality. . . . Homosexuality means the death of society because homosexuals can recruit, but they cannot reproduce."[13] In that same literary opus, Hagee prophesied, "It [gay marriage] will open the door to incest, to polygamy, and every conceivable marriage arrangement demented minds can possibly conceive."[14]

And John McCain is in bed with these hatemongers. Metaphorically, that is. He's not literally in bed with them. I meant that in a male, macho, stag, studly, not-at-all-gay way. Just like when George W. Bush holds hands with the king of Saudi Arabia.

McCAIN ANGRY.
McCAIN WILL CUT
CHILDREN'S HEALTH CARE.

9

HEALTH CARE: THE McCAIN PLAN WON'T EVEN COVER McCAIN

Like most Americans, I go see my doctor fairly frequently.

—*John McCain*[1]

One of my concerns is that the health care not be as good as it can possibly be.

—*George W. Bush, on military benefits, Tipp City, Ohio, April 19, 2007*[2]

GOVERNMENT HEALTH CARE IS EVIL—EXCEPT FOR ME

George W. Bush is, physically speaking, the picture of health. With all the mountain biking and jogging, the weight training and brush clearing—and don't forget the naps—President Bush is fit as a fiddle. Oh, sure, he passed out while undertaking the onerous challenge of eating a pretzel, has had some noncancerous polyps removed from his colon, and beat back a bout of Lyme disease, but overall his doctors have pronounced him in "superior" medical condition.[3] Overall cholesterol is 170, resting heart rate is 52 beats per minute, and his body fat is an astonishingly low 16.6 percent.[4]

John McCain, on the other hand, well, what can I say? If elected, he will be seventy-two at his inauguration in 2009, making him the oldest first-term president in history.[5] But age is not everything. Ask any used car salesman and you'll hear, "It's not the years, it's the mileage." Sadly, McCain's chassis has seen some hard miles. He has had four melanomas, described by the physician-journalist Lawrence K. Altman of the *New York Times* as "a potentially fatal form of skin cancer."[6] In 2000, McCain underwent a five-hour operation to remove a melanoma. In May 2008, his doctors released a statement that said in part, "We continue to find no evidence of metastasis or recurrence of the invasive melanoma as we approach the eighth anniversary of that operation."[7] The doctors—of the Mayo Clinic in Scottsdale, Arizona—also shared the good news that Senator McCain "has no evidence of melanoma."[8] He has also been treated for kidney stones and bladder stones and had some benign enlarged prostate tissue removed.[9] McCain also takes the following medications:

- Simvastatin, a cholesterol-lowering medicine
- Hydrochlorothiazide, for kidney stone prevention
- Amiloride, to preserve potassium in the bloodstream
- Aspirin, for blood-clot prevention
- Zyrtec, an antihistamine for nasal allergies as necessary
- Ambien CR, for sleep when traveling as necessary
- A multiple vitamin tablet[10]

Oh, yeah, McCain's docs note in their dry-as-dust summary that he broke both arms and a leg while ejecting from his plane over North Vietnam and was subsequently tortured and beaten repeatedly for five and a half years. His orthopedic injuries left him "with significantly reduced range of motion of his shoulders, arms, and right knee. He does not complain of bone or joint pain and does not take pain medication."[11]

If anyone deserves government-guaranteed medical care,

it's John McCain. John McCain just doesn't think you deserve it, too.

And that's where Bush and McCain are—once again—identical twins. While one is as fit as anyone his age, and the other has been through hell, each opposes guaranteeing that all American citizens have the same access to affordable, high-quality health care that they have. In fact, if possible, McCain would be even worse than Bush. Lest you think that's hyperbole, consider this: while George W. Bush has merely fiddled while health-care costs have burned out of control, John McCain would actually destroy the link between work and health-care benefits—the link that has defined what it means to have a good job and a secure future.[12]

Senator John McCain has enjoyed taxpayer-funded access to health care since birth.[13] You might believe that John McCain would want to share this privilege with the rest of us. But it turns out he would rather keep it for himself. Whereas some military heroes—retired four-star army general Wesley Clark comes to mind—want all Americans to have the same guaranteed health care they've had, McCain is different. He rails against government health care for you, even as he accepts it for himself.[14]

After all, with the U.S. government footing the bill, John McCain visits the Mayo Clinic in Scottsdale, Arizona, every few months to get a thorough checkup[15] and state-of-the-art medical care. They make sure he's in the best health a seventy-two-year-old man who's had cancer four times can be. According to documents released by his campaign, the highly skilled doctors of America's finest medical institutions have been employed on tasks ranging from removing several malignant melanomas[16] to removing excess earwax.[17] When it comes to health care for everyone else, however, McCain wants to prop up big insurance and leave ordinary people to fend for themselves.[18] McCain wants to cut benefits for children[19] and for seniors[20] while CEOs receive extraordinary profits and protections.[21] If McCain gets elected and his health-care plan passes, he'll be able to see his doctor even more frequently—because no one else will be in the waiting room.

Most Americans would like to see their doctor as regularly as John McCain, but few can afford that kind of care. In fact, one in six Americans—over forty-five million people—lack health insurance. Nearly nine million children have no health-care protection whatsoever.[22] That's right: nothing. Even middle-class families "lucky" enough to have coverage face rising health-insurance costs as benefits from their employers decline.[23]

Even before he'd read it, McCain blasted Senator Hillary Clinton's health-care proposal. "I haven't seen it," he told reporters, "but if it's anything like the last time around where they wanted to have a complete government takeover of the health-care system in America with a huge number of new bureaucracies being invented for government, I will oppose it vigorously."[24] In fact, Senator Clinton's proposal—like Barack Obama's health-care plan—builds on the private health-care system. It's only powerful politicians like John McCain who get fully socialized health insurance.

DR. NO

It shouldn't come as a surprise to anyone that John McCain has no interest in helping Americans get health care. He has spent nearly his entire career as Dr. No, voting to deny nearly every group of Americans coverage.

If you are elderly, John McCain has voted to cut, restrict, and underfund your Medicare at least twenty-eight times.[25] In 2005, McCain voted to cut Medicare by $6.4 billion.[26] In 2003, he voted against funds to treat heart disease, Alzheimer's, and cancer.[27] If nothing else, he has been consistent. In 1996, he voted in favor of cutting Medicare by $158.1 billion.[28] And in 1995, McCain voted twice to cut Medicare by $270 billion.[29] The list goes on and on.

He also voted against Medicare prescription drug coverage

at least twenty-eight times.[30] He even voted against ensuring drug coverage for cancer patients.[31] Think about that: *John McCain is a cancer survivor who voted against medicine for cancer patients.* McCain might have cast even more votes against helping seniors pay for their prescriptions, but he skipped five votes on the subject.[32]

It's not just the elderly. McCain has voted to cut, restrict, and underfund Medicaid at least seven times.[33] McCain voted against veterans' health care at least 27 times.[34] When it came time to take a stand on the Patients' Bill of Rights, John McCain voted against patients—twice.[35] He also voted to weaken consumer protections, access, and safety in the Patients' Bill of Rights at least twelve times.[36] McCain even voted to cut, eliminate, or restrict health-insurance coverage for poor children and pregnant mothers at least six times.[37]

So, after saying no, as a senator, to health care for nearly everyone except the rich, what is John McCain's health-care plan now that he wants to be president? It looks like he cribbed off of W's paper. McCain—who admits that he's underexperienced in economic issues[38]—promises a "genuinely conservative vision for health-care reform."[39]

When it comes to health care, we've tasted the compassionate conservative dish before. I've been waiting eight years to return it to the kitchen and fire the chef. Thanks, but no thanks.

BREAKING THE BOND BETWEEN WORK AND BENEFITS

What's the first thing your friends and relatives ask you when you take a new job? "Does it have good benefits? Does it include health care?" The link between work and health benefits was forged in the Second World War, and it has been at the heart of our conception of health care ever since.[40] In fact, 60 percent of all non-elderly Americans—one hundred fifty-eight million of us—get health care through our employers.[41]

But John McCain, following George W. Bush's lead, wants to break that bond. In John McCain's America, you're on your own. Just you, alone, against the big insurance companies. He has promised to eliminate the tax break for employers who provide health insurance.[42] His health-care proposal would effectively strip individuals of their employer-provided insurance. He'll break the link between work and health care by pressuring corporations to abandon work-provided health insurance, leaving workers to buy insurance on their own.[43] He intends to "lure workers away from their company health plans"[44] by eliminating the incentives for companies to provide health insurance for their workers.[45] That's right. John McCain wants to make employer-provided health insurance *more expensive.* So if you think the answer to our current health-care challenges is to make employer-provided health insurance more expensive—so expensive that nearly all employers will abandon their employees—then John McCain is your man.

Your employer will essentially be forced to drop employee health coverage, and you'll be forced into the largely unregulated individual market. Costs will go up, coverage will go down.[46]

Don't just take my word for how similar McCain's and Bush's visions for health care are. Describing McCain's health-care plan, the *Washington Post* wrote, "Senator John McCain on Tuesday rejected calls by his Democratic opponents for universal health coverage, instead offering a market-based solution with an approach similar to a proposal put forth by President Bush last year."[47] McCain also proposed health savings accounts, which were "a centerpiece of Bush's health-care efforts."[48] In addition, the *New York Times* wrote, "His proposal to move away from employer-based coverage was similar to one that President Bush pushed for last year."[49]

Think about that. One hundred fifty-eight million Americans would be in danger of suddenly losing their health benefits.[50] They'll flood the individual market, where we would all be at the tender mercies of the big insurance companies and the multinational pharmaceutical firms.

John McCain is still drinking the Bush Kool-Aid. He makes the Bush argument on the subject: that the market is more "efficient," that it will find a balance of high quality for low cost. Right. The Bush-McCain take on health care involves almost no oversight or protections.[51] Big health-insurance companies will control your health even more than they do now—and both quality and cost will suffer. That is a scary thought.

Instead of giving employers a tax break to buy insurance for their workers, McCain is proposing giving a tax credit to individuals in the hopes that they will buy private insurance on their own. The problem is, the tax credit would be just twenty-five hundred dollars for an individual and only five thousand dollars for families.[52] That's just not enough. The Kaiser Family Foundation reports that the most popular employer-provided health-insurance plans cost an average of $11,765 per year—and that's with the massive bargaining power that big employers have.[53] When you remove that bargaining power, that figure will go through the roof. You'll be left trying to buy a twelve-thousand-dollar health insurance policy with a five-thousand-dollar voucher. Good damn luck.

Even McCain's senior economic adviser, Douglas Holtz-Eakin, has said that for some people McCain's health-care plan won't be able to cover the costs insured with the elimination of the employer-based system.[54] Employer-provided health insurance keeps costs down by sharing risks between the healthy and the sick. Thus, in today's system, workers enjoy lower costs, while employers can write off the health-care premiums as a business expense. McCain's plan, on the other hand, would tax employers for the health coverage they provide. At the same time, by luring people out of the employer-based system, McCain would effectively decrease the pool and thereby increase the costs for everyone in the system.[55]

Furthermore, McCain's senior economic adviser *brags* that his plan to eliminate the employer-based health-care system would raise approximately $3.6 trillion in revenues.[56] What that means is McCain wants to make Americans pay $3.6 trillion more for health insurance. That would be the mother of all tax increases. Jonathan B. Oberlander, a political scientist at the University of North Carolina at Chapel Hill, remarked of McCain's health-care plan, "Any way you cut it, if you make health benefits subject to taxation, that's a tax increase."[57]

McCAIN'S PLAN WOULD NOT EVEN COVER JOHN McCAIN

One of the most pernicious aspects of the current health-insurance system is the so-called preexisting condition rule. It's not as complicated as, say, the infield fly rule, but if the preexisting condition rule pops up in your file, you're out.

According to a study by the Center for American Progress Action Fund, "The individual market . . . plays by different rules. Individual insurers in most states can exclude people with pre-existing conditions directly by denying them coverage or indirectly by charging them exorbitant premiums."[58] People don't choose to get sick if they could be healthy, just as they don't choose to be poor if they could be wealthy. Under the McCain-Bush plan, being sick—or even having been sick in the past—means you have precisely two chances of getting affordable health coverage: slim and none.

If you happen to be diagnosed with a disease—say, skin cancer . . . four times; and you're not sitting on a family fortune—say, $100 million; and you're not a powerful federal official—say, a senator who is covered by the Federal Employees' Health Benefit Plan, the McCain-Bush plan counts you out.

Okay, let's take a little quiz:

(1) Who needs health care? Is it:

a. John S. McCain III: male, age 62 (circa 1998)

b. Tiny Tim Cratchit: male, age 7

c. Elizabeth Edwards: female, age 58

d. All of the above

(2) Who is the most likely to be left out of the Bush-McCain health-care plan? Is it:

a. John S. McCain III

b. Tiny Tim Cratchit

c. Elizabeth Edwards

d. All of the above

The answer to both is (d)—All of the above.

Why would a cancer survivor propose a health plan that doesn't cover people who have had cancer? McCain is one of millions of people who have gotten a bad bill of health, which would keep them from getting affordable care in the individual market. Preexisting conditions are a tremendous barrier to getting insured. Karen Pollitz of Georgetown University points out, "Those with cancer, diabetes, heart disease, HIV, epilepsy, and other more serious problems are rejected outright 99 percent of the time."[59] In the market, with its bottom-line mentality, people with serious illnesses are simply liabilities, risks, not worth covering. All those sick folks, kids, and grandparents just aren't "cost efficient."

Of course, McCain isn't just making it harder for people to get insurance; he's also making it easier for insurance companies to deny coverage. Another key component of the McCain-Bush "deregulation" plan includes eliminating the laws that require patients to buy their insurance from in-state providers, who abide by state standards. The idea is that by letting people buy insurance from companies in other states they can find a cheaper plan. Unfortunately, as the *New York Times* pointed out, "That could lead some insurers to relocate from highly regulated states to states that would allow them to cover fewer services."[60]

McCain's plan would essentially shut down the state-run health-care market and push consumers into a nationwide pool. McCain, Bush, and other Republicans tout this policy as a chance to let people shop around for the insurance market that best fits them. The problem is that it's also a chance for insurance companies to shop around for their best market. Once the starting gate is lifted, they would race to the states with the lowest standards of care.

In a system that doesn't guarantee coverage for all, the first people to be excluded are the ones who would be most expensive to insure: sick kids, grandparents, and people with lesser means. That's how the market works. The people who have the easiest time getting insurance are the ones who are least likely to need it. You don't have to take my word on this. Even the *Wall Street Journal* concluded, "The [McCain] plan isn't expected to make a major dent in the number of uninsured Americans." The *Journal* also noted "questions remain about how the plan would help older, sicker people who can't find insurance on the open market."[61] In a nutshell, what McCain is suggesting is a plan that ups the costs for the middle class, taxes employers who provide health care trillions of dollars, doesn't decrease the number of people who are uninsured, doesn't help the old and sick, and excludes anyone who's ever had a serious illness or injury.

Other than that, it's a great plan.

Elizabeth Edwards, like John McCain, is a cancer patient. But unlike John McCain, she both knows a lot about health care and cares a lot about people who need it. When she pointed out that Senator McCain's so-called plan would not cover her or McCain himself, the McCain campaign hemmed and hawed and came up with a "Guaranteed Access Plan." First, note the name. Even in the Orwellian Bushspeak of the Bush-McCain GOP, some hint of the contents can be gleaned from the title. It's guaranteed *access*, not guaranteed health insurance. Hell, I have *access* to a Ferrari. I have *access* to Pamela Anderson. That doesn't mean I can actually get either. Just that I have the chance to get it. A second clue is in the acronym: McCain proposes a Guaranteed Access Plan—or a GAP. And if you have a preexisting condition, you're going to fall through that GAP.[62]

According to the *New Republic*'s Jonathan Cohn, "More than

thirty states already have programs almost exactly like the one Mr. McCain just sketched out. They are called 'high-risk pools' . . . and the idea is pretty straightforward: Private insurers agree to sell policies directly to individuals, even those with preexisting medical conditions, as long as the state helps subsidize the cost. But the whole reason conservatives like Mr. McCain prefer this approach to universal coverage is that it involves minimal government regulation. As a result, private insurers have enormous leeway in setting high prices. A few years ago, a Commonwealth Fund study found that, on average, state high-risk pools offered coverage that was two-thirds more expensive than regularly priced coverage. In some states, the high-risk coverage was actually twice as high as regular coverage. (In Texas, for example, state law requires the risk pool to set rates twice as high as the standard risk rate charged by major insurers for individual coverage.)"[63]

In other words, if you have a preexisting condition, you'll be priced out of the market by McCain's GAP.

"SUFFER THE CHILDREN . . ." AND THE SENIORS

Nine million kids in America don't have insurance, but just like George W. Bush, John McCain's solution to this problem is for them to grow up.[64] In 2007, McCain actually went to the Senate floor and argued *against* covering millions of kids.[65] Then after his speech, he voted to deny health coverage to 3.2 million uninsured children and not to renew coverage for 6 million children insured by the Children's Health Insurance Program because he said he felt the bill would cover too many children.[66] Despite McCain's opposition, the bill passed both houses of Congress and made it to the president's desk. Bush vetoed it—and McCain praised President Bush for making "the right call."[67]

Similarly, McCain has also voted consistently against seniors. In a page straight out of the Bush playbook, McCain is seeking to raise the premiums that some seniors will have to pay for their Medicare prescription drug plans.[68] This is an idea that George W. Bush has been pushing for a couple of years now—it was part of his budget submissions in 2006 and 2007—to the chagrin of the AARP, among others.[69]

And that's not all. Besides forcing our grandparents to pay more for their prescription drugs, John McCain is likely to leave many elderly people without a health-care plan at all. As the *Wall Street Journal* reported, McCain's plan to force Americans to purchase their own insurance "could be problematic for older people and those in poor health, who are routinely denied health insurance on the individual market, or charged very expensive premiums, because insurance companies know they will be costly to care for."[70]

INSURANCE COMPANIES UBER ALLES

In his assessment of McCain's health-care plan, Robert Gordon, one of the resident geniuses of the Center for American Progress Action Fund, compares McCain's health-care plan to the credit card free-for-all of the late 1970s. Releasing insurance companies to sell across state lines would not only increase costs but would also degrade quality and scope of health coverage. In the current system, in states where standards of care are high, insurance companies can and must offer fair, affordable policies to the sick without losing their competitive edge in the market. McCain would make sure that's not true anywhere.

Let's look at what would happen in New York and Arizona. New York is one of eighteen states that prohibit charging higher rates for people who are already sick. At the other end of the spectrum is McCain's state, Arizona, which allows insurers to increase charges as they see fit to those who are sick—or deny them coverage completely. If McCain gets his way, insurers from New York and seventeen other states will be forced to lower their standards to compete with companies in Arizona and other states where insurers can keep their costs low by denying services to those in need.[71]

Gordon warns that with McCain's plan, "it's as though the rafts are reserved for people who already have life preservers. . . . Americans with preexisting conditions . . . through no fault of their own . . . would end up without insurance [while] insurers would improve their own profits by offering targeted policies to people with the fewest health expenses. . . . [I]t's Robin Hood in reverse."[72]

McCain's plan proves itself to be not only morally wrong but also economically unsound. Denied care, sick people get sicker. The market-based system does sick Americans a disservice by leaving them without access to affordable health care; additionally, as Gordon points out, "When more [of the sickest] Americans go uninsured, skip checkups, and land in the emergency room, they end up costing taxpayers more. . . . Apart from the obvious injustice, this approach could add to spiraling health costs."[73] The employer-based insurance system, on the other hand, places "young, healthy workers into the same risk pool as colleagues who are older or sicker . . . employer-based coverage supports cost-sharing: . . . We pay relatively more in premiums for what we get when we're young but relatively less when we're old."[74] Pooling risks and sharing costs between the healthy and the sick offer people with preexisting conditions a chance at affordable health care—and it saves Americans money. Neither is true of the market-based system. The exclusion of sick Americans ultimately takes its toll on the ethics and pocketbooks of all of us.

Don't worry, though. This isn't a total lose-lose situation. The old, the young, the sick, and the middle class might fare worse under the McCain-Bush plan. But there are a few big winners here—insurance companies.

While regular families scrape the bottom of the barrel to pay for their basic needs, not least of which include health care, the ten largest health insurance companies are hitting the jackpot. According to a detailed analysis by the Center for American Progress Action Fund, those insurance companies stand to make nearly $2 billion from the McCain-Bush plan. The experts write,

"For the ten largest American health insurance companies, the McCain plan is worth nearly $2 billion a year. . . . UnitedHealth Group alone would receive a $700 million tax cut. The tax breaks come in addition to the benefits of McCain's health-care plan for insurance companies."[75] Putting it in perspective, they add, "More bad news for regular families today: the median family income is down and income inequality is up. But although John McCain's tax plan costs a total of $2 trillion, it gives little or nothing to most families. Instead, McCain chose to earmark 80 percent of his tax relief proposals for corporations."[76] McCain wants to continue the trend Bush set: do as little as possible for average Americans, and do as much as possible for big corporations. If McCain gets his way on health care, for once he and Bush can declare "Mission Accomplished."

If all this sounds a bit familiar, that's because it is. McCain has just copied Bush when it comes to health care. In an article outlining his health-care plan, the *New York Times* wrote, "[McCain's] proposal to move away from employer-based coverage was similar to one that President Bush pushed for last year, to little effect."[77]

McCain is peddling a Bush idea about health care. He would pit each of us individually against Aetna and would remove group-based protections and savings, forcing individuals to navigate the spider's web of powerful insurance providers. McCain doesn't cover everyone, and he leaves the rest of us alone to battle the insurance giants. What is even more amazing is that the McCain plan will actually result in a big tax increase for the middle class.

McCain's not just offering a third term of Bush's ignorant policies; he's also giving us a chance for another go-round at Bush's hypocrisy and indifference. With all the fuss he's making about the glories of private health care over the degradation of government-provided insurance, you'd think he had been a long and loyal consumer of private insurance. Not so. In fact, not even close.

Although he rails against it, McCain has enjoyed government-provided health insurance *for his entire life*. *American Prospect* tells the story: "Born the son of a Navy admiral, he was cared for by Navy physicians during his childhood. After graduating from high school, he enrolled in the U.S. Military Academy, and the military's care continued until he retired from the service in 1981. In 1982, he won a seat in Congress, ushering him into the Federal Employee Health Benefits Program, and in 2001, he qualified for Medicare." They conclude, *"When he says, 'We have the highest quality of health care in the world in America,' he is speaking as a man who has enjoyed a lifetime of government-run care."*[78]

John McCain earned that government health care by years of service and sacrifice. I honor that service and I revere that sacrifice. But I cannot for the life of me understand why someone who has had such excellent health care courtesy of the government would think that the best solution for civilians is to be left to the tender mercies of unregulated health insurance corporations.

HERE'S LOOKING AT YOU, KID.
I WISH I DIDN'T LOVE YOU SO MUCH!

10

ENVIRONMENTAL CON JOB

I certainly think that there are areas off our coasts that should be open to [oil] exploration and exploitation.

—*John McCain*[1]

I'm a strong proponent of the restoration of the wetlands, for a lot of reasons. There's a practical reason, though, when it comes to hurricanes: The stronger the wetlands, the more likely the damage of the hurricane.

—*George W. Bush*[2]

John McCain would like you to believe he's an environmentalist. And I would like you to believe I have a full head of hair. Sure, McCain is better than some of the worst elements of his party. And it's also true that I have more hair than James Carville. That still doesn't mean I have a full head of hair, and it damn sure doesn't mean McCain is an environmentalist. Being better on the environment than some other Republicans is about as difficult as looking chaste next to Paris Hilton. You don't have to do much. So McCain has taken a few baby steps in an attempt to be seen as environmentally friendly—for example, he "acknowledges" that climate change exists.[3]

The Republicans have made it easy for McCain to distinguish himself. The GOP is so bass-ackwards on climate change that McCain has nowhere to go but up from their ranks. After all, their first in command on the Senate's Environment Committee is one of America's chief climate change deniers, Senator James Inhofe (R-ExxonMobil).[4] This is the guy who said that global warming is "the greatest hoax ever perpetrated on the American people."[5]

McCain wants "acknowledging" global warming to be enough to qualify him as a bona fide environmentalist. As we say back home in Texas, that dog won't hunt. Acknowledging that climate change is real is like agreeing that the sun rises in the east. It's a start, but it's not going to keep you from getting a sunburn. McCain's record—his real record, not his rhetoric—shows that when it comes to the environment, he shares many of the same radical pro-corporate, antienvironment views as George W. Bush.

Senator McCain has a long and troubling record on the environment. Whether the issue is climate change or water quality, McCain has a knee-jerk hostility to any kind of federal regulation of polluters; he instinctively opposes protecting American lives and American families from corporate polluters. He waves on corporations as they pollute our environment, and he has voted against requiring big businesses to tell their communities when they cause a serious toxic spill or accident.[6] McCain has even abetted big donors and lobbyists seeking to restrict, gut, and destroy the Environmental Protection Agency.[7]

He is knee-deep in contributions from the oil and gas industry and their lobbyists. And he's offering up a tax plan that is a nearly $4 billion big wet kiss to oil companies.[8]

Of course, John McCain still travels the country saying with a straight face that he's a "different kind of Republican."[9] Sounds familiar. Back in 2000, Americans heard all about a different kind of Republican promising to govern differently in Washington. George W. Bush called it "compassionate conservatism."[10] Running against Al Gore in 2000, Bush even pledged to limit carbon dioxide emissions from power plants, which would have been an important step in fighting global warming. During the campaign he said, "We will require all power plants to meet clean-air standards in order to reduce emissions of sulfur dioxide, nitrogen dioxide, mercury and carbon dioxide within a reasonable period of time." The pledge impressed moderate and independent voters, and no doubt helped Bush, who was, after all, running against the foremost environmentalist in American political life. But just weeks after the five thieves in black robes installed him as president, Bush reversed himself. He wrote a letter to a group of Republican senators, including Jesse Helms and Larry "Wide Stance" Craig, in which he stated, "I do not believe, however, that the government should impose on power plants mandatory emissions reductions for carbon dioxide, which is not a 'pollutant' under the Clean Air Act."[11] Now, just like Bush, it is McCain who is trying to play the election-year environmentalist. But his real record tells a very different story.

A LONG HISTORY OF BAD POLICY POSITIONS

Over his twenty-five years in Washington, John McCain has cast quite a few votes on the environment. Fortunately for us, groups like the nonpartisan, nonprofit League of Conservation Voters keep track of environmental votes and rate politicians based on what they actually do, not on what they say.[12] McCain has earned a 24 percent lifetime rating on environmental issues. Twenty-four percent. In 2007, McCain received a zero. He voted with environmentalists exactly zero times.[13] That's right, in 2007, on every issue affecting the environment, McCain either skipped the vote or voted the wrong way. Now, to be fair to McCain, he skipped an awful lot of votes in 2007. But given the fact that he votes against the environment three-fourths of the time when he does vote, maybe that's not the worst thing.

It's been a while since I was in school, but I do teach, and 24 percent would be an F–. Even grading on a curve, it's an F. That's a grade George W. Bush would recognize. But McCain got his F the old-fashioned way: he earned it.

PROTECTING POLLUTERS' RIGHT TO POISON IN SECRET

Way back in 1985, some members of Congress were pushing a commonsense environmental law that would have required polluters to publicly report any leaks or spills of cancer-causing or hazardous chemicals.[14] Simply put, this law would require companies to let Americans know if we are drinking, breathing, or being exposed to harmful poisons like asbestos, benzene, or dioxin. Laws like this one make sure local officials, firefighters, police officers, and other first responders can take action to protect public health when a community is exposed to a harmful substance. But McCain voted against making polluters tell communities if they have been exposed to toxins—the same position Bush took when he came to Washington.

Ten years later, McCain sided with corporate polluters over American families again.[15] Environmentalists in Congress were pushing legislation that would have required community water systems serving more than ten thousand people to issue a yearly report on the level of contaminants in their drinking water. It wasn't even strict. The law would let states opt out of the requirement if they told citizens the reason for doing so.[16] But McCain voted against this "right to know" legislation as well. What McCain did not want to acknowledge is that what you don't know really can hurt you.

McCain has voted against improving water quality quite a few times. That's fine, perhaps, if you're worth tens of millions of dollars like John McCain: Let them drink Perrier! But many Americans—and this might shock some Bush-McCain Republicans—get their drinking water right from the tap. McCain voted against protecting our water from waterborne illnesses, against ensuring that there isn't radon—yes, radon—in drinking water, and against federal assistance for states so that they could meet Clean Water Act standards.[17] I'll drink to that.

McCain has displayed knee-jerk hostility to environmental protection over and over again. It's the same attitude as George W. Bush's. Those two would have Americans believe that fewer protections against polluters would somehow make corporations more honest when they dump chemicals in our water, cause an industrial accident, or accidentally poison a neighborhood. Call me a junkie, but I am addicted to things like air and water. And I expect my government to protect my family from corporate polluters.

So when John McCain says he's been there for you in the fight for our environment, keep this in mind: he's only been on our side 24 percent of the time.

McCAIN CAMPAIGN, BROUGHT TO YOU BY EXXONMOBIL

John McCain is the kind of politician the oil and gas industry loves. He talks a good game to the public, but he's in the tank for oil and gas, just like George W. Bush and Dick Cheney. According to a Campaign Money Watch analysis of campaign finance data provided by the nonpartisan Center for Responsive Politics, John McCain has accepted at least $1,069,854 from the oil and gas industry since 1989.[18] Of course, oil and gas executives aren't giving McCain money out of the goodness of their hearts—if they have hearts. They're standing with someone who they think will stand with them.

As we have seen elsewhere in this book (check out the chapter "If McCain's a Reformer, I'm a Hasidic Diamond Merchant"), McCain's campaign is run by lobbyists, many of them for the oil and gas industry. In fact, the former cochairman of McCain's campaign was a lobbyist for numerous oil companies and the government of Saudi Arabia. All told, McCain has at least twenty-two oil and gas industry lobbyists working or fundraising for his campaign.

McCain has proposed a Big Windfall for Big Oil. He says if

elected president he will ask Congress to cut the corporate tax rate from 35 percent to 25 percent.[19] This tax cut alone would reduce taxes for the five largest U.S. oil companies by $3.8 billion a year.[20] With gasoline going for four dollars a gallon, with Big Oil racking up record profits, with corporate CEOs walking away with golden parachutes, does anyone really think that what corporate America needs is a break? Why not give consumers a break, Senator McCain?

Then there's McCain's proposed "gas tax holiday." It would not reduce gas prices—it would just cost American jobs and take away funding from roads and bridges.[21] The federal revenue from the gas tax goes right into the federal highway trust fund. If we slashed the gas tax for the summer, as McCain has proposed, it would cost the federal highway trust fund at least $11 billion.[22] It would also mean fewer construction jobs for Americans struggling to get out of the George W. Bush recession. Oh, I can almost hear my Republican friends saying, "But Paul, Hillary Clinton supports a gas tax holiday as well." Yes, but under Hillary's plan, consumers get a tax cut but oil companies have to make up the revenue so the highway trust fund would be held harmless. McCain, on the other hand, asks nothing of Big Oil. He just asks everyone who drives to endure deteriorating roads and bridges and more traffic and more potholes. Moreover, nothing in McCain's plan prevents oil companies from simply raising their prices and consuming the bulk of the subsidy. Much of the eighteen-cent gas-tax subsidy McCain wants could end up in the pockets of ExxonMobil and other corporations. Keep in mind these titans of Big Oil are already getting $18 billion from the federal government through subsidies that McCain supports.[23]

BIG WELFARE FOR BIG OIL

McCain has spent his twenty-five years in Congress on the wrong side of environmental issues. When he had a chance to redirect more than $18 billion in subsidies for oil companies to investment in renewable energy, he didn't take it—he sunk the bill. He was the only senator to miss the vote. The bill failed by exactly one vote—McCain's.[24]

On measure after measure, when Big Oil's bottom line was at risk, McCain had their back. He voted against a measure that would have provided an income tax rebate to Americans by taxing enormous oil company profits temporarily on the sale of crude above $40 a barrel.[25] He voted against an amendment to impose a temporary tax on oil company profits from the sale of crude oil. The funds would be used to provide every taxpayer with a one-hundred-dollar tax credit for each person in their household.[26] He also voted against an amendment that would impose a temporary 50 percent tax on oil company profits from the sale of crude oil. Funds collected from the tax would be used to provide a consumer tax credit to offset the crippling cost of gas, home heating oil, and other petroleum products.[27]

FAIR-WEATHER FRIEND OF FUEL EFFICIENCY

With gas prices out of control, you would think increasing fuel efficiency would be priority numero uno for any truly pro-environment legislator. When cars use less gas, Americans save money, pollute less, and become less dependent on foreign oil sources. It's good for everyone—except Big Oil. But when it comes to standing up to Big Oil, you can't count on John McCain.

From time to time, McCain has expressed support for increasing the corporate average fuel economy standards for cars and trucks. In 2002, for example, there was an amendment to limit increases in the fuel economy standards. Siding with environmentalists, McCain voted against the measure.[28] On the same day he also voted with environmentalists against delaying tactics that would have slowed down congressional action on fuel standards.[29] Good for him.

But when environmentalists—and consumers—who want cars that are more fuel efficient really need him, McCain is not always there. In 2003, McCain voted against an amendment that would have mandated an increase in fuel economy standards. Passenger vehicles made before 2006 would have had to average 25 miles per gallon. After that, the standard would gradually increase to 40 miles per gallon by model year 2015. Nonpassenger vehicles made before 2006 would have to average 17 miles per gallon. By model year 2015, they would have to average 27.5 miles per gallon.[30]

And on the most important energy vote of the last several years, McCain was nowhere to be found. In 2007, the Senate was debating a Democratic bill that represented a giant step toward energy independence. The proposed law would require new corporate average fuel economy standards of 35 miles per gallon for cars and light trucks, and require the production and use of 36 billion gallons of biofuels by 2022. It would direct the Energy Department to set new energy efficiency standards. It would also require utilities to produce 15 percent of their electricity from alternative sources by 2020, and provide $21.8 billion in tax incentives for alternative energy. Those tax incentives would be paid for in part by eliminating or reducing $13 billion in subsidies for major oil and gas companies.

The battle lines were drawn. The Republicans, ever the obstructionists, launched a filibuster. Senate Majority Leader Harry Reid (D-NV), the former boxer and miner, was ready to fight. Summoning all his legendary legislative legerdemain, Reid rallied the Democrats, who stood firm with him against Big Oil. Knowing he needed sixty votes to break the GOP filibuster, he reached across the aisle and persuaded several Republicans. Observers thought the good guys were about to win one. But they fell one vote short: fifty-nine to forty. John McCain failed to show up.

How a man renowned for his physical courage could fail to stand up and be counted on one of the most important issues of our time is beyond me. Ninety-nine other senators—none of whom had stood up to torture in Hanoi the way John McCain had—voted. But not McCain. Perhaps it didn't matter, though.

Through a spokesman he said he would not have supported breaking the filibuster.[31]

What does McCain's inconstancy portend for a McCain presidency? Well, one of his advisers left us a hint. Douglas Holtz-Eakin, his most prominent economist, recently told an energy trade publication that when it comes to fuel economy requirements, "You might want to take them off the books."[32] That would certainly complete the flip-flop-flip, wouldn't it? Oppose fuel economy standards, then support them, then take them off the books entirely. Only in McCainland.

McDRILLING

After collecting over a million dollars from the oil industry—and no doubt listening to all those oil company lobbyists who are advising him—John McCain went to Houston, the beating heart of the American oil patch, and showed the courage to pander. He called for lifting the ban on offshore drilling.[33] That means drilling off the coast of Florida. It means drilling off the coast of California. It means savaging pristine waters off the East Coast. It means giving Big Oil a license to drill—and a license to kill any habitat that stands in its way.

The ban on offshore drilling was imposed by President Ronald Reagan in 1981. It has been renewed by every president since—even the veteran oilman George H. W. Bush and the failed oilman George W. Bush. Republicans and Democrats alike for twenty-seven years have acted to protect our coastlines. But not John McCain. When Big Oil says, "Jump," he's already in the air before he asks how high.

DRILLING IN ALASKA'S WILDERNESS: BOTH SIDES NOW

One of the most contentious environmental issues of the last ten years has been the fight over oil drilling in Alaska's Arctic National Wildlife Refuge. Keep in mind that this refuge is what it sounds like—one of the last remaining areas of pristine wilderness in North America. Preserving it means it will stay in pristine condition for our children, grandchildren, and generations to come. It's a pretty simple issue, really. Either you support allowing Big Oil to drill in this wilderness refuge, or you don't. Unless you're John McCain. On drilling in the Alaska wilderness, McCain has been firmly, squarely, decidedly on both sides of the fence. The man who created the Straight Talk Express has instead been Senator Straddle. Good luck trying to make sense of these votes:

- May 24, 1995: Democrats offered an amendment prohibiting oil drilling in ANWR. McCain voted no, thus supporting drilling.[34]

- October 27, 1995: Senate Democrats introduced an amendment that would have disallowed drilling in the ANWR. McCain voted to kill it.[35]

- April 18, 2002: McCain voted to prohibit oil and gas development in ANWR, thus *opposing* drilling there.[36]

- November 3, 2005: McCain voted against the establishment of an oil and gas leasing program in ANWR, thus, once again, opposing the drilling he had supported in the 1990s.[37]

- December 21, 2005: McCain voted to support the FY 2006 Defense Appropriations bill, which included $50 billion for operations in Iraq and Afghanistan. In addition, the bill allowed drilling in ANWR, so now McCain was voting to allow the drilling he had voted against a month earlier. In McCain's defense, this was likely due to McCain's support for keeping U.S. troops in Iraq indefinitely—a position he has never wavered on, no matter what the cost, no matter how high the casualties, no matter how flawed the strategy, no matter how dishonest the rationale. So perhaps we can't call this vote a vote to drill in Alaska.[38]

- A few hours later, though, McCain skipped the vote on specifically removing the pro-drilling provision. That was a pro-drilling move, since the environmentalists needed McCain's vote and he did not come through.[39]

- April 6, 2000: McCain voted to count $1.2 billion in projected revenue from ANWR drilling in the budget. Most senators who genuinely opposed drilling in the refuge voted not to count the projected revenue, so environmentalists count this as a pro-drilling, antienvironmental vote.[40]

- McCain has also voted to despoil other protected lands, like national parks. In 2001, McCain voted to kill an amendment prohibiting the use of funds for the pre-leasing or leasing of oil and gas, or other exploration activities within lands designated as national monuments.[41]

McCain is at best an election-year environmentalist, not the kind of guy you'd bet your life—or our ecosystem—on. When the League of Conservation Voters asked McCain to fill out a questionnaire on environmental issues, McCain had this to say about drilling in ANWR "I do not support drilling in the ANWR *at this time.*"[42] I added the emphasis because it is the furthest thing from straight talk. Those are weasel words designed to give McCain an out if—heaven forbid—he were to become president and Big Oil came a-knockin'. He caved on offshore drilling even before the election. What makes you think he won't cave on Alaska drilling after the election?

THE EPA, McSAME-STYLE

McCain has voted to gut, weaken, undermine, or cut off funding for the Environmental Protection Agency at least ten times. That's right—the government agency that is responsible for enforcing the Clean Water and Clean Air acts, monitoring toxic spills, and setting standards for environmental safety is a favorite punching bag of John McCain. Just as it has been under George W. Bush.

Back in 1990, McCain actually voted against a measure to provide tax credits to companies that comply with provisions of the Clean Air Act.[43] It's one of the few corporate tax breaks that he opposes—and one of the few that would reward corporations for doing the right thing. He also voted against the enforcement of penalties against serious polluters.[44] There is no doubt that his corporate backers would like nothing more than ensuring that the agency they are most afraid of is weakened and ineffective. This, of course, was a favorite goal of George W. Bush as well.

Let's take a look at some of McCain's greatest hits during his war on the EPA.

- He voted to allow natural gas companies to shift the cost of fines for violating environmental law onto consumers by raising prices.[45] If your gas company is breaking the law, McCain thinks you should pay the price.

- He voted to undermine the power of the EPA and the ability of states to regulate the nuclear power industry.[46]

- He voted to prevent the EPA from enforcing the Clean Water Act, weakening its oversight of the oil industry and delaying the cleanup of toxic sites.[47]

- He voted to keep the EPA from being able to respond to health risks from waterborne microbes in drinking water.[48]

- He supported the creation of an enormous loophole for serial toxic pollution emitters.[49] It would have allowed corporations to avoid reporting serious toxic emissions to the EPA, thus keeping Americans in the dark about the toxins in their community.

I've taught my boys that if they make a mess, they have to clean it up. The four of them get it, but George W. Bush and

John McCain don't—they don't think that their polluting buddies should have to follow a rule that every kindergartner understands. McCain has voted to charge taxpayers to clean up the mess polluters are making. That's right, if Pollution Industries dumps hazardous waste, or if Smog, Inc., has an industrial accident, McCain thinks you should pay for it.

He has consistently been on the wrong side of the Superfund law, also known as the "Polluter Pays Law" and Comprehensive Environmental Response, Compensation, and Liability Act (CERCLA).[50] The Superfund law allows the EPA to compel companies to clean up a toxic site or to reimburse the EPA for cleanup costs. It was enacted after the discovery of toxic waste dumps across the country, such as the infamous Love Canal site.[51]

There are Superfund sites in every state. These hazardous sites aren't a hazard to wildlife alone; they're a hazard to every living thing in the area. In Love Canal's case, a chemical company filled in an old waste site and sold it to the city of Niagara Falls. A working-class neighborhood sprang up there. The true gravity of the situation became clear when the *New York Times* began investigating the area's high occurrence of cancer, birth defects, and miscarriages. The *Times* wrote, "Twenty-five years after the Hooker Chemical Company stopped using the Love Canal here as an industrial dump, eighty-two different compounds, eleven of them suspected carcinogens, have been percolating upward through the soil, their drum containers rotting and leaching their contents into the backyards and basements of one hundred homes and a public school built on the banks of the canal."[52] The Love Canal story is an American tragedy that should never be repeated.

Superfund sites endanger the communities surrounding them, but McCain has consistently opposed cleaning up these sites. He'd rather expose Americans to carcinogens than inconvenience a corporate polluter.

McCain's on the wrong side of intervention for smaller disasters too. A brownfield is what the EPA calls a hazardous site that is dangerous, but not quite as disastrous as a Superfund site.[53] Most brownfields occur on land that was used for an industrial purpose but has long since been abandoned and is uninhabitable. McCain repeatedly voted against cleaning up brownfield sites.[54] Not only did McCain vote against having the government clean them up but he also voted against tax incentives for private individuals to clean up and redevelop them.[55] He has repeatedly voted to gut Superfund resources and against forcing corporate polluters to pay into the program to clean up the messes they've made.[56]

Polluters know that it pays to have friends, and they have good ones in John McCain and George W. Bush.

McCAIN'S TOXIC ADVISER

Take Nancy Pfotenhauer, please. Ms. Pfotenhauer has been designated by the McCain campaign as their "public face" on television. Officially, she is listed on McCain's website as one of his economic advisers. Her role extends to advising, and spinning, all fiscal, regulatory, and energy matters.[57]

According to Senate lobbying disclosure records, Nancy Pfotenhauer was a registered lobbyist for Koch Industries, one of the worst environmental polluters of the last three decades. She formerly served as the head of two lobbying firms: Americans for Prosperity, which has actively lobbied against nearly every environmental achievement of the last decade, and Citizens for a Sound Economy, an embarrassment of an organization that flacks for corporate interests.

Ms. Pfotenhauer's deep love of pollution was, perhaps, developed during her time at Koch Industries.

While she was director of Koch's Washington office, the federal government sued the company for eight hundred oil spills that dumped an estimated three million gallons of oil into various lakes and streams across six states.[58] Damn that big, bad federal government. You spill a few drops of poison—okay, three million gallons—into lakes and streams in a half-dozen places and they get in your grill. Self-righteous tree-huggers. Thank goodness a woman of courage and conviction like Nancy Pfotenhauer was in Koch's corner.

Koch ignored a warning from its employees that a massive line repair and replacement was necessary. Then in October 1994, pressure built up in a corroded pipe and caused a hole to rip through an underground pipeline, spilling ninety thousand gallons of crude oil into a creek outside Corpus Christi, Texas. The resulting oil slick was twelve miles long.[59]

Nancy also helped Koch through a ninety-seven-count indictment for releasing benzene, a carcinogen, into the air outside Corpus Christi at fifteen times the legal limit.[60] Koch settled the two suits only after paying what was described as the largest civil penalty ever secured under federal environmental laws. The settlement forced the company to admit that it had vented benzene directly into the air and that it had concealed its noncompliance with requirements of the Clean Air Act.[61] In plain English, Koch admitted that it was willfully breaking the law and knowingly exposing Americans to cancer-causing chemicals. Here is where it gets personal for me. Four generations of my family have fished Corpus Christi Bay and hunted in that part of Texas. And it kind of chaps me when mega-polluters like Koch Industries poison the habitat where those redfish swim and whitetail deer live.

Now Ms. Pfotenhauer has gone from advising Koch on how to avoid responsibility for its pollution to advising John McCain on how to avoid responsibility for his lousy environmental record. Should McCain become president, we can all look forward to people like Nancy Pfotenhauer protecting our land and air and water and children against corporate polluters. Just like Bush, John McCain would put foxes in charge of guarding the henhouse.

★ ★ ★

Sniff
Sniff
Sniff
SMELLS LIKE FOUR MORE YEARS TO ME!

THE JOHN McCAIN QUIZ

1. What does John McCain say is "one of the best things that's happened to America"?
2. Which of the following locations that John McCain has recently visited HAS NOT been the recipient of a congressional earmark?
   - a) Villanova University
   - b) Gee's Bend ferry
   - c) Lehigh Valley Hospital
   - d) H. Lee Moffitt Cancer Center & Research Institute
   - e) None of the above—they have ALL been recipients of earmarks McCain would cut as president
3. John McCain has made many predictions regarding the length of the war in Iraq. Match his predictions with the date he made them:

A few months	May 2007
One hundred years	February 2004
One year	November 2006
The end is very much in sight	February 2005
Months	November 2003
Ten years	April 2003
Two years	January 2007

I don't have a date	June 2005
Five years	January 2008

4. Which of the following Third World dictators was NOT represented by a McCain adviser?

    a) Somali dictator Mohamed Siad Barre. Between 1988 and 1990, Barre's Somali Army killed forty thousand to fifty thousand unarmed civilians.
    b) Philippine dictator Ferdinand Marcos, who stole between $5 billion and $10 billion from the country and implemented martial law for fourteen years.
    c) Ugandan dictator Idi Amin Dada. Human rights groups estimate one hundred thousand to five hundred thousand Ugandans were killed as a result of his regime.
    d) Zairean dictator Mobutu Sese Seko, who amassed a personal fortune estimated to be as much as $5 billion while tens of thousands of children in his nation starved to death.

5. What did Carly Fiorina, the "face" of John McCain's economic team, say was her biggest mistake during her tenure as CEO of Hewlett-Packard?

6. Which of the following McCain lobbyists works for which client?

Anthony Principi	a) Dubai (which was facing a class-action lawsuit over alleged enslavement of boys as jockeys in camel races)
Thomas Loeffler	b) Saudi Arabia
John Green	c) Go Daddy
Steve Perry	d) ExxonMobil
Kerry Cammack	e) U.S. Smokeless Tobacco
Peter Madigan	f) Pfizer

7. Which of the following WAS NOT said by Charlie Black?

   a) "I've got access to just about anybody in the government."
   b) "As long as you comply with all the rules and regulations, your past activities shouldn't be criticized."
   c) "Those who favor rights for homosexuals have no place in the Republican Party."
   d) "The Democrats will regret the day they crossed my path."

8. Who said this about John McCain? "The thought of his being president sends a cold chill down my spine. He is erratic."

   a) Republican senator Thad Cochran of Mississippi
   b) Democratic House Speaker Nancy Pelosi
   c) Independent former governor Jesse Ventura
   d) Socialist senator Bernie Sanders of Vermont
   e) Green Party candidate Ralph Nader
   f) Libertarian presidential candidate Bob Barr

9. How many homes do the McCains own?

   a) 2
   b) 4
   c) 6
   d) Ummm . . . 9?
   e) Come on, that's ridiculous. Nobody owns 9 homes.

10. Who did John McCain describe as "my base"?

    a) Moderate Republicans
    b) The national media
    c) Veterans
    d) Corporate lobbyists

Bonus Question: Name the special interest NOT represented by a lobbyist that is working for, advising, or raising money for John McCain's campaign.

1. Answer: The war in Iraq.

McCain said war in Iraq was "one of the best things that's happened to America." During an appearance on NBC's *Meet the Press,* John McCain said about the war in Iraq, "[C]ould I just say again, keep our nerve here, keep our nerve here. We're going to be all right. We're going to prevail and we will win and it'll be one of the best things that's happened to America and the world in a long time 'cause it'll reverberate throughout the Middle East." [NBC, *Meet the Press,* 3/30/03]

2. Answer: E

Villanova

On April 15, 2008, Senator McCain visited Villanova University in Philadelphia, Pennsylvania. [*Villanovan,* 4/17/08] According to the White House Office of Management and Budget, Villanova University received an earmark to develop technologies for future naval capabilities. Villanova University and Pennsylvania State University Applied Research Laboratory and Naval Surface Warfare Center-Carderock Division–Philadelphia split the earmark of $1,254,000. [White House Office of Management and Budget, accessed 5/1/08]

Gee's Bend, Alabama

On April 21, 2008, Senator McCain visited Gee's Bend, Alabama, and stopped at the town's ferry. McCain said, "I have heard of this wonderful place and I know that it has a place in history. I know Dr. [Martin Luther] King was here before the march in Selma, so they stopped running the ferry. Now the ferry is running and I intend to ride the ferry back." Ironically, *it was a FY 2005 earmark that allowed the ferry to reopen.* The Associated Press reported, "A federal grant allowed the ferry to reopen in 2006." [Associated Press, 4/20/08] Senator McCain voted against the Consolidated Appropriations Bill that included that earmark. [Conference Report, accessed 4/30/08; H.R. 4818, *Vote #215,* 11/20/2004]

Lehigh Valley Hospital

On April 30, 2008, Senator McCain appeared at the Lehigh Valley Hospital. [JohnMcCain.com, accessed 4/30/08] According to the White House Office of Management and Budget, Lehigh Valley Hospital received a $694,000 earmark to purchase equipment for its Cath Laboratory. The funding was earmarked in the FY 2005 Labor-HHS Appropriations Bill. That legislation was included in the FY 2005 Consolidated Appropriations Bill, which McCain voted against. [OMB, accessed 4/30/08; HR 4818, *Vote #215,* 11/2/2004]

H. Lee Moffitt Cancer Center

On April 29, 2008, Senator McCain gave his health policy speech at the H. Lee Moffitt Cancer Center and Research Institute. [JohnMcCain.com, 4/29/08] The H. Lee Moffitt Cancer Center and Research Institute received a $3 million earmark in the FY 2004 Consolidated Appropriations Bill for construction and renovation, including equipment. Senator McCain voted against the Consolidated Appropriations Bill. [Conference Report, accessed 4/30/08; HR 2673, Vote #3, 1/22/2004]

3. Matching on Iraq

A few months: November 2003 [MSNBC, *Buchanan & Press*, 11/6/03]

One hundred years: January 2008 [Town Hall meeting in Concord, New Hampshire, 1/3/08]

One year: February 2005 [CBS, *The Early Show*, 2/3/05]

The end is very much in sight: April 2003 [ABC, *Good Morning America*, 4/9/03]

Months: November 2006 [NBC, *Meet the Press*, 11/12/06]

Ten years: January 2007 [*Houston Chronicle*, 1/30/07]

Two years: June 2005 [NBC, *Meet the Press*, 6/19/05]

I don't have a date: May 2007 [NBC, *Meet the Press*, 5/13/07]

Five years: February 2004 [MSNBC, *Hardball*, 2/25/04]

McCain said, "I don't have a date" when asked about the end of the war. While discussing the war in Iraq on *Meet the Press,* McCain said, "If it is only in a role that is of support and American casualties are minimal, then I think it's probably worth the investment. If the level of casualties stays where it is, and we do not have success, then we know that that will be a condition that we cannot stand before." Tim Russert then asked, "By when?" to which McCain replied, "*I don't have a date.* I think that the important thing is whether we assess as we move along."

McCain said, "Listen, my friend, we're going to have to be there for five or six years." While discussing the war in Iraq on *Hardball*, McCain said, "Listen, my friend, we're going to have to be there for five or six years. A little straight talk. We're going. We're going to have to be there for quite a while."

4. Answer: C

Black Enlisted to Improve Marcos's Image. [*The Globe and Mail*, 12/20/85; FARA Database, accessed 3/2008]

Black's Firm Lobbied for Somalia's Dictator Mohamed Siad Barre. [*Common Cause* magazine, Winter 1993; FARA Database, accessed 3/2008]

Black Lobbied for Zaire's Dictator Mobutu Sese Seko. [*Common Cause* magazine, Winter 1993; Department of Justice, FARA database, accessed 2/26/08]

5. Answer: Not firing more people more quickly.

18,000 Hewlett-Packard employees were laid off or fired during her tenure. Fiorina suggests her biggest mistake was not firing more people more quickly. "I would have done them all faster. Every person that I've asked to leave, whether it's been clear publicly or not, I would have done faster." [*Fortune,* 2/7/05]

6. Lobbyist matching

McCain fund-raiser Anthony Principi—Pfizer

Adviser Thomas Loeffler—Saudi Arabia

McCain congressional liaison John Green—U.S. Smokeless Tobacco
McCain fund-raiser Steve Perry—Go Daddy
McCain fund-raiser Kerry Cammack—ExxonMobil
McCain fund-raiser Peter Madigan—Dubai

Anthony Principi Has Lobbied for Pfizer. [Senate Lobbying Disclosure Database, accessed 4/2008]

Loeffler Lobbies for Saudi Arabia. [ABC News, 2/1/08]

U.S. Smokeless Tobacco Company Public Affairs (UST Public Affairs) Paid Green and His Firm $920,000 to Lobby from 1999 to 2005. [Senate Lobbying Disclosure Database, accessed 5/2008]

Steve Perry Has Lobbied for Go Daddy. [Senate Lobbying Disclosure Database, accessed 4/2008]

Kerry Cammack Has Lobbied for ExxonMobil. Cammack is a top McCain fund-raiser. [Senate Lobbying Disclosure Database, accessed 4/2008]

Madigan Hired to Fight Child Enslavement Claims. [ABC News, 2/1/08; *Hill*, 4/4/07]

7. Answer: D. Black actually said the other three.

"I've got access to just about anybody in the government." —Charlie Black [*Washington Post*, 8/12/89]

"As long as you comply with all the rules and regulations, your past activities shouldn't be criticized."—Charlie Black [Associated Press, 9/29/93]

"Campaign official Charles Black and Pat Buchanan have both said in the last twenty-four hours, 'Those who favor rights for homosexuals have no place in the Republican Party.' " [*MacNeil/Lehrer NewsHour*, 8/19/92]

8. Answer: A.

Republican senator Thad Cochran said of McCain, "The thought of his being president sends a cold chill down my spine. He is erratic." [*Boston Globe*, 1/27/08]

9. Answer: D.

The McCains indeed own nine homes. [San Diego County Property Records; Maricopa County Property Records; Yavapai County Property Records; Arlington County Property Records; *GQ*, 3/18/08]

10. Answer: B.

McCain calls the national media "my base." [Michael Scherer, "McCain Takes the Press for a Bumpy Ride," *Salon*, March 18, 2007]

Bonus: You got me. I couldn't think of a single special interest who doesn't have an in with the McCain campaign. Can you?

THINGS JOHN McCAIN IS OLDER THAN

John McCain was born in 1936. That makes him older than . . .

- **The nylon toothbrush.** The nylon toothbrush was invented in 1938.
- **The Republic of Iceland.** The Republic of Iceland was formed in 1944.
- **The ballpoint pen.** The ballpoint pen was invented by the Hungarian journalist Laszlo Biro in 1938.
- **Teflon.** PTFE, or polytetrafluoroethylene, marketed as Teflon, was discovered on April 6, 1938, by Dr. Roy Plunkett at the DuPont research laboratories in New Jersey.
- **The Margarita.** Sometime in 1938 or '39, bartender Carlos Herrera of Tijuana decided to mix a jigger of white tequila with lemon juice, shaved ice, triple sec, and—the crowning touch—salt.
- **LSD.** LSD was invented in 1938 by the Swiss chemist Albert Hoffman, who was interested in developing medicines from compounds in ergot, a fungus that attacks rye.

- **Israel.** The State of Israel was born in 1948.

- **Fiberglass.** Fiberglass was invented in 1938 by Dale Kleist, Dr. Russell Games Slayter, and John T. "Jack" Thomas of the Owens-Corning Company.

- **M&M's.** M&M's were first marketed to the public in 1941.

- **Penicillin.** Penicillin was first mass produced in 1942, when the U.S. Northern Regional Research Laboratory in Peoria, Illinois, isolated *Penicillium chrysogenum* from a moldy melon and solved the perplexing problem of penicillin's previously prohibitively short shelf life.

- **Color television.** Color TV was first demonstrated on February 5, 1940, when engineers from RCA showed members of the FCC a television receiver producing color images in Camden, New Jersey.

- **Spray paint.** In 1949, canned spray paint was invented by Edward Seymour. It was Seymour's wife, Bonnie, who came up with the idea. Seymour got the credit, however.

- **The atom bomb.** The first atomic bomb was detonated in New Mexico on July 16, 1945.

- **The credit card.** The first credit card—Diners Club—was introduced in 1950 by Frank X. McNamara.

APPENDIX

McCain Has at Least 134 Lobbyists Running His Campaign and Raising Money for Him

The individuals in this chart are all current or former lobbyists who either serve as fund-raisers for McCain's campaign or as senior aides or advisers. There are currently 134 lobbyists working for or raising money for McCain's campaign.

Last Name	First Name	Firm/Employer	Campaign Role	Select List of Clients
Aiken	Robert	Pinnacle West Capital Corporation	Fund-raiser	Pinnacle West Capital Corporation
Aldonas	Grant	Split Rock International	Economic Adviser	Corning Mittal Steel USA
Anderson	Philmore B.	DC Navigators LLC	Fund-raiser	Aetna American Council of Life Insurers AT&T BellSouth Hartford Life PG&E Corp. Visa
Anderson	Rebecca "Becky"	Williams & Jensen	Women for McCain Steering Committee	AstraZeneca Pharmaceuticals Cigna Cox Communications Novartis Sunoco Time Warner Wyeth

Last Name	First Name	Firm/Employer	Campaign Role	Select List of Clients
Anderson	Stanton	McDermott Will & Emery	Fund-raiser Lawyers for McCain	Chiquita Brands Electronic Industries Assoc. of Japan Northwest Airlines Union Telephone U.S. Chamber of Commerce
Andres	Susan Auther	Union Pacific	Women for McCain Steering Committee	Union Pacific
Asher	Robert	WMPI Pty	Fund-raiser	Jefferson Health System WMPI Pty
Bailey	William J. III	XM Satellite Radio	Fund-raiser	Padgett Business Services XM Satellite Radio
Ball	William III	Loeffler Group	National Security Adviser	American Beverage Association EADS Introgen Therapeutics Qualcomm Southwest Airlines
Beightol	David	Dutko Worldwide	Fund-raiser	Amerigroup Corporation Amgen IDT Corporation
Bentz	Rhonda A.	Visa	Fund-raiser Women for McCain Steering Committee	Visa
Berman	Wayne	Ogilvy Government Relations	National Finance Cochair Fund-raiser	AIG American Petroleum Institute AmeriChoice AT&T Chevron Texaco Motorola NRA Reliant Energy Verizon Visa
Betts	Steve	Gallagher & Kennedy	Fund-raiser	William Lyon Homes

Last Name	First Name	Firm/Employer	Campaign Role	Select List of Clients
Black	Charlie	BKSH & Associates	Senior Adviser	Accenture Fluor General Electric Capital Services General Motors GTech Johnson & Johnson JP Morgan NADA Occidental Petroleum Corp. Philip Morris United Technologies U.S. Smokeless Tobacco Washington Mutual Bank Yukos Oil
Black	Judy	Brownstein Hyatt Farber & Schreck	Fund-raiser Women for McCain Steering Committee	AT&T Clear Channel Comcast Genworth Financial IBM Merrill Lynch National Cable & Telecom Association
Blalock	Kirk	Fierce Isakowitz & Blalock	Fund-raiser	American Insurance Association America's Health Insurance Plans Coalition for a Competitive Pharma Market Coca-Cola EADS North America MCI Miller Brewing Sprint Nextel Time Warner Yahoo!

Last Name	First Name	Firm/Employer	Campaign Role	Select List of Clients
Bonilla	Carlos	Washington Group	Economic Adviser	Bangladesh BellSouth Bio Marin Pharmaceutical BioPure Corp. Cox Communications E-Trade Exelon Fleming & Co. Pharmaceuticals Heyl Chem-Pharm Fabrik Motorola NADA National Cable & Telecom Association Panama Ranbaxy Pharmaceuticals Sanofi Pasteur Teva Pharmaceuticals Watson Pharmaceuticals
Burgeson	Christine	CitiGroup Inc.	Fund-raiser Women for McCain Steering Committee	CitiGroup
Burgeson	Eric Robert	Barbhur Griffith & Rogers	Fund-raiser Energy Adviser	BP Cellular Telecommunications & Internet Association Government of Kurdistan Lockheed Martin NRA
Cammack	Kerry	Kerry N. Cammack, P.C.	Fund-raiser	ExxonMobil SAP America
Chadwick	Kirsten Ardleigh	Fierce Isakowitz & Blalock	Fund-raiser Women for McCain Steering Committee	American Insurance Association America's Health Insurance Plans APRIA Healthcare Coca-Cola EADS North America Fannie Mae Ford Home Depot MCI Sprint Nextel Time Warner

Last Name	First Name	Firm/Employer	Campaign Role	Select List of Clients
Chamberlin	Rob	McBee Strategic Consulting	Fund-raiser	American Airlines Babcock & Wilcox Boeing Delta Airlines Expedia FedEx General Dynamics Northrop Grumman United Technologies
Charlton	Susan	Gallagher & Kennedy	Fund-raiser	William Lyon Homes
Clerici	John	McKenna Long	Fund-raiser	Acambis DOR Bio EMD GMH Sanofi
Cooper	Josephine "Jo"	Toyota	Women for McCain Steering Committee	Alliance of Automobile Manufacturers Toyota
Courter	James	Verner Liipfert Bernhard McPherson & Hand	National Finance Committee Cochairman	Lockheed Martin NBC PhRMA SBC Verizon
Crane	David	Washington Group	Senior Policy Adviser	Bank of America Beacon Capital Partners BellSouth Bio Martin Pharmaceutical BioPure Corp. Chamber of Commerce Cox Communications Delta E-Trade Exelon Fleming & Co. Pharmaceuticals Heyl Chem-Pharm Fabrik Hyundai Microsoft Ranbaxy Pharmaceuticals State Farm Insurance Teva Pharmaceuticals Theragenics Corp. Watson Pharmaceuticals

Last Name	First Name	Firm/Employer	Campaign Role	Select List of Clients
Crippen	Dan	Washington Counsel	Senior Policy Adviser	Aetna GE Capital Assurance General Electric Co. General Motors Group Health Hewlett-Packard Merrill Lynch Mutual of Omaha
Culvahouse	Arthur	O'Melveny & Myers	Heading V.P. Search Lawyers for McCain	Civil Justice Reform Group Fannie Mae Lockheed Martin Time Warner
Cunning-ham	Bryan	Barbour Griffith & Rogers	Fund-raiser	AT&T Services Eli Lilly Motorola Pfizer Republic of India Verizon
D'Amato	Alfonse	Park Strategies	Fund-raiser	Lockheed Martin News Corporation United Technologies
Davenport	Doug B.	DCI Group	Regional Campaign Manager Fund-raiser	AT&T GM Goldman Sachs Intel Lockheed Martin Mortgage Insurance Companies of America Verizon Visa
Davis	Ashley	Blank Rome	Women for McCain Steering Committee	Bearing Point Boeing Mylan Laboratories Prudential Financial
Davis	Kurt	Hamilton, Gullett, Davis & Roman	Fund-raiser	Translational Genomics Research Institute Yavapai Ranch
Davis	Rick	Davis, Manafort	Campaign Manager	BellSouth GTech SBC Telecommunications Verizon

Last Name	First Name	Firm/Employer	Campaign Role	Select List of Clients
Dawson	Mimi	Wiley Rein	Fund-raiser Women for McCain Steering Committee	Amazon.com Holdings Colorado Gaming Association General Motors Motorola Sirius Satellite Radio Verizon Wireless
Diamond	John	Washington Capital Group	Economic Adviser	KSOLV
Donatelli	Frank	McGuire Woods	Deputy RNC Chairman	AT&T Blue Cross Blue Shield Dominion Resources ExxonMobil Knoll Pharmaceutical PhRMA Verizon
Edwards	Melissa "Missy"	Washington Group	Fund-raiser Women for McCain Steering Committee	Amgen Assoc. of Corporate Credit Unions Bangladesh BellSouth Cox Communications Delta Airlines E-Trade Microsoft Motorola National Automobile Dealers Assoc. Panama
Fay	Kevin	Alcalde & Fay	Fund-raiser	3M Corporation
Ferry	Christian	Davis, Manafort	Deputy Campaign Manager	SBC Telecommunications Verizon
Fidler	Chris	Petrizzo Strategic Group	Fund-raiser	America's Health Insurance Plans (AHIP) Boehringer IngelHeim DirecTV GlaxoSmithKline NewsCorp Stratus Pharmaceuticals
Fiorentino	Thomas Jr.	Fiorentino & Hewett	Fund-raiser	United Airlines
Furman	Sally	Furman Group	Women for McCain Steering Committee	Pinnacle West Capital Corporation

Last Name	First Name	Firm/Employer	Campaign Role	Select List of Clients
Geduldig	Samuel K.	Clark Lytle & Geduldig	Fund-raiser	AT&T Ernst & Young Fidelity Investments Prudential Qwest Verizon
Ginsberg	Ben	Patton Boggs	Fund-raiser	Lucent Technologies Venetian Casino Resort
Girard-diCarlo	David	Blank Rome	Fund-raiser	American Financial Group FastShip Mylan Laboratories
Glassner	Michael	IDT Corp.	Fund-raiser	IDT Corp.
Glover Weiss	Juleanna R.	Ashcroft Group	Fund-raiser Women for McCain Steering Committee	Adelphia AT&T Aventis Pharmaceuticals Coors Brewing Company Eli Lilly Freddie Mac Novartis PhRMA
Gorton	Slade	Kirkpatrick & Lockhart Preston Gates	Honorary Chairman, Washington State	Allstate Insurance American Nuclear Insurers Babcock & Wilcox Delta Airlines Microsoft Safeco Starbucks T-Mobile USA
Gramm	Phil	UBS	Fund-raiser Economic Adviser	UBS Americas

Last Name	First Name	Firm/Employer	Campaign Role	Select List of Clients
Green	John	Ogilvy Government Relations	Congressional Liaison Fund-raiser	AHIP Amerada-Hess AmeriChoice AT&T BellSouth Blackstone Group Chevron Texaco CitiGroup EADS Hoffman-La Roche Motorola NRA Pfizer Philip Morris Time Warner U.S. Smokeless Tobacco Company U.S. Telecom Association Verizon
Grissom	Janet M.	Johnson, Madigan, Peck, Boland & Stewart	Women for McCain Steering Committee	Accenture Alliance of Auto Manufacturers Amgen Ford NYSE Group
Gullett	Wes	Hamilton, Gullett, Davis & Roman	Fund-raiser Arizona Campaign Coleader	Translational Genomics Research Institute Yavapai Ranch
Gullott	Kristen	Brown Rudnick Berlack Israels	Women for McCain Steering Committee	American Gas Association AT&T Bristol-Myers Squibb Introgen Therapeutics PhRMA Toyota Yamaha Motor Corporation
Hance	Kent	Hance Scarborough Wright Woodward & Weisbart	Fund-raiser	Stanford Financial Group
Harding	Robert	Greenberg Traurig	Fund-raiser	Home Source Inc. Stellar Management

Last Name	First Name	Firm/Employer	Campaign Role	Select List of Clients
Hart	Vicki	Hart Health Strategies	Women for McCain Steering Committee	Amgen CitiGroup Eli Lilly Johnson & Johnson Lehman Brothers Lockheed Martin Merrill Lynch New York Stock Exchange PhRMA United Health Group Vaxgen Verizon Visa Vitas Healthcare Corporation
Hartwell	Robert van Laer	Hartwell Capitol Consulting/ Hartick LLC	Fund-raiser	BLR Aerospace National Association of Chain Drug Stores
Hawley	Buzz	Van Scoyoc Associates	Virginia Steering Committee	ELSAG North America
Heubusch	John D.	Waitt Family Foundation	Fund-raiser	Gateway
Hilleary	William "Van"	Sonnenschein Nath & Rosenthal	State Cochairman, Tennessee	AmSurg MILITEC SMS Holdings Corporation
Hohlt	Deborah	Self-Employed	Women for McCain Steering Committee	State of Indiana
Hohlt	Richard	Hohlt and Associates	Fund-raiser	Bristol-Myers Squibb Chevron JP Morgan Chase Nuclear Energy Institute SBC Communications Time Warner
Hughey	Gaylord T. Jr.	Self-Employed	Fund-raiser	Heartland Security Insurance Group
Huntsman	Peter	Huntsman International LLC	Fund-raiser	Huntsman International LLC

Last Name	First Name	Firm/Employer	Campaign Role	Select List of Clients
Hyland	James "Jim"	Pennsylvania Avenue Group	Fund-raiser Virginia Steering Committee	American Insurance Association BP America Citigroup eBay Federal Home Loan Mortgage Corp. General Motors Independent Fuel Terminal Operators Association Merrill Lynch Mortgage Investors Corporation New York Stock Exchange Occidental Petroleum Corp. Raytheon Viacom Visa
Jarvis	Aleix	Fierce Isakowitz & Blalock	Fund-raiser	EADS MCI National Cable & Telecom Association Sprint Nextel Time Warner Viacom
Jenner	Greg	American Council of Life Insurers	Economic Adviser	American Council of Life Insurers Edison Electric Institute JG Wentworth
Johnson	Edwin "Ned"	McNair Law Firm	Fund-raiser	Fuji Porter Technologies
Johnson	Mary Kate	Cassidy & Associates	Women for McCain Steering Committee	Blue Cross/Blue Shield of S.C. Boeing
Johnson	Nancy	Berman, Caldwell & Berkowitz	Fund-raiser	Verizon
Jones	Christine	Go Daddy Group Inc.	Fund-raiser	Go Daddy
Kahn	Charles N. III	Federation of American Hospitals	Fund-raiser	Federation of American Hospitals

Last Name	First Name	Firm/Employer	Campaign Role	Select List of Clients
Kilberg	William	Gibson, Dunn & Crutcher	Fund-raiser	Investment Co. Institute
Kuykendall	Steve	Strategic Marketing Innovations	Fund-raiser	Cercom SMI Techfinity
Lesher	William "Bill"	Lesher, Russell & Barron	Fund-raiser	Kraft Foods Pepsico Philip Morris
Lichten-stein	Jack	Asis Intl.	Fund-raiser	Asis Intl.
Loeffler	Thomas	Loeffler Group	National Campaign Cochair Fund-raiser	AT&T Bristol-Myers Squibb Capital One Financial Edison Electric Institute Motorola PhRMA Saudi Arabia Toyota
MacKinnon	Gail	Time Warner	Women for McCain Steering Committee	CBS National Cable & Telecom Association Time Warner Viacom
Madigan	Peter	Johnson, Madigan, Peck, Boland & Stewart	Fund-raiser	Accenture Alliance of Auto Manufacturers Amgen Arthur Andersen Bank of New York BellSouth Charles Schwab Dubai Goldman Sachs Merrill Lynch Microsoft Peruvian Asparagus Institute Philip Morris Shell Oil U.S. Telecom Association United Technologies Verizon

Last Name	First Name	Firm/Employer	Campaign Role	Select List of Clients
Manaigo	Aaron	Fenner, Gray & Associates	National Coalitions Director	Center for Financial Literacy Quixotic Solutions Inc. U.S. Fast Food Coalition U.S. Hydrogen Energy Coalition
Mann	Mary	International Paper	Women for McCain Steering Committee	International Paper
Martino	Paul	Alston & Bird	Fund-raiser	AT&T Charles Schwab Morgan Stanley Dean Witter
McAuliffe	Mary	Union Pacific	Fund-raiser Women for McCain Steering Committee	Union Pacific
McGovern	John	McGovern & Smith	Fund-raiser	Intelsat Global Service Neuren Pharmaceuticals 10 Tanker Air Carrier LLC
McKay	Mike	Federal Strategy Group	Fund-raiser	American Airlines Verizon
McKeag	Jana	Lowry Strategies	Fund-raiser	Alliance Central California Leadership Alliance Prairie Island Indian Community Sodak Gaming Venture Catalyst Viejas Band of Kumeyaay Indians
McKone	Timothy	AT&T	Fund-raiser	AT&T ComSat Corp. Fruit of the Loom SBC Telecommunications
McSlarrow	Alison H.	McSlarrow Consulting	Fund-raiser Women for McCain Steering Committee	American Trucking Association Fannie Mae Hartford Microsoft Nextel Northwest Airlines
McSlarrow	Kyle E.	National Cable & Telecom Association	Fund-raiser	National Cable & Telecom Association

Last Name	First Name	Firm/Employer	Campaign Role	Select List of Clients
Meece	Michael E.	Meece Group	Fund-raiser	Coca-Cola Comcast Dubai Mercantile Exchange
Metzner	David A.	American Continental Group	Fund-raiser	Association of American Railroads Cisco Systems Edison Electric Institute Ernst & Young Exelon Intel PepsiCo Prudential Insurance
Molinari	Susan	Washington Group	Women for McCain Steering Committee	AAI Pharma Amgen Bangladesh BellSouth Bio Marin Pharmaceutical BioPure Corp. Cox Communications E-Trade Exelon Heyl Chem-Pharm Fabrik Hyundai Motor America Microsoft Motorola NADA National Cable & Telecom Association Panama Ranbaxy Pharmaceuticals Sanofi Pasteur SBC Communications Teva Pharmaceutical Verizon Watson Pharmaceuticals
Munger	John	Munger Chadwick PLC	Fund-raiser	Clear Channel Outdoor Inc.
Nahigian	Ken	Nahigian Strategies	Fund-raiser	Discover America Partnership

Last Name	First Name	Firm/Employer	Campaign Role	Select List of Clients
Nelson	Susan	Loeffler Group	National Finance Director	American Health Insurance Plans AmeriChoice AT&T Toyota Verizon
Oliver	Jack	Bryan Cave Strategies	Fund-raiser	Ameren Anheuser-Busch Ernst & Young Financial Services Forum Northwest Airlines Shell Oil Union Pacific Verizon
Perry	Steve	Dutko Worldwide	Fund-raiser	Amazon.com AT&T/AT&T Wireless Charles Schwab Go Daddy IDT Corporation TiVo
Pfautch	Roy	Civic Service	National Finance Committee Cochairman	Assoc. of Clinical Endocrinologists International Fuel Technology Japan Federation of Construction Contractors MetCor Nippon Telegraph & Telephone Corp. NTT Docomo USA Inc. Sanwa Bank Shandwick International
Pfoten-hauer	Nancy Mitchell	Koch Industries	Economic Adviser	Koch Industries
Phillips	Steve	DLA Piper	Fund-raiser	Amazon.com BellSouth BP America eBay General Motors Lockheed Martin Merrill Lynch Staples Time Warner

Last Name	First Name	Firm/Employer	Campaign Role	Select List of Clients
Pickering	Elise	Mehlman Vogel Castagnetti	Women for McCain Steering Committee	American Clinical Laboratory Assn. American Health Insurance Plans Amgen Amylin Ascension Healthcare AstraZeneca Pharmaceuticals eBay Edison Electric Institute IBM Intel Pepsi PhRMA Procter & Gamble Sprint Nextel Wal-Mart Yahoo!
Pitts	James L.	DC Navigators	Fund-raiser	Aetna American Council of Life Insurers AT&T BellSouth Council of Insurance Agents andBrokers PG&E Corp.
Powers	Timothy	Artemis Strategies	Fund-raiser	Caspian Energy Alliance Cricket Communications Islamic Republic of Pakistan Motorola Pakistan Human Development Fund Teva Pharmaceuticals
Principi	Anthony	Pfizer	Fund-raiser	Pfizer
Racy	Michael	Munger Chadwick	Fund-raiser	Clear Channel
Rappoport	Sloan W.	Downey McGrath Group	Fund-raiser	Manufacturers Association of Haiti Pharmed Group Preferred Care Partners Thorium Power
Rill	James	Collier Shannon Scott	Economic Adviser	Intel

Last Name	First Name	Firm/Employer	Campaign Role	Select List of Clients
Roman	Steve	Hamilton, Gullett, Davis & Roman	Fund-raiser	Translational Genomics Research Institute
Rudman	Warren	Paul, Weiss, Rifkind, Wharton & Garrison	Cochairman, National Exploratory Committee	Intelsat
Salmon	Matt	Greenberg Traurig	Fund-raiser	American Capital Holdings ArmorWorks Dillion Aero El Paso Pipeline Group Nien Made Enterprises
Samora	Joseph	Case New Holland	Fund-raiser	Case New Holland
Scheune-mann	Randy	Scheunemann and Associates	Defense and Foreign Policy Coordinator	BP Amoco Lockheed Martin NRA
Seaton	Jon	Associated Builders & Contractors	Regional Campaign Manager (OH & PA)	Associated Builders & Contractors
Shanahan	Kathleen M.	Public Strategies	2008 McCain Victory Florida Finance Committee	New York Stock Exchange
Stahl	Katie	Brownstein Hyatt Farber Schreck	Fund-raiser	Life Medical Technologies Medical Device Manu-facturers Association Sanofi-Aventis
Stanges	Milly	TIAA-CREF	Women for McCain Steering Committee	TIAA-CREF Bell Atlantic Mobile
Suarez	Aquiles	National Association of Industrial & Office Properties	Economic Adviser	Fannie Mae National Association of Industrial & Office Properties
Sundquist	Don	Sundquist & Anthony	State Cochair, Tennessee	The Hartford Scotts Company U.S. Smokeless Tobacco
Symington	Fife	Symington Group LLC	Fund-raiser	Diversified Energy Corporation
Thompson	Jeri	Verner Liipfert Bernhard McPherson & Hand	Fund-raiser	American Insurance Association

Last Name	First Name	Firm/Employer	Campaign Role	Select List of Clients
Timmons	John	Cormac Group	Fund-raiser & Adviser	America West Airlines AT&T Time Warner Telecom U.S. Airways
Van Dongen	Dirk W.	National Association of Wholesalers-Distributors	Fund-raiser	National Association of Wholesalers-Distributors
Vennett	David	Toyota	Fund-raiser	Toyota
Villamil	J. Antonio	Washington Economics Group	Florida Advisory Committee	PSEG Global
Wagner	Raymond T. Jr.	Enterprise Rent-A-Car	Fund-raiser	Enterprise Rent-A-Car
Weiss	Jeffrey	BKSH	Fund-raiser	Alcoa Inc. JP Morgan NFIB U.S. Airways Group Yukos Oil Company
Wiley	Richard "Dick"	Wiley Rein	Fund-raiser Cochairman, Lawyers for McCain	CBS Gannett Co. General Motors
Williams	Tony	Washington2 Advocates	Fund-raiser	National Mining Association
Woolsey	James	Shea & Gardner	Energy and National Security Adviser	North American Industrial Hemp Council
Wright	Joseph	Panamsat Corp.	Economic Adviser	Panamsat Corp.
Zeidman	Fred	Greenberg Traurig	Fund-raiser	Sprenger & Lang
Zimmer	Richard "Dick"	Gibson Dunn & Crutcher	Honorary Vice Chairman, New Jersey	Business Roundtable T-Mobile USA

Source: Senate Lobbying Disclosure Records

NOTES

1 THE HUG

1. Judy Keen, "Bush: Kerry Repeatedly Flip-Flops on Iraq War," *USA Today*, 8/10/04.
2. Peter Baker, "For McCain, Bush Has Both Praise, Advice," *Washington Post*, 2/11/08.
3. *Dallas Morning News*, 12/2/99.
4. Sarah Baxter, "Republicans Turn to McCain the Maverick," *Times of London*, 11/20/05.
5. Jake Tapper, "Getting Ugly," Salon.com, 11/14/00.
6. Jake Tapper, "Straight Talk, No Smiles," Salon.com, 2/18/00.
7. Allison Mitchell, "The 2000 Campaign: McCain Catches Mud, Then Parades It," *New York Times*, 2/16/00.
8. Dana Goldstein, "Baby on Board," *New Republic*, 1/19/08.
9. "Rove Responds to 2000 South Carolina Campaign Allegation," CNN.com, 3/16/07.
10. Bill Moyers, quoted in *The Johnson Years: The Difference He Made* (Austin: University of Texas Board of Regents, 1993).
11. Joshua Green, "Karl Rove in a Corner," *Atlantic*, November 2004.
12. John McCain Press Release: "Statement regarding final tax reconciliation bid," May 26, 2001.
13. Bob Cusack, "Democrats Say McCain Nearly Abandoned GOP," *Hill*, 3/28/07.
14. "McCain Denies Party Switch and Presidential Run," CNN.com, 6/2/01.
15. Author's interview with a participant in the conversation, 5/20/08.
16. Ibid.

17. Maria Newman, "Bush and McCain Campaign Together in West," *New York Times*, 6/18/04.
18. "President Bush Salutes Soldiers in Fort Lewis, Washington," Official Remarks of the President, Whitehouse.gov, accessed 6/18/04.
19. Mike Allen, "Bush, McCain Look Beyond Differences," *Washington Post*, 6/19/04.
20. Judy Keen, "Bush: Kerry Repeatedly Flip-Flops on Iraq War," *USA Today*, 8/10/04.
21. Todd S. Purdum, "Bearhug Politics: Careful Steps to a New Bush-McCain Alliance," *New York Times*, 8/21/04.
22. Ibid.
23. Jonathon Martin, "Nicole Wallace to Team McCain," *Politico*, 4/24/08.

2 McSAME OLD THING

1. *Chicago Tribune*, 4/14/06.
2. Campaign event in Central Point, Oregon, 10/14/04.
3. CQ Voting Studies, accessed 5/15/08.
4. Ibid.
5. George H. W. Bush Official Biography, accessed 6/10/08.
6. John McCain, *Faith of My Fathers* (New York: Random House, 1999).
7. *Arizona Republic*, 3/1/07.
8. NBC News, 4/2/08.
9. *San Antonio Express-News*, 11/30/97.
10. *Boston Globe*, 6/7/05.
11. *Washington Post*, 7/26/99.
12. *Atlanta Journal-Constitution*, 11/4/00.
13. *Charleston Gazette*, 4/12/08.
14. *Time*, 4/3/08.
15. ABC News, 4/1/08.
16. *Arizona Republic*, 3/1/07.
17. *Capital*, 3/31/08.
18. John McCain, *Worth the Fighting For* (New York: Random House, 2003).

19. *New York Times*, 5/30/08.
20. *Los Angeles Times*, 8/29/05.
21. *St. Petersburg Times*, 8/14/05.
22. Center for Responsive Politics via Opensecrets.org, accessed 4/2/08.
23. *Wall Street Journal*, 4/17/08.
24. San Diego County property records.
25. Ibid.
26. *Arizona Republic*, 10/26/06; Maricopa County property records.
27. Yavapai County property records.
28. Arlington County property records.
29. *GQ*, 3/18/08; Maricopa County property transfer records.
30. National Association of Realtors, *Single Family*, 4th Quarter 2007.
31. *Vanity Fair*, February 2007.
32. Town Hall Meeting in Concord, New Hampshire, 1/3/08.
33. Ibid.
34. David L. Phillips, *Losing Iraq* (New York: Basic Books, 2005), 101.
35. *The Hugh Hewitt Show*, 3/17/08.
36. *Washington Post*, 3/18/08.
37. Ibid.
38. MSNBC, *Hardball*, 11/7/07.
39. CNN, 5/30/08.
40. Reuters, 5/30/08.
41. Ibid.
42. Agence France-Presse, 6/3/08.
43. BBC, 6/4/08.
44. *New York Times*, 6/5/08.
45. Ibid.
46. *Washington Post*, 10/21/04.
47. NBC, *Today*, 3/20/03.
48. MSNBC, 9/29/02.
49. McCain, Town Hall in Houston, Texas, 2/28/08.
50. *Washington Post*, 3/14/08.
51. Bill Bennett's *Morning in America*, 3/26/07.
52. "The Swamp," *Chicago Tribune*, 8/10/07.

53. McCain, rally in Hilton Head Island, South Carolina, 1/18/08.
54. McCain, Town Hall in West Palm Beach, Florida, 1/24/08.
55. *Newsweek*, 4/7/08.
56. *Hill*, 2/12/08.
57. *Arizona Republic*, 11/5/99.
58. NBC, *Meet the Press*, 1/30/00.
59. *Arizona Republic*, 11/5/99.
60. HR 2658, *CQ Vote #287*, 7/17/03.
61. HR 2658, *CQ Vote #284*, 7/16/03.
62. HR 2658, *CQ Vote #283*, 7/16/03.
63. HR 2658, *CQ Vote #279*, 7/16/03.
64. *Times-Picayune*, 8/29/08.
65. *Times-Picayune*, 8/30/05.
66. White House, 8/27/05.
67. CNN, 8/29/05.
68. *Times-Picayune*, 8/29/08.
69. CBS, *Face the Nation*, 8/28/05.
70. NBC, *Today* show, 8/29/05; *Times-Picayune*, 8/30/05.
71. *Kansas City Star*, 8/29/05.
72. Associated Press, 8/30/05.
73. *Los Angeles Times*, 9/1/05.
74. CNN, *Anderson Cooper 360*, 9/1/05.
75. Statement of Sen. John McCain, *U.S. Fed News*, 9/1/2005.
76. Ibid.
77. CNN, *Anderson Cooper 360*, 9/1/05.
78. *Dallas Morning News*, 9/7/05.
79. HR 2862, *CQ Vote #229*, 9/14/2005.
80. HR 4297, *CQ Vote #6*, 2/2/2006.
81. HR 2862, *CQ Vote #228*, 9/14/05; S 1042, *Vote #316*, 11/10/05.
82. HR 2862, *CQ Vote #234*, 9/15/2005.
83. S 1932, *CQ Vote #285*, 11/3/2005.
84. *Hill*, 3/8/06; Associated Press, 3/10/06.
85. Associated Press, 3/10/06.
86. *Washington Post*, 4/21/08.
87. CBS News, 4/24/08.
88. *Dallas Morning News*, 12/24/07.

89. *Clarion-Ledger*, 9/8/07.
90. Associated Press, 5/14/08.
91. NPR, *Fresh Air*, 9/18/06.
92. *Wall Street Journal*, 7/27/06.
93. NPR, *Fresh Air*, 6/2/08.
94. *Newsday*, 2/29/00.
95. *Washington Post*, 5/14/06.
96. *Dallas Morning News*, 2/28/08.

3 NEWS STORIES FROM THE McCAIN PRESIDENCY

1. Al-Arabiya TV, via CQ, 1/6/08; Dan Froomkin, "Bush's Messiah Complex," WashingtonPost.com, 1/7/08.
2. Charlie Savage, "John McCain Q & A," *Boston Globe*, 12/20/07.
3. CBS, "From the Road" blog, 4/24/08.
4. Benjamin Pimentel, "HP Sued Over Fiorina's $42 Million in Exit Pay," *San Francisco Chronicle*, 3/8/06.
5. *San Francisco Chronicle*, 1/9/04.
6. *Rust v. Sullivan*, 500 U.S. 173 (1991).
7. Julia Eilperin, "For McCain, Views on Abortion Come to the Fore," *Washington Post*, 1/18/08.

4 ECONOMY: McWORSE THAN BUSH

1. McCain Town Hall in West Palm Beach, Florida, 1/24/08.
2. Mark Silva, "Bush: 'Fundamentals of Our Economy Are Strong,' " *Chicago Tribune*, 8/10/07.
3. Bureau of Labor Statistics, accessed 6/12/08.
4. Ibid.
5. Paul Krugman, "Job Creation?" The Conscience of a Liberal blog, *New York Times*, 6/11/08.
6. *New York Times*, 6/7/08.
7. Joint Economic Committee, *The Way We Were: Comparing the Bush Economy with the Clinton Economy*, March 2007.
8. Ibid.
9. Ibid.

10. Andrew Leckey, "Stressing the negative: Consumers feel lousy," *Hartford Courant*, 6/8/08.
11. Joint Economic Committee, *The Way We Were: Comparing the Bush Economy with the Clinton Economy*, March 2007.
12. Ibid.
13. Associated Press, 2/12/08.
14. Associated Press, 12/3/07.
15. Clinton, remarks on the budget, 12/28/00.
16. *USA Today*, 12/3/07.
17. *Los Angeles Times*, 2/2/08; emphasis added.
18. CNN, 1/22/08; emphasis added.
19. CBS News, 2/28/08; emphasis added.
20. Fox News, GOP Debate, South Carolina, 1/10/08; emphasis added.
21. *Los Angeles Times*, 2/2/08.
22. Fox News, GOP Debate, South Carolina, 1/10/08; emphasis added.
23. *Wall Street Journal*, 1/15/08.
24. *Hartford Courant*, 4/10/08.
25. TheStreet.com, 4/9/08.
26. Knight Ridder, 4/10/08.
27. Buffett, interview with CNBC's *Squawk Box* 3/3/08.
28. Gallup, 3/19/08.
29. McCain, question-and-answer session at Associated Press annual meeting, 4/14/08.
30. *Wall Street Journal*, 4/17/08.
31. McCain, Town Hall in West Palm Beach, Florida, 1/24/08.
32. ABC, *This Week*, 11/19/06.
33. NBC, *Meet the Press*, 5/16/04.
34. NBC, *Today*, 3/20/03.
35. Economic Policy Institute, *Costly Trade With China*, 10/9/07, accessed 05/06/08.
36. *New Republic*, 1/31/08.
37. NBC, *Meet the Press*, 1/27/08.
38. Cal Thomas, op-ed, *New York Sun*, 3/7/06.
39. *Washington Post*, 2/6/08.
40. ABC, *This Week*, 2/17/08.
41. Political Intelligence, *Boston Globe*, 12/18/07.

42. John McCain, economic speech in Santa Ana, California, 3/25/08.
43. Fox News, Republican debate, 1/10/08.
44. MSNBC, *Hardball*, 2/25/04.
45. *Roll Call*, 6/20/02.
46. *Wall Street Journal*, 4/17/08.
47. CNN, Republican primary debate, 1/30/08.
48. Bloomberg TV, 4/17/08.
49. Gallup, 3/19/08.
50. Gallup, 4/25/08.
51. Gallup, 6/3/08.
52. President Bush, speech at the NRCC dinner, 3/17/08.
53. CNN, 3/14/08.
54. McCain, remarks on the economy at Carnegie Mellon University, 4/15/08.
55. *Washington Post*, 4/15/08.
56. *National Journal*, CongressDaily, 3/7/08.
57. *Washington Post*, 1/2/08.
58. Ibid.
59. *London Observer*, 2/13/05.
60. *New York Times*, 6/6/08.
61. *International Herald Tribune*, 2/12/05; *Washington Post*, 3/29/02.
62. *Washington Post*, 3/29/02.
63. *London Observer*, 2/13/05.
64. Associated Press, 2/9/05.
65. *New Yorker*, 2/19/07.
66. Bloomberg TV, 5/28/08.
67. *San Francisco Chronicle*, 1/9/04.
68. Associated Press, 2/9/05.
69. *New York Times*, 6/6/08.
70. *Washington Post*, 1/2/04.
71. "Trading With the Enemy," *Forbes*, 4/19/04.
72. Hewlett-Packard Q1 2003 Earnings, conference call, Fair Disclosure Wire, 2/25/03.
73. CNNMoney.com, 2/12/05.
74. McCain, economy speech, 4/15/08.
75. McCain, remarks to AIPAC policy conference, 6/2/08.

76. CNN, 2/19/08.
77. *Fortune,* 2/19/08.
78. *American Banker*, 3/11/08.
79. *Washington Post*, 4/2/08.
80. Ibid.
81. Associated Press, 3/19/08.
82. *American Banker*, 9/20/00.
83. *Texas Observer*, 5/30/08.
84. Sen. Phil Gramm, qouted by Patricia Kilday Hart in "John McCain's Gramm Gamble," *Texas Observer,* May 30, 2008.
85. "Buffett warns on investment 'time bomb,' " BBC News, 3/4/03.
86. *Houston Chronicle*, 7/29/01.
87. *Washington Post*, 4/2/08.
88. *Houston Chronicle*, 7/29/01.
89. *American Banker*, 3/5/01.
90. *Politico*, 3/28/08.
91. MSNBC, *Countdown with Keith Olbermann*, 5/27/08.
92. S 420, *CQ Vote #18*, 3/8/2001.
93. McCain, housing speech, 3/25/08.
94. *New York Times*, 3/27/08.
95. *Seattle Times*, 3/26/08.
96. McCain, housing speech, 3/25/08.
97. *Plain Dealer,* 3/28/08.
98. *Plain Dealer,* 2/7/08.
99. McCain, housing speech, 4/10/08.
100. *Washington Post,* 4/11/08.
101. *New York Times*, 4/11/08.
102. *Wall Street Journal*, 4/11/08.
103. McCain, economy speech, 4/15/08.
104. FactCheck.org, 5/14/08.
105. *American Prospect*, 3/17/08.
106. Reuters, 3/10/08.
107. *Congressional Quarterly Weekly*, 6/1/01.
108. Associated Press, 5/19/04.
109. McCain, letter to President Bush, 3/18/03.
110. Ibid.

111. NBC, *Meet the Press*, 1/27/08.
112. SCR 23, *CQ Vote #62*, 3/20/03; HR 8, *CQ Vote #151*, 6/12/02; HR 1863, *CQ Vote #170*, 5/26/01.
113. *Roll Call*, 6/5/06.
114. HR 8, *CQ Vote #164*, 6/8/06.
115. Krugman, op-ed, *New York Times*, 6/5/06.
116. *National Review*, 3/5/07.
117. *New York Times*, 1/18/08.
118. "Supply-side Spin," FactCheck.org, 6/11/07.
119. Ibid.
120. Ibid.
121. *New York Times*, 10/16/1995.
122. HR 2264, *CQ Vote #247*, 8/6/93.
123. HR 2491, *CQ Vote #556*, 10/28/95.
124. HR 2491, *CQ Vote #584*, 11/18/95.
125. S 1357, *CQ Vote #501*, 10/26/95.
126. S. Con. Res. 95, *CQ Vote #39*, 3/1/04.
127. Center for American Progress Action Fund, 3/27/08.
128. Center for American Progress Action Fund, "Five Easy Pieces and Two Trillion Dollars," March 2008.
129. Ibid.
130. U.S. Department of the Treasury, "Approaches to Improve the Competitiveness of the U.S. Business Tax System for the 21st Century," 12/20/07.
131. Center for American Progress Action Fund, "Five Easy Pieces and Two Trillion Dollars," March 2008.
132. *New Republic*, "The Illusionist," 6/2/08.
133. Center on Budget and Policy Priorities, 3/28/08.
134. Ibid.
135. *New Republic*, "The Illusionist," 6/2/08.
136. *Wall Street Journal*, 3/14/08.
137. *Washington Post*, 4/16/08.
138. *Economist*, 4/19/08.
130. Center for American Progress Action Fund, 4/16/08.
140. *Wall Street Journal*, 3/14/08.
141. *Wall Street Journal*, 4/16/08.

142. *Tribune-Star*, 2/23/08.
143. *Politico*, 4/16/08.
144. Center for American Progress, "McCain's Plan to Cut Earmarks Would Eliminate Aid to Israel," *Think Progress*, 4/16/08.
145. States News Service, 3/31/87.
146. PBS, *MacNeil/Lehrer NewsHour*, 1/22/90.
147. Ibid.
148. *New York Times*, 2/12/00.
149. *New York Times*, 2/18/08.
150. Presidential campaign press materials, 11/23/99.
151. *New York Times*, 2/18/08.
152. States News Service, 6/13/91.
153. *Arizona Republic*, 4/6/08.
154. FactCheck.org, 5/13/08.
155. *Wall Street Journal*, 4/22/08.
156. Ibid.
157. Ibid.
158. Jared Bernstein, on McCain's economic policy, 4/25/08.
19. *Wall Street Journal*, 4/22/08.
160. SJR 41, *CQ Vote #47*, 3/1/94; S 1, *CQ Vote #52*, 1/26/95; S 1, *CQ Vote #83*, 2/28/95; HJR 122, *CQ Vote #578*, 11/16/95; S 1664, *CQ Vote #82*, 4/24/96; SJR 1, *CQ Vote #22*, 2/27/97; SCR 86, *CQ Vote #53*, 4/1/98; *Healthcare Financial Management*, 2/98; SCR 86, *CQ Vote #58*, 4/1/98; SCR 86, *CQ Vote #69*, 4/2/98; S 2260, *CQ Vote #222*, 7/22/98; SCR 20, *CQ Vote #59*, 3/24/99; SCR 20, *CQ Vote #61*, 3/24/99; HCR 68, *CQ Vote #84*, 4/13/99; 1429, *CQ Vote #227*, 7/29/99; *Washington Post*, 6/7/99; SCR 101, *CQ Vote #65*, 4/7/00; HR 4577, *CQ Vote #162*, 6/29/00; SCR 95, *CQ Vote #33*, 3/9/04.
161. HR 4577, *CQ Vote #162*, 6/29/00.
162. HR 1836, *CQ Vote #137*, 5/22/01; SCR 23, *CQ Vote #93*, 3/25/03; SCR 23, *CQ Vote #58,* 3/18/03; SCR 18, *CQ Vote #47*, 3/15/05; HR 1836, *CQ Vote #137*, 5/22/01; HR 1836, *CQ Vote #122*, 5/21/01; S 1429, *CQ Vote #236*, 7/30/99; S 1429, *CQ Vote #228*, 7/29/99; SCR 20, *CQ Vote #66*, 3/25/99.
163. S 1429, *CQ Vote #228*, 7/29/99.

164. SCR 20, *CQ Vote #66*, 3/25/99.

165. Bob Davis, "McCain's Economic Platform: Big Tax Cuts, With Caveats," *Wall Street Journal*, 3/3/08.

166. McCain, speech, *Weekly Compilation of Presidential Documents*, Tucson, Arizona, 3/21/05.

167. Associated Press, 3/22/05.

168. Editorial, "Shame on John McCain," *St. Petersburg Times*, 3/25/05.

169. HR 1836, *CQ Vote #137*, 5/22/01; HR 4577, *CQ Vote #162*, 6/29/00; S 1429, *CQ Vote #228*, 7/29/99; HCR 68, *CQ Vote #84*, 4/13/99; SCR 20, *CQ Vote #66*, 3/25/99; SCR 20, *CQ Vote #61*, 3/24/99; SCR 20, *CQ Vote #59*, 3/24/99; S 947, *CQ Vote #125*, 6/25/97; S 947, *CQ Vote #124*, 6/25/97.

170. S 947, *CQ Vote #112*, 6/24/97; S 947, *CQ Vote #115*, 6/25/97.

171. S 1932, *CQ Vote #363*, 12/21/05; S 1932, *CQ Vote #303*, 11/3/05; S 1, *CQ Vote #253*, 6/26/03; S 1, *CQ Vote #247*, 6/26/03; SCR 23, *CQ Vote #89*, 3/25/03; HJR 2, *CQ Vote #21*, 1/23/03; HJR 2, *CQ Vote #21*, 1/23/03; HCR 83, *CQ Vote #73*, 4/5/01; HCR 178, *CQ Vote #156*, 5/23/1996; HCR 178, *CQ Vote #159*, 6/13/96; HCR 178, *CQ Vote #159*, 6/13/96; HCR 178, *CQ Vote #156*, 5/23/96; SCR 57, *CQ Vote #117*, 5/16/96; HR 2491, *CQ Vote #584*, 11/17/95; HR 2491, *CQ Vote #556*, 10/27/95; HCR 67, *CQ Vote #296*, 6/29/95; SCR 13, *CQ Vote #232*, 5/25/95; S 1357, *CQ Vote #499*, 10/26/95; SCR 13, *CQ Vote #173*, 5/22/95; HR 2491, *CQ Vote #584*, 11/17/95; HR 2491, *CQ Vote #556*, 10/27/95; S 1357, *CQ Vote #524*, 10/27/95; S 1357, *CQ Vote #499*, 10/26/95; HCR 67, *CQ Vote #296*, 6/29/95; SCR 13, *CQ Vote #232*, 5/25/95; SCR 13, *CQ Vote #218*, 5/25/95; SCR 13, *CQ Vote #173*, 5/22/95.

172. *Wall Street Journal*, 3/3/08.

173. Center for American Progress Action Fund, "The Wonk Room" blog, 5/15/08.

174. *Wall Street Journal*, 4/22/08.

175. Center for American Progress Action Fund, "The Wonk Room" blog, 5/16/08.

5 IRAQ: BUSH ON STEROIDS

1. *Newsweek*, 4/19/2004.
2. ABC News, 10/24/04.
3. *Economist*, 2/7/08.
4. McCain, Town Hall in Concord, New Hampshire, 1/3/08.
5. McCain, rally in Florence, South Carolina, 01/18/08.
6. *Washington Post*, 9/9/07.
7. S.J.RES.46, 10/3/02.
8. *Asheville Citizen-Times*, 10/13/02.
9. NBC, *Today*, 3/20/03.
10. NBC, *Meet the Press*, 9/22/02.
11. NBC, *Meet the Press*, 3/30/03.
12. ABC, *Good Morning America*, 4/9/03.
13. NBC, *Meet the Press*, 3/3/03.
14. ABC, *This Week*, 3/7/04.
15. ABC News, 10/24/04.
16. Bill Bennett's *Morning in America*, 3/26/07.
17. NBC, *Nightly News*, 4/1/07.
18. Fox News, *The Big Story*, 5/10/04.
19. Ibid.
20. Fox News, *Hannity & Colmes*, 5/12/04.
21. Ibid.
22. *East Valley Tribune*, 4/15/2006.
23. MSNBC, *Hardball*, 11/7/07.
24. *Los Angeles Times*, 4/7/08.
25. *Washington Post*, 3/14/08.
26. McCain, Remarks, 5/15/08.
27. *New York Observer*, 4/11/07.
28. McCain, Town Hall in Concord, New Hampshire, 1/3/08.
29. CBS, *Face the Nation*, 1/6/08.
30. TIME.com, 4/1/08.
31. *Washington Post*, 9/9/07.
32. *Marine Corps Times*, 4/19/07; CNN, *Anderson Cooper 360*, 11/20/06.
33. *National Journal*, 5/3/08.
34. *Washington Post*, 3/18/08.

35. Bloomberg TV, 3/12/08.
36. Ibid.
37. United Press International, 4/19/07.
38. *National Interest*, 2/4/08; *Huffington Post*, 2/4/08.
39. NBC, *Today*, 2/6/08.
40. *Columbia Journalism Review*, 4/10/08.
41. McCain, speech to the Florida Association of Broadcasters, 6/20/07.
42. Bloomberg TV, 3/12/08.
43. Dion Nissenbaum, "Syria, Israel Announce Search for 'Comprehensive Peace,' " McClatchy Newspapers, 5/21/08.
44. Sir Winston Leonard Spencer Churchill, Remarks at a White House luncheon, June 26, 1954, reported in *New York Times*, 6/27/54.
45. Fox News, *Hannity & Colmes*, 10/5/06.
46. Salon.com, 3/21/08.
47. *New York Times*, 12/3/07; Salon.com, 3/7/08.
48. Bolton, address to CPAC, 2/8/08.
49. Salon.com, 8/29/07.
50. Fox News, 3/29/07.
51. *Guardian*, 1/15/06.
52. CQ Floor Votes; HR 1585, *CQ Vote #341*, 9/19/07.
53. S 1689, *CQ Vote #390*, 10/17/03.
54. S 762, *CQ Vote #116*, 4/2/03.
55. Z. Byron Wolf, "McCain, Military Oppose Expanding G.I. Bill," ABC News, 4/14/08.
56. *Hill*, 2/13/08.
57. S. Amdt. 4764 to H.R. 980, *CQ Vote #127*, 5/14/08.
58. HR 2642, *CQ Vote #137*, 5/22/08.
59. Peter R. Orszag, Director of the Congressional Budget Office, Letter to Sen. Judd Gregg, Ranking Member, Senate Budget Committee, 5/8/08.
60. HR 4939, *CQ Vote #111*, 5/4/06; HR 4939, *CQ Vote #98*, 4/26/06; SCR 83, *CQ Vote #70*, 3/16/06; SCR 83, *CQ Vote #67*, 3/16/06; SCR 83, *CQ Vote #63*, 3/16/06; SCR 83, *CQ Vote #41*, 3/14/06; HR 4297, *CQ Vote #15*, 2/13/06; S 2884, *CQ Vote #226*, 8/4/90; S 2020, *CQ Vote #343*, 11/17/05; HR 2863, *CQ Vote #251*,

10/5/05; HR 2528, *CQ Vote #242*, 9/22/05; HR 2361, *CQ Vote #165*, 6/29/05; HR 2361, *CQ Vote #166*, 6/29/05; HR 2361, *CQ Vote #168*, 6/29/05; HR 1268, *CQ Vote #90*, 4/12/05; HR 1268, *CQ Vote #89*, 4/12/05; SCR 95, *CQ Vote #40*, 3/10/04; SCR 95, *CQ Vote #34*, 3/9/04; S 1689, *CQ Vote #379*, 10/14/03; SCR 23, *Vote #81*, 3/25/03; HCR 83, *CQ Vote #84*, 4/6/01; HR 2684, *CQ Vote #292*, 9/24/99; HR 2684, *CQ Vote #286*, 9/22/99; HR 2684, *CQ Vote #285*, 9/22/99; S 1429, *CQ Vote #243*, 7/30/99; S 2168, *CQ Vote #185*, 7/7/98; S 2057, *CQ Vote #175*, 6/25/98; SCR 86, *CQ Vote #76*, 4/2/98; S 936, *CQ Vote #168*, 7/10/97; S 1664, *CQ Vote #95*, 4/30/96; HR 3666, *CQ Vote #276*, 9/5/96; HR 3666, *CQ Vote #275*, 9/5/96; HR 2099, *CQ Vote #466*, 9/27/95; HR 4624, *CQ Vote #256*, 8/4/94; HR 1335, *CQ Vote #97*, 4/1/93; HR 2519, *CQ Vote #132*, 7/17/91; HR 4297, *CQ Vote #7*, 2/2/06.

61. Salon.com, 3/21/08.
62. HR 4297, Vote #15, 2/13/06.
63. HR 1268, Vote #90, 4/12/05.
64. S 2020, Vote #343, 11/17/05.
65. SCR 83, *CQ Vote #63*, 3/16/06.
66. HR 2099, *CQ Vote #470*, 9/27/95; HR 2099, *CQ Vote #465*, 9/27/95; S 1, *CQ Vote #76*, 2/22/95; HR 4624, *CQ Vote #306*, 9/27/94; SCR 83, *CQ Vote #70*, 3/16/06; SCR 86, *CQ Vote #76*, 4/2/98; HR 3666, *CQ Vote #275*, 9/5/96; HR 1335, *CQ Vote #97*, 4/1/93; HR 4624, *CQ Vote #256*, 8/4/94.
67. S 2400, *Vote #136*, 6/23/04; Salon.com, 3/21/08.
68. S 869, *CQ Vote #259*, 11/20/91.
69. CQ Floor Votes; S 1042, *CQ Vote #307*, 11/8/05.
70. HR 4939, *CQ Vote #111*, 5/4/06.
71. *Arizona Daily Star*, 8/28/03.
72. "Iraq Reconstruction Passes 1,000 Project Milestone," Department of Defense Press Release No. 1246-04, 12/3/04.
73. Special Inspector General for Iraq Reconstruction (SIGIR) Project Assessment, 10/22/07.
74. SIGIR Project Assessment, 10/23/07.
75. *Conference Report*, accessed 4/30/08; HR 2673, *CQ Vote #3*, 1/22/04.

76. *Conference Report*, accessed 4/30/08; HR 2673, *CQ Vote #3*, 1/22/04; CNN, 5/26/08.
77. *Conference Report*, accessed 4/30/08; HR 2673, *CQ Vote #3*, 1/22/04.
78. Ibid.
79. Ibid.
80. Ibid.
81. "Iraq Reconstruction Passes 1,000 Project Milestone," Department of Defense Press Release No. 1246-04, 12/3/04.
82. CNN.com, 4/30/07.
83. SIGIR Report, 1/8/07.
84. SIGIR Report, 9/12/06.
85. *Conference Report*, accessed 4/30/08; HR 2673, *CQ Vote #3*, 1/22/04.
86. Ibid.
87. Ibid.
88. Ibid.
89. Ibid.
90. McCain, Senate press release, 11/20/04.
91. John McCain, "Statement Of Senator John McCain On The FY 04 Omnibus," press release, 1/22/04.
92. *Congressional Quarterly Weekly*, 9/26/03.
93. "Iraq Reconstruction Passes 1,000 Project Milestone," Department of Defense Press Release No. 1246-04, 12/3/04.
94. Report of the Special Inspector General for Iraq Reconstruction, 1/22/08 and 7/24/06.
95. *Conference Report*, HR 2673, *Vote #3*, 1/22/04.
96. Report of the Special Inspector General for Iraqi Reconstruction.
97. "Army engineers near 4,000 complete Iraqi projects," Press Release from Multi-National Force–Iraq, 8/5/07.
98. *Iraq Reconstruction Report*, Office of the Assistant Secretary of the Army for Acquisition, Logistics and Technology, 4/30/07.
99. *Conference Report*, HR 2673.
100. Special Inspector General for Iraq Reconstruction Project Assessment, 4/21/08.
101. Ibid.

102. Special Inspector General for Iraq Reconstruction Report, 4/5/06.
103. Special Inspector General for Iraq Reconstruction Project Assessment, 1/14/08.
104. S 1, *Vote #108*, 5/16/01.
105. HR 4577, *Vote #159*, 6/28/00.
106. SCR 27, *Vote #79*, 5/22/97.
107. HR 2646, *Vote #90*, 4/21/98.
108. HR 2660, *Vote #329*, 9/5/03.
109. Special Inspector General for Iraq Reconstruction Project Assessment, 4/26/07.
110. Special Inspector General for Iraq Reconstruction Project Assessment, 7/24/06.
111. Special Inspector General for Iraq Reconstruction Project Assessment, 7/25/06.
112. HR 4567, *Vote #169*, 9/9/04.
113. S 2673, *Vote #3*, 1/22/04.
114. *Washington Post*, 10/6/04.
115. Dana Hedgpeth, "Spending on Iraq Poorly Tracked," *Washington Post*, 5/23/08.
116. Center for Corporate Policy, "Cracking Down on War Profiteering," 6/13/06.
117. *New York Times*, 7/28/07.
118. *Conference Report*, accessed 4/30/08; HR 2673, *CQ Vote #3*, 1/22/2004.
119. Associated Press, 8/29/07.
120. Joseph Stiglitz, with Linda Bilmes, *The Three Trillion Dollar War: The True Cost of the Iraq Conflict*, (New York: Norton, 2008).
121. "1 billion hogs on earth," howstuffworks.com. Average weight of a domesticated hog is 272 pounds, according to "US: Production of Pork, Red Meat Up," *Pig Progress*, 1/30/08. Hog price of $23 per live hundredweight from "Pork Prices Increase Despite Surplus Supplies," *American Agriculturalist*, 5/28/08.
122. Andrew Taylor, "Report: Wars Cost US $12 Billion a Month," Associated Press, 7/9/07.
123. *Nation*, 10/4/07.
124. Center for Responsive Politics, accessed 4/9/08.

125. *Army Times*, 2007; Senate Lobbyist Disclosure Records, accessed 2/29/08.
126. Senate Lobbying Disclosure Records, accessed 4/8/08.
127. Senate Lobbying Disclosure Records, accessed 3/08.
128. CNN, 1/31/05.
129. CNN, "Audit: US Lost Track of $9 Billion in Iraq Funds," 1/31/05.
130. *Los Angeles Times* op-ed, 4/23/08.
131. *National Review*, 4/5/08.

6 IF McCAIN'S A REFORMER, I'M A HASIDIC DIAMOND MERCHANT

1. McCain Federalist Society speech, 11/16/06.
2. Jake Tapper, "How Dubya Got His Groove Back," Salon.com, 2/10/00.
3. Marc Ambinder, *Atlantic*, 5/10/08; *New York Times*, 5/11/08.
4. *Washington Post*, 5/9/08.
5. *New York Times*, 2/22/08.
6. *National Journal*, 3/8/96.
7. Congressional Record, S 198, 1/22/97.
8. *Los Angeles Times*, 1/19/06.
9. Molly Ivins, *Molly Ivins Can't Say That, Can She?* (New York: Random House, 1991).
10. Ibid.
11. Texans for Public Justice via *Talking Points Memo*, 2/20/02.
12. Ibid.
13. *Newsweek*, 5/26/08.
14. *Saudi Publications on Hate Ideology Invade American Mosques*, Freedom House, Center for Religious Freedom, January 28, 2006.
15. Ibid.
16. "Saudi Arabia: End Suffering, End Secrecy," Amnesty International, accessed 6/16/08.
17. Ibid.
18. *Newsweek*, 5/26/08.
19. Ibid.
20. Ibid.

21. ABC News, 2/1/08.
22. Jack O'Dwyer's Newsletter, 1/15/92.
23. *Boston Herald*, 12/26/92.
24. *New Yorker*, 6/7/04.
25. Ibid.
26. *New Yorker*, 2/16/04.
27. *Washington Post*, 2/22/08.
28. Associated Press, 2/22/08.
29. *Politico*, 7/11/07.
30. Senate Lobbying Database, accessed 3/12/08; Senate Commerce Committee, accessed 3/12/08.
31. *New York Times*, 2/22/08.
32. Associated Press, 3/8/05.
33. Ibid.
34. Ibid.
35. *Harper's*, May 2008.
36. Associated Press, 3/8/05.
37. *New York Times*, 4/30/06.
38. *Newsweek*, 3/3/08.
39. *Boston Globe*, 1/9/00.
40. Ibid.
41. *Washington Post*, 12/31/07.
42. *Newsweek*, 3/3/08.
43. *Associated Press*, 3/23/08.
44. *New York Times*, 2/21/08.
45. *Boston Globe*, 1/9/00.
46. *USA Today*, 1/10/06.
47. *USA Today*, 1/10/06.
48. *"Gimme Five"—Investigation of Tribal Lobbying Matters*, final report, Senate Committee on Indian Affairs, 6/22/06.
49. Associated Press, 11/17/05.
50. Ibid.; *Washington Post*, 9/1/05.
51. *Boston Globe*, 1/5/00.

7 MCNASTY

1. Washintonpost.com, "Capitol Briefing" blog, 5/18/07.
2. Lois Romano and George Lardner, Jr., "Bush's Life-Changing Year," *Washington Post*, 7/25/99.
3. John McCain, *Worth the Fighting For* (New York: Random House, 2002).
4. Mike Leahy, "McCain: A Question of Temperament," *Washington Post*, 4/20/08.
5. Ibid.
6. Ibid.
7. Ibid.
8. Ibid.
9. Ed O'Keefe, "McCain the 'Punk' goes back to school," ABC News, 4/1/08.
10. Dan Nowiscki and Bill Muller, "At the Naval Academy," *Arizona Republic*, 3/1/07.
11. Ibid.
12. O'Keefe, "McCain the 'Punk.' "
13. *Los Angeles Times*, 5/25/07.
14. *Boston Globe*, 1/27/08.
15. *Washingtonian*, September 2006; *Washingtonian*, September 2004; *Washingtonian*, September 2000; *Washingtonian*, July 1998.
16. *Newsweek*, 2/11/08.
17. *Boston Globe*, 1/27/08.
18. Associated Press, 12/2/99.
19. "Political Intelligence," *Boston Globe*, 2/3/08.
20. Fox News, *Hannity & Colmes*, 2/19/08.
21. *Arizona Republic*, 11/5/99.
22. CBS News, 1/23/08.
23. Scott Thomson, "McCain's Temper May Become an Issue," Associated Press, 10/31/99.
24. Bill Minutaglio, *First Son: George W. Bush and the Bush Family Dynasty* (New York: Random House, 1999).
25. *Washingtonian*, 2/97; *Newsweek*, 2/11/08.

26. Brett Hovell, "McCain Loses Cool With New York Times Reporter," ABC News Political Radar, 3/7/08.
27. *New York Post*, 5/19/07.
28. *Newsweek*, 2/21/00.
29. Jake Tapper, "How Tough Is John McCain?" Salon.com, 5/14/99.
30. Ibid.
31. *Arizona Republic*, 11/5/99.
32. Mike Leahy, "McCain: A Question of Temperament," *Washington Post*, 4/20/08.
33. *Arizona Republic*, 11/5/99.
34. Leahy, "McCain: A Question of Temperament."
35. Ibid.
36. *Newsweek*, 2/11/08.

8 CRAZY BASE WORLD

1. Comedy Central, *The Daily Show with Jon Stewart*, 4/4/06.
2. "Bush: McCain a 'True Conservative,' " Associated Press, 2/10/08.
3. *Kansas City Star*, 5/28/05.
4. *CQ* Voting Studies, accessed 5/15/08.
5. *Dallas Morning News*, 2/28/08.
6. *Kansas City Star*, 5/28/05.
7. *Chattanooga Times Free Press*, 4/5/08; *Huffington Post*, accessed 6/14/08.
8. HR 3706, *Vote #289*, 8/2/83; CQ 1983.
9. Sam Stein, *Huffington Post*, 4/1/08.
10. NPR, *Morning Edition*, 9/8/97.
11. *Washington Post*, 1/14/1987; *Phoenix Gazette*, 4/13/1987.
12. *Phoenix Gazette*, 5/2/1989.
13. *Phoenix Gazette*, 10/28/1992.
14. S 2104, *CQ Votes #304*, 10/24/90; *#276* and *275*, 10/16/90 and *#161*, 7/18/90.
15. Sam Stein, "McCain Won't Apologize for Vote Against Civil Rights Act," *Huffington Post*, 4/11/08.
16. Ralph Neas, letter to John McCain, People for the American Way, 2/17/00.

17. *Southern Partisan*, Fall 1983; "Partisan View," *Southern Partisan*, Winter 1989.
18. *New York Times*, 2/8/00; Associated Press, 2/18/00.
19. Jacob Weisberg, "The Pot and Kettle Primary," *Slate*, 2/26/00.
20. "McCain's Tricky History with the MLK Holiday," *Mother Jones*, MoJo Blog, 4/4/08.
21. Elisabeth Bumiller and John Broder, "Day on the Campaign Trail to Remember Dr. King," *New York Times*, 4/5/08.
22. Will Thomas, "McCain Booed at Martin Luther King Speech," *Huffington Post*, 4/4/08.
23. National Women's Law Center, accessed 6/14/08.
24. *Ledbetter v. Goodyear Tire and Rubber Company*, 550 U.S., 127 (2007).
25. Ibid.
26. Associated Press, 4/24/08.
27. *Washington Post*, "The Trail" blog, 5/7/08.
28. McCain, speech at Wake Forest University, 5/6/08.
29. Ibid.
30. American Institute of Biological Sciences, accessed 6/14/08.
31. *Ledbetter v. Goodyear Tire and Rubber Company*, 550 U.S., 127 (2007).
32. *American Prospect*, 12/27/07.
33. McCain, speech at Wake Forest University, 5/6/08.
34. McCain, remarks in Cedar Rapids, Iowa, 8/6/07.
35. *Houston Chronicle*, 5/12/03.
36. Ibid.
37. *Minneapolis Star Tribune*, 11/13/03.
38. *Houston Chronicle*, 5/12/03.
39. *Fort Worth Star-Telegram*, 7/11/02.
40. APT 194, *Vote #128*, 5/25/05.
41. *Washington Post*, 4/11/03; *Atlanta Journal-Constitution*, 5/6/03.
42. *Charleston Gazette*, 6/30/03.
43. "Bush Court Nominee William Pryor: Outside the American Mainstream," AFL-CIO News Archive, 7/9/03.
44. Ibid.
45. *Indianapolis Star*, 9/18/03.

46. *Washington Post*, 4/11/03.
47. APT 512, *Vote #441*, 11/6/03.
48. *San Francisco Chronicle*, 10/26/03.
49. *Philadelphia Jewish Voice,* accessed 6/14/08.
50. APT 201, *Vote #131*, 6/8/05.
51. *New York Times,* 5/3/06.
52. Ibid.
53. NPR, *All Things Considered*, 6/26/07.
54. Ibid.
55. APT 1179, *Vote #159*, 5/26/06.
56. Associated Press, 10/2/87.
57. *Kansas City Star*, 5/28/05.
58. NBC News, 4/2/06.
59. *Lynchburg News & Advance,* 3/28/06.
60. McCain, remarks in Cincinnati, Ohio, 2/26/08.
61. *Columbus Dispatch*, 2/27/08.
62. *Atlanta Journal-Constitution,* 3/23/08.
63. Ibid.
64. Ibid.
65. Rod Parsley, World Harvest Church sermon, People for the American Way.
66. People for the American Way, 2/2/07.
67. McCain, remarks in Cincinnati, Ohio, 2/26/08.
68. People for the American Way, accessed 6/14/08.
69. People for the American Way, accessed 5/22/08.
70. *Boise Weekly,* 11/8/06.
71. People for the American Way, accessed 5/22/08.
72. Parsley, speech to the War on Christians and Values Voters Conference, 3/28/06.
73. *New York Times*, 4/8/08.
74. *Washington Post*, 8/13/99.
75. Associated Press, 5/14/08.
76. CNN, 5/22/08.
77. Catholic League Release, 2/28/08.
78. McCain, speech in Round Rock, Texas, 2/29/08.
79. *San Antonio Express,* 2/28/08.

80. *U.S. News & World Report*, 5/31/07.
81. John Hagee, appearance on BVOV TV, date unknown, accessed 6/14/08.
82. Ibid.
83. Catholic League Release, video, 2/28/08.
84. Bill Bennett's *Morning in America*, via Think Progress, 3/11/08.
85. Hagee, *What Every Man Wants in a Woman*, via Media Matters, accessed 5/12/08.
86. John Hagee, "Bible Positions on Political Issues."
87. Hagee, *What Every Man Wants in a Woman*.
88. NPR, *Fresh Air*, 9/18/06.
89. Ibid.
90. *The Dennis Prager Show*, 4/22/08.
91. CNN, 5/22/08.
92. Ibid.
93. *Washington Post*, 8/24/99.
94. *National Review*, 5/17/99.
95. *Washington Post*, 4/14/99.
96. *National Review*, 3/5/07.
97. Julie Rovner, "Misperceptions About McCain's Abortion Stance," NPR, 2/2/08.
98. S. Amdt. 258 to S 3, *Vote #45*, 3/11/03.
99. HR 1757, *Vote #105*, 4/28/98.
100. S 1956, *Vote #231*, 7/23/96.
101. HR 1298, *Vote #180*, 5/16/03.
102. *New York Times*, 7/18/07.
103. *Boston Globe*, 3/17/05.
104. *New York Times*, "Caucus Blog," 3/16/07.

SIDEBAR: SOME AMERICANS ARE MORE EQUAL THAN OTHERS

1. S 2056, *CQ Vote #281*, 9/10/96.
2. S 2400, *CQ Vote #114*, 6/15/04; S 625, *CQ Vote #147*, 6/11/02; S 2549, *CQ Vote #136*, 6/20/00.
3. Mary Leonard, "McCain Character Loyal to a Fault," *Boston Globe*, 3/4/00.

4. 2005 State of the Union Speech, 2/2/05.
5. http://www.youtube.com/watch?v=j7DHscURg3E.
6. MSNBC, " 'Hardball's' College Tour with John McCain," *Hardball*, October 18, 2006.
7. Ibid.
8. Todd S. Purdum, "Prisoner of Conscience," *Vanity Fair*, February 7, 2007.
9. *Lynchburg News & Advance*, 3/28/06.
10. *Tucson Citizen*, 2/25/04; Senate floor statement, 7/13/04; *Boston Herald*, 4/1/04; *Washington Post*, 7/15/04; Associated Press, 6/7/06; Senate vote #163, S.J.Res.1, 6/7/06, failed 49-48, McCain "Nay"; *Richmond Times Dispatch*, 6/6/06; *San Jose Mercury News*, 6/11/06.
11. *The Ellen DeGeneres Show*, 5/22/08.
12. People for the American Way, 9/17/07.
13. Hagee, *What Every Man Wants in a Woman*, via Media Matters, accessed 5/12/08.
14. Ibid.

9 HEALTH CARE: THE McCAIN PLAN WON'T EVEN COVER McCAIN

1. Associated Press, 3/10/08.
2. MSNBC, *The News with Brian Williams*, 5/9/00.
3. *Chicago Tribune*, 1/15/02; *New York Times*, 7/29/07; Associated Press, 5/19/08.
4. CBS News, 8/8/07.
5. *Los Angeles Times*, 5/24/08.
6. *New York Times*, 3/9/08.
7. "Statement Of Health Status Prepared By Mayo Clinic At The Request Of Senator John McCain," JohnMcCain.com, accessed 6/11/08.
8. Ibid.
9. Ibid.
10. Ibid.
11. Ibid.
12. *Washington Post*, 4/30/08.

13. *American Prospect*, 4/30/08.
14. McCain, speech at Miami's Children Hospital, 4/28/08.
15. Associated Press, 5/23/08.
16. McCain website, accessed 5/29/08.
17. Associated Press, 5/23/08.
18. *New York Times*, 5/1/08.
19. SCR 27, *CQ Vote #76*, 5/21/97; S 949, *CQ Vote #149*, 6/27/97; HR 4810, *CQ Vote #204*, 7/17/00; HR 976, *CQ Vote #307*, 8/2/07; S 3, *CQ Vote #45*, 3/11/03; HR 3963, *CQ Vote #401*, 10/31/07; CNN, *The Situation Room*, 10/3/07.
20. McCain, remarks on the economy at Carnegie Mellon University, 4/15/08.
21. Center for American Progress, 4/9/08.
22. U.S. Census Bureau, *Income, Poverty, and Health Insurance Coverage in the United States: 2006*, accessed 4/3/08.
23. *Health Business Week*, 6/1/07.
24. CNN Political Ticker, 9/17/07.
25. S 1932, *CQ Vote #363*, 12/21/05; S 1932, *CQ Vote #303*, 11/3/2005; S 1, *CQ Vote #253*, 6/26/03; S 1, *CQ Vote #247*, 6/26/03; SCR 23, *CQ Vote #89*, 3/25/03; HJR 2, *CQ Vote #21*, 1/23/03; HJR 2, *CQ Vote #21*, 1/23/03; HCR 83, *CQ Vote #73*, 4/5/01; HCR 83, *CQ Vote #73*, 4/5/01; SCR 86, *CQ Vote #53*, 4/1/98; HCR 178, *CQ Vote #156*, 5/23/96; HCR 178, *CQ Vote #159*, 6/13/96; HR 2491, *CQ Vote #584*, 11/17/95; HR 2491, *CQ Vote #556*, 10/27/95; HCR 67, *CQ Vote #296*, 6/29/95; SCR 13, *CQ Vote #232*, 5/25/95; S 1357, *CQ Vote #499*, 10/26/95; HCR 178, *CQ Vote #159*, 6/13/96; HCR 178, *CQ Vote #156*, 5/23/96; S 1357, *CQ Vote #524*, 10/27/95; S 1357, *CQ Vote #499*, 10/26/95; HCR 67, *CQ Vote #296*, 6/29/95; SCR 13, *CQ Vote #232*, 5/25/95; SCR 13, *CQ Vote #218*, 5/25/95; SCR 13, *CQ Vote #173*, 5/22/95; HR 2491, *CQ Vote #584*, 11/17/95; HR 2491, *CQ Vote #556*, 10/27/95; S 1932, *CQ Vote #363*, 12/21/05; SCR 13, *CQ Vote #173*, 5/22/95.
26. S 1932, *CQ Vote #363*, 12/21/05.
27. S 1, *CQ Vote #253*, 6/26/03.

28. HCR 178, *CQ Vote #156*, 5/23/1996; HCR 178, *CQ Vote #159*, 6/13/1996.
29. HR 2491, *CQ Vote #584*, 11/17/95; HR 2491, *CQ Vote #556*, 10/27/95.
30. S 1, *CQ Vote #262*, 6/26/03; S1, *CQ Vote #259*, 6/26/03; S 1, *CQ Vote #254*, 6/26/03; S 1, *CQ Vote #253*, 6/26/03; S 1, *CQ Vote #250*, 6/26/03; S 1, *CQ Vote #240*, 6/24/03; S 1, *CQ Vote #229*, 6/19/03; S 1, *CQ Vote #227*, 6/18/03; S 1932, *CQ Vote #363*, 12/21/05; S 1932, *CQ Vote #302*, 11/3/05; S 1054, *CQ Vote #159*, 5/15/03; SCR 23, *CQ Vote #89*, 3/25/03; SCR 23, *CQ Vote #82*, 3/25/03; SCR 23, *CQ Vote #63*, 3/20/03; S 812, *CQ Vote #199*, 7/31/02; S 812, *CQ Vote #187*, 7/23/02; S 812, *CQ Vote #186*, 7/23/02; S 812, *CQ Vote #182*, 7/18/02; HCR 83, *CQ Vote #66*, 4/3/01; HCR 83, *CQ Vote #65*, 4/3/01; HR 4810, *CQ Vote #206*, 7/17/00; HR 8, *CQ Vote #186*, 7/13/00; HR 4577, *CQ Vote #144*, 6/22/00; SCR 101, *CQ Vote #52*, 4/5/00; S 1429, *CQ Vote #231*, 7/29/99.
31. S 1, *CQ Vote #250*, 6/26/03.
32. S 1, *CQ Vote #246*, 6/25/03; SCR 20, *CQ Vote #79*, 3/25/99; S 1, *CQ Vote #244*, 6/25/03; S 1, *CQ Vote #245*, 6/25/03.
33. HJR 2, *CQ Vote #21*, 1/23/03; HCR 178, *CQ Vote #159*, 6/13/96; HCR 178, *CQ Vote #156*, 5/23/96; SCR 57, *CQ Vote #117*, 5/16/96; HCR 67, *CQ Vote #296*, 6/29/95; SCR 13, *CQ Vote #173*, 5/22/95; S 947, *CQ Vote #124*, 6/25/97; S 947, *CQ Vote #111*, 6/24/97; HCR 67, *CQ Vote #296*, 6/29/95.
34. SCR 83, *CQ Vote #70*, 3/16/06; SCR 83, *CQ Vote #67*, 3/16/06; SCR 83, *CQ Vote #63*, 3/16/06; SCR 83, *CQ Vote #41*, 3/14/06; HR 4297, *CQ Vote #15*, 2/13/06; HR 4297, *CQ Vote #7*, 2/2/06; S 2020, *CQ Vote #343*, 11/17/05; HR 2863, *CQ Vote #251*, 10/5/05; HR 2528, *CQ Vote #242*, 9/22/05; HR 2361, *CQ Vote #165*, 6/29/05; HR 2361, *CQ Vote #166*, 6/29/05; HR 2361, *CQ Vote #168*, 6/29/05; HR 1268, *CQ Vote #90*, 4/12/05; HR 1268, *CQ Vote #89*, 4/12/05; SCR 95, *CQ Vote #40*, 3/10/04; S 1689, *CQ Vote #379*, 10/14/03; SCR 23, *CQ Vote #81*, 3/25/03; S 2168, *CQ Vote #185*, 7/7/98; S 936, *CQ Vote #168*, 7/10/97; HR 3666, *CQ Vote #276*, 9/5/96; HR 3666, *CQ Vote*

#275, 9/5/96; HR 2099, *CQ Vote #466*, 9/27/95; HR 4624, *CQ Vote #256*, 8/4/94; HR 1335, *CQ Vote #97*, 4/1/93; S 2884, *CQ Vote #226*, 8/4/90; HR 2519, *CQ Vote #132*, 7/17/91.

35. SCR 86, *CQ Vote #73*, 4/2/98; S 1233, *CQ Vote #182*, 6/22/99.
36. S 1344, *CQ Vote #210*, 7/15/99; S 1344, *CQ Vote #209*, 7/15/99; S 1344, *CQ Vote #208*, 7/15/99; S 1344, *CQ Vote #206*, 7/15/99; S 1344, *CQ Vote #205*, 7/14/99; S 1344, *CQ Vote #203*, 7/14/99; S 1344, *CQ Vote #202*, 7/13/99; S 1344, *CQ Vote #201*, 7/13/99; S 1344, *CQ Vote #200*, 7/13/99; S 1344, *CQ Vote #199*, 7/13/99; S 1233, *CQ Vote #181*, 6/22/99; HR 4250, *CQ Vote #311*, 10/9/98.
37. SCR 27, *CQ Vote #76*, 5/21/97; S 949, *CQ Vote #149*, 6/27/97; HR 4810, *CQ Vote #204*, 7/17/00; HR 976, *CQ Vote #307*, 8/2/07; S 3, *CQ Vote #45*, 3/11/03; HR 3963, *CQ Vote #401*, 10/31/07.
38. *Boston Globe*, Political Intelligence, 12/18/07; *Washington Post*, 2/6/08; *New Republic*, 1/31/08.
39. John McCain, op-ed, *Union Leader*, 12/28/07.
40. *Time*, 11/8/07.
41. Roger Hickey, "The McCain Health Plan: Millions Lose Coverage, Health Costs Worsen, and Insurance and Drug Industries Win," Campaign for America's Future, 4/29/08.
42. *New York Times*, 4/30/08.
43. *New York Times*, 5/1/08.
44. *Washington Post*, 4/30/08.
45. According to the *New York Times*, McCain's health-care plan calls "for eliminating the tax breaks that currently encourage employers to provide health insurance for their workers." *New York Times*, 4/30/08.
46. *New York Times*, 5/1/08; *Wall Street Journal*, 4/30/08.
47. *Washington Post*, 4/30/08.
48. *Washington Post*, 4/30/08.
49. *New York Times*, 4/30/08.
50. *New York Times*, 5/4/08.
51. *New York Times*, 4/30/08.
52. *USA Today* reported that McCain's plan included "tax credits to encourage people to buy private insurance. The credits would be

$2,500 annually for individuals and $5,000 for families." *USA Today*, 4/29/08.

53. Roger Hickey, "The McCain Health Plan: Millions Lose Coverage, Health Costs Worsen, and Insurance and Drug Industries Win," Campaign for America's Future, 4/29/08.
54. *New York Times*, 5/1/08.
55. Center for American Progress Action Fund, 4/29/08.
56. Associated Press, 4/29/08.
57. *New York Times*, 5/1/08.
58. Center for American Progress Action Fund, 4/29/08.
59. *Wall Street Journal*, 4/30/08.
60. *New York Times*, 4/30/08.
61. *Wall Street Journal*, 4/30/08.
62. *National Journal*, 6/7/08.
63. *Dallas Morning News*, 5/19/08.
64. CNN Political Ticker, 9/17/07.
65. McCain not only voted against the State Children's Health Insurance Program (SCHIP), he went to the Senate floor to argue against covering millions of additional children, saying "the program has expanded beyond what Congress first intended. In some cases, SCHIP coverage has been extended to middle-income children." *Congressional Record*, 8/2/07.
66. HR 976, *CQ Vote #307*, 8/2/07; *Knight Ridder*, 8/2/07.
67. CNN.com, 10/3/07.
68. The *Washington Post* reported, "Sen. John McCain will propose today that affluent seniors pay more for government-provided drug benefits as a way to control health-care spending," adding that "the proposal is similar to a controversial one put forth last fall by President Bush, in which married retirees who make more than $160,000 a year would pay increasingly higher costs for the newly established Medicare prescription drug plans." *Washington Post*, 4/15/08.
69. The *Washington Post* wrote of McCain's plan to increase premiums wealthy seniors must pay for their prescription drug benefit: "That idea has been part of Bush's budget submissions for the past two years. It has been greeted coldly by both Congress and AARP, which says it erodes the delicate deal that Republicans brokered in

creating the popular prescription drug benefit in 2003." *Washington Post*, 4/15/08.

70. *Wall Street Journal*, 4/30/08.
71. *Slate*, 5/19/08.
72. Ibid.
73. Ibid.
74. *National Journal*, 5/17/08.
75. Center for American Progress Action Fund, 4/9/08.
76. Ibid.
77. *New York Times*, 4/30/08.
78. *American Prospect*, 4/30/08 [emphasis added].

10 ENVIRONMENTAL CON JOB

1. McCain Media Availability in Arlington, Virginia, via CQ Transcriptions, 6/16/08.
2. Bush, address in New Orleans, 3/1/07.
3. Global Warming and Energy Solutions Conference, Manchester, N.H., 10/13/07.
4. Senator James Inhofe, floor statement, 07/28/03; http://inhofe.senate.gov/pressreleases/climateupdate.htm.
5. Think Progress, 7/24/06.
6. S 343, *CQ Vote #306*, 7/13/95.
7. HCR 83, *CQ Vote #77*, 4/5/01; SCR 57, *CQ Vote #125*, 5/22/96; HR 3019, *CQ Vote #37*, 3/19/96; HR 4404, *CQ Vote #64*, 4/26/90.
8. Center for American Progress, 3/27/08.
9. Federal News Service, 5/13/08; Knight Ridder Washington Bureau, 6/6/08; CNN, *American Morning*, 6/11/08.
10. *Economist*, 7/29/00.
11. *Philadelphia Inquirer*, 3/14/01.
12. LCV.org, accessed 6/9/08.
13. League of Conservation Voters Scorecard, accessed 4/3/08.
14. HR 2817, *CQ Vote #408*, 12/10/85.
15. S 1316, *CQ Vote #587*, 11/29/95.
16. Ibid.

17. HR 5679, *CQ Vote #195*, 9/9/92.
18. Center for Responsive Politics, via Campaign Money Watch.
19. Associated Press, 1/17/08.
20. Center for American Progress, 3/27/08.
21. *Time*, 4/15/08.
22. CAPAF, 4/15/08; http://thinkprogress.org/wonkroom/2008/04/15/mccain-econ-speech/.
23. LCV.org, accessed 6/12/08.
24. HR 6, *CQ Vote #425*, 12/13/07.
25. S 2020, *CQ Vote #331*, 11/17/05; S 2020, *CQ Vote #341*, 11/17/05; *Houston Chronicle*, 11/17/05; *Las Vegas Review-Journal*, 11/18/05; *Environment and Energy Daily*, 11/18/05.
26. S 2020, *CQ Vote #341*, 11/17/05.
27. S 2020, *CQ Vote #331*, 11/17/05.
28. S 517, *CQ Vote #48*, 3/13/03.
29. S 517, *CQ Vote #47*, 3/13/02.
30. S 14, *CQ Vote #309*, 7/29/03.
31. Forbes.com, 12/13/07.
32. "McCain Adviser Questions Democrats' Push for More Than Cap and Trade," *E & E (Environment and Energy Daily)*, 3/23/08.
33. Michael D. Shear and Juliet Eilperin, "McCain Seeks to End Offshore Drilling Ban," *Washington Post*, 6/17/08.
34. S 13, *CQ Vote #190*, 5/24/95.
35. S 1357, *CQ Vote #525*, 10/27/95.
36. S 517, *CQ Vote #71*, 4/18/02.
37. S 1932, *CQ Vote #288*, 11/3/05.
38. HR 2863, *CQ Vote #364*, 12/21/05.
39. SCR 74, *CQ Vote #365*, 12/21/05.
40. SCR 101, *CQ Vote #58*, 4/6/00.
41. HR 2217, *CQ Vote #229*, 7/11/01.
42. League of Conservation Voters questionnaire.
43. S 1630, *CQ Vote #45*, 3/28/90.
44. S 1630, *CQ Vote #44*, 3/27/90.
45. HR 1722, *CQ Vote #87*, 6/13/89.
46. S 1630, Vote #30, 3/7/90.
47. HR 2861, *CQ Vote #449*, 11/12/03.

48. SCR 13, *CQ Vote #211*, 5/25/95.
49. S 343, *CQ Vote #306*, 7/13/95.
50. HR 2099, *CQ Vote #469*, 9/27/95; HJR 2, *CQ Vote #27*, 1/23/03; SCR 23, *CQ Vote #97*, 3/25/03; HJR 2, *CQ Vote #27*, 1/23/03; S 1637, *CQ Vote #84*, 5/5/04.
51. EPA.gov, accessed 6/17/08.
52. *New York Times*, 8/1/78.
53. EPA.gov, accessed 6/17/08.
54. S 1637, *CQ Vote #84*, 5/5/04; HJR 2, *CQ Vote #27*, 1/23/03; HJR 2, *CQ Vote #27*, 1/23/03.
55. S 2733, *CQ Vote #126*, 6/23/92.
56. HR 2099, *CQ Vote #469*, 9/27/95; HJR 2, *CQ Vote #27*, 1/23/03; SCR 23, *CQ Vote #97*, 3/25/03; HJR 2, *CQ Vote #27*, 1/23/03; S 1637, *CQ Vote #84*, 5/5/04.
57. JohnMcCain.com, accessed 5/7/08; *Politico*, 5/2/08.
58. PublicIntegrity.org, accessed 6/2/08.
59. Associated Press, 7/23/01.
60. PublicIntegrity.org, accessed 6/2/08.
61. *Washington City Paper*, 3/14/02.

ACKNOWLEDGMENTS

If, as my friend Hillary Clinton likes to say, it takes a village to raise a child, then it took a small city to research this book. I have been blessed to work with the most talented, energetic, creative, and hardworking researchers in the business. They examined nearly every vote John McCain has ever taken, analyzed nearly every speech McCain has ever given, scrutinized nearly every dime McCain has ever taken. They are remarkable, and this book would not exist without them.

First among equals is Rebecca Buckwalter-Poza. She organized the work, led the team of researchers, kept things on track, and brought this effort to a successful conclusion. I have never worked with anyone whose ratio of brains to ego was more inversely proportional—at least, not in the favorable sense.

Martine Apodaca, Elizabeth Baylor, Peter Bondi, Cammie Croft, Sara DuBois, Chris Harris, Bradley Herring, Jenni Lee, Ian B. Mandel, Jason Rosenbaum, Eddie Vale, and Melinda Warner all put their hearts and minds into this book—not to mention a lot of sweat. Their research and writing were indispensable. Attentive readers may have already seen their research and writing at various progressive sites. This book would not exist without them, and I am proud to have gathered and collected their genius in one place. Ari Rabin-Havt created the cartoons, movie posters, and graphics that enliven this tome. The team was assembled by Tom Matzzie and Tara McGuinness, as part of an effort led by David Brock, Susan McCue, Stan Greenberg, and John Podesta. And the glue that held us together was the unsinkable Steve Bing. I thank all of them, I thank each of them, and I appreciate every one of them. Their passion for progressive change is matched only by their fidelity to the truth. I am confident that every word in this book is backed up by the documented public record, because so many people worked so hard for so long to make sure that was so. Still, whatever errors or omissions are in this book are mine and mine alone.

My publisher, David Rosenthal of Simon & Schuster, was, as he has been through four previous books, a source of enduring support and endless good cheer. Ruth Fecych was a careful, thoughtful, and extraordinarily helpful editor. Elisa Rivlin of Simon & Schuster's legal department was enormously helpful. Bob Barnett has been my attorney, counselor, and friend for sixteen years and through three careers (so far). I am indebted to him for his advocacy and advice. Mark Weiner remains an inspiration, both as a Democrat and even more so as a man. The folks at CNN—from network president Jon Klein to Bureau Chief David Bohrman to political guru Sam Feist to ace producer Pat Reap—have been supportive, as have all the smart and interesting people who make up the best f^%$#*&ing political team in television. Harry Rhoads, Jr., and the talented, supportive crew at the Washington Speakers Bureau have allowed me to travel the country and test my theories on real voters on a continuing basis. Several times each day I talk with James Carville and Rahm Emanuel, two of the most hyperactive—and brilliant—political minds in America. If some of the thoughts, words, and phrases seem familiar to them, it is because I stole them. Jon Macks has, for twenty-two years, made me laugh nearly every day. I've never known anyone with as sharp a mind or as quick a wit.

My assistant, Laurelie Wallace, is entitled to special thanks. She has been almost more family than assistant, and I appreciate her greatly.

It's been said, "If you ever see a turtle on a fence post, you know one thing: it didn't get there on its own. Someone had to put it there." The people named herein put this unlikely turtle up on a high fence post. But I would not be on any fence post, anywhere, if Bill Clinton and Hillary Clinton had not taken a chance on an untested young man from Missouri City, Texas. I owe them a debt I can never repay.

Finally, thanks to my large and loving family. My mother, Peggy Howard, and her husband, Jerry. My dad, David Begala, my sister Kathleen, and her husband, Yves Istel. My brother David, his wife, Becky, and their kids: Sam, Grace, and Catherine. My brother Chris, his wife, Jeanie, and their children, Nicole and Christopher. And my brother Michael. My in-laws, Dean and Jean Friday, are an inspiration. Through fifty years of marriage, eighteen moves, two tours of duty in Vietnam, four children, and ten grandchildren, they are shining examples of real patriotism and true family values.

Most of all, I want to thank my boys: John, Billy, Charlie, and Patrick. They are my world. And especially the incomparable Diane Friday Begala. Why I proposed to her nineteen years ago is obvious to all. Why she said yes remains a mystery.

INDEX

Page numbers in *italics* refer to tables.

McCain's Lobbyists

brought to you by

9 781439 102138